"War Governor of the South"

NEW PERSPECTIVES ON THE HISTORY OF THE SOUTH SERIES

UNIVERSITY PRESS OF FLORIDA / STATE UNIVERSITY SYSTEM

Florida A&M University, Tallahassee
Florida Atlantic University, Boca Raton
Florida Gulf Coast University, Ft. Myers
Florida International University, Miami
Florida State University, Tallahassee
University of Central Florida, Orlando
University of Florida, Gainesville
University of North Florida, Jacksonville
University of South Florida, Tampa
University of West Florida, Pensacola

NEW PERSPECTIVES ON THE HISTORY OF THE SOUTH

Edited by John David Smith

Charles H. Stone Distinguished Professor of American History
at the University of North Carolina at Charlotte

"In the Country of the Enemy": The Civil War Reports of a Massachusetts Corporal,
    edited by William C. Harris (1999)
The Wild East: A Biography of the Great Smoky Mountains, by Margaret L. Brown
    (2000; first paperback edition, 2001)
*Crime, Sexual Violence, and Clemency: Florida's Pardon Board and Penal System
    in the Progressive Era,* by Vivien M. L. Miller (2000)
*The New South's New Frontier: A Social History of Economic Development
    in Southwestern North Carolina,* by Stephen Wallace Taylor (2001)
Redefining the Color Line: Black Activism in Little Rock, Arkansas, 1940–1970,
    by John A. Kirk (2002)
The Southern Dream of a Caribbean Empire, 1854–1861, by Robert E. May (2002)
Forging a Common Bond: Labor and Environmental Activism during the BASF Lockout,
    by Timothy J. Minchin (2003)
*Dixie's Daughters: The United Daughters of the Confederacy and the Preservation
    of Confederate Culture,* by Karen L. Cox (2003)
*The Other War of 1812: The Patriot War and the American Invasion of Spanish East
    Florida,* by James G. Cusick (2003)
*"Lives Full of Struggle and Triumph": Southern Women, Their Institutions, and Their
    Communities,* edited by Bruce L. Clayton and John A. Salmond (2003)
German-Speaking Officers in the United States Colored Troops, 1863–1867,
    by Martin W. Öfele (2004)
Southern Struggles: The Southern Labor Movement and the Civil Rights Struggle,
    by John A. Salmond (2004)
Radio and the Struggle for Civil Rights in the South, by Brian Ward (2004)
Luther P. Jackson and a Life for Civil Rights, by Michael Dennis (2004)
*Southern Ladies, New Women: Race, Region, and Clubwomen in South Carolina,
    1890–1930,* by Joan Marie Johnson (2004)
Fighting against the Odds: A Concise History of Southern Labor since World War II,
    by Timothy J. Minchin (2004)
*"Don't Sleep with Stevens!": The J. P. Stevens Campaign and the Struggle to Organize
    the South, 1963–1980,* by Timothy J. Minchin (2005)
"The Ticket to Freedom": The NAACP and the Struggle for Black Political Integration,
    by Manfred Berg (2005)
"War Governor of the South": North Carolina's Zeb Vance in the Confederacy,
    by Joe A. Mobley (2005)

"War Governor of the South"
North Carolina's Zeb Vance in the Confederacy

JOE A. MOBLEY

Foreword by John David Smith, Series Editor

UNIVERSITY PRESS OF FLORIDA

Gainesville · Tallahassee · Tampa · Boca Raton · Pensacola

Orlando · Miami · Jacksonville · Ft. Myers

Copyright 2005 by Joe A. Mobley
Printed in the United States of America on recycled, acid-free paper
All rights reserved

10 09 08 07 06 05   6 5 4 3 2 1

A record of cataloging-in-publication data is available from the Library of Congress.
ISBN 0-8130-2849-3

The University Press of Florida is the scholarly publishing agency
for the State University System of Florida, comprising Florida A&M University,
Florida Atlantic University, Florida Gulf Coast University, Florida International University,
Florida State University, University of Central Florida, University of Florida, University
of North Florida, University of South Florida, and University of West Florida.
University Press of Florida
15 Northwest 15th Street
Gainesville, FL 32611-2079
http://www.upf.com

For Kay

CONTENTS

ILLUSTRATIONS

FOREWORD

Historians and writers from Ulrich Bonnell Phillips, C. Vann Woodward, and Howard Zinn to Wilbur J. Cash, William Faulkner, and Lee Smith have underscored the South's distinctiveness. For many persons the South signifies more than a region. For them it represents an idea, an abstraction, even an ideology. For some the South has become an obsession. Since the colonial period, the South has been both connected to and distanced from the rest of North America. Its settlement pattern, its crops, and, most significantly, its commitment to racial slavery earmarked the Old South as different from the rest of the nation. As Woodward noted in 1960, the South has many "burdens." Its defeat in the Civil War and its experiences during and after Reconstruction left an indelible blot on the fabric of southern history. Yet in the twenty-first century, the South seems very much "American"—more like the rest of the country, not some mythic land apart.

Since the 1880s, historians and critics have defined and redefined southern history in innumerable ways. The "Nationalist" historians, the "Dunning School," the "Agrarians," the "Revisionists," the "Post-Revisionists," the Marxists, and, today, all manner of postmodernists have tried to squeeze some contemporary meaning from southern history. Historians and others regularly interpret the region's history and culture in such varied journals and magazines as the *Journal of Southern History, Southern Review, Southern Humanities Review, Southern Living, Southern Exposure,* and *Southern Cultures.* In 1979 the *Encyclopedia of Southern History* appeared, followed ten years later by the *Encyclopedia of Southern Culture.* Both within and beyond the region, there seems to be an insatiable appetite for information on the South and its people.

In fact, no region in America, including New England and the West, has received as much in-depth analysis and reflection as has the American South. Insiders (native southerners) and outsiders (nonsoutherners, including an unusually large number of northern and European specialists on the South) agree that the Southland has a particular weltanschauung, one loaded with irony, pathos, paradox, and racial and class conflict. In some universities southern history long has reigned as a major research specialty. They confer doctorates in the field. Many academic publishers consider "southern studies" a strong part of their lists. Books about the South sell on both sides of the Mason-Dixon line and overseas. Associations and institutions sponsor regular symposia and conferences regionally, nationally, and internationally on the South's past.

In the last century, when the South ranked as "the nation's economic problem No. 1," sociologists dissected the region's pathologies, especially its historic race problem and poverty. Today, social scientists and economists marvel at the "Sun Belt"—its thriving and alluring prosperity (built atop longstanding antiunion sentiment), its daunting skyscrapers, its rapid transit systems, its social and racial progress. Atlanta, the region's bourgeois Mecca, has numerous lesser rivals throughout the former Confederacy—Dallas, New Orleans, Miami, Nashville, Charlotte, Raleigh, and Richmond. Cable television, chain restaurants, New York department stores, "malls" and their accompanying outlet shops—even the *New York Times'* "national edition" (printed in several southern cities and delivered to the doorsteps of thousands of southerners)—dot the southern landscape like the proverbial cotton plants of old.

An appreciation of the South's distinctiveness and its diversity lies at the heart of the University Press of Florida's New Perspectives on the History of the South series. This broadly based series publishes the highest quality new scholarship on the history of the American South. The books cover all aspects and periods of the southern past, with special emphasis on the region's cultural, economic, intellectual, and social history.

Joe A. Mobley's *"War Governor of the South": North Carolina's Zeb Vance in the Confederacy*, the latest volume in the series, looks carefully and critically at the role of Zebulon Baird Vance (1830–1894) as North Carolina's Civil War governor. In 1925 the influential southern historian Frank L. Owsley cited Vance as "a shining example of the governors who neither raised local Confederate troops nor transferred the state troops to the Confederacy." Owsley added: "If a monument is ever erected as a symbolical gravestone over the 'lost cause' it should have engraved upon it . . .

'Died of State Rights.'" Explaining how and why Vance behaved during the war, Mobley clarifies Vance's relationship with the Confederate government and convincingly revises Owsley's states' rights thesis. Mobley, for example, cautions historians not to question Vance's commitment to the Confederacy and its independence. Whereas Owsley faulted Vance for independently supplying North Carolina troops, Mobley interprets the governor's "willingness to accept the responsibility of keeping the state's soldiers well equipped and in the fight" as evidence of both the central Confederate government's inefficiency and Vance's dedication to the cause. Mobley dubs as inaccurate "the persistent Owsley portrait of Vance as the Scrooge of the Confederacy, whose miserly withholding of supplies helped bring about Southern defeat." Answering criticism that Vance fashioned his states' rights policies in response to his war-weary constituents, Mobley writes: "If he was to lead his state in the struggle for Confederate independence, he had to retain the support of a majority of North Carolinians." Mobley also argues that vitriolic exchanges between Vance and Confederate president Jefferson Davis resulted more from their individual personalities than from essential disagreements over Confederate nationalism. Careful reading of the evidence convinces Mobley that "neither Davis nor Vance ever denounced the other as a demagogue, and Davis never openly questioned Vance's loyalty to the cause of a free and independent Confederate States of America."

More than any previous scholar, Mobley links Vance's fears of President Abraham Lincoln's Emancipation Proclamation and the Union's recruitment of black troops to his support of the Confederacy. "In large part," Mobley explains, Vance "was motivated by an absolute belief that, after Lincoln issued his Emancipation Proclamation, the only way slavery would survive was for the Confederacy to achieve its independence. If the Confederate nation collapsed, so too would the South's social and economic system, based on black servitude. Racial warfare might result."

Vance's commitment, then, to white supremacy and states' rights reinforced his devotion to the Confederacy. Readers will find Mobley's deeply researched, well-argued, and gracefully written book an original and significant contribution to southern and Civil War history.

John David Smith
Series Editor

ACKNOWLEDGMENTS

I am indebted to a number of institutions and individuals for their assistance in the completion of this work. I have the good fortune to reside in an area of North Carolina rich in documentary resources related to Civil War governor Zebulon B. Vance and his contemporaries. The helpful repositories include the State Archives, North Carolina Office of Archives and History, Raleigh; the Southern Historical Collection, University of North Carolina Library, Chapel Hill; and the Special Collections, Duke University Library, Durham. I express my appreciation to the staffs of those institutions and to the editors Gordon McKinney and Richard McMurry for the microfilm edition *The Papers of Zebulon Vance*.

The editors of the *North Carolina Historical Review* kindly granted me permission to quote material from my article on Vance that appeared in the October 2000 issue of that journal. Sarah Caroline Thuesen and Martin K. Winchester, once summer interns on the Vance Papers project at the North Carolina Office of Archives and History and now scholars in their own fields, contributed valuable labor and insight in evaluating and transcribing Vance documents. A note of thanks goes to Mary Moulton Barden for allowing me to quote from an unpublished brief autobiographical sketch by Vance that has been owned by her family for generations.

I must extend my gratitude to William C. Harris for reading a portion of the draft and, as always, offering sage advice. As my teacher, mentor, and friend, he ignited in me an enthusiasm for the history of the Civil War and Reconstruction that has never waned. For that I will always be grateful to him. I also owe a special note of thanks to John David Smith, who urged me to complete this study and to offer it to the University Press of Florida for the series New Perspectives on the History of the South. John is the best of scholars and a prodigious worker who, nevertheless, always finds time to encourage his students and friends.

My greatest debt is to my wife, Kathleen B. "Kay" Wyche. She took time from her own busy career to proofread and correct the draft. Her skill and thoroughness saved me from many an editorial pitfall. I thank her for this and all her other acts of kindness over the years. She is the best of editors and the best of companions, and this book is dedicated to her.

INTRODUCTION

Frequently neglected in Civil War historiography is the role of Southern governors in the war effort of the Confederate States of America. Every year, Civil War scholars introduce new material, insight, and interpretation to familiar topics. Generals are assessed and reassessed, revised, denounced, and defended. Battles are reexamined in large monographs that might cover only a day or two of fighting. New hypotheses are offered for the significance and inevitability of battle outcomes. In recent years, the writing of Civil War history has expanded considerably to include such topics as the role of women and blacks, the social upheaval resulting from the conflict, the nature of Confederate nationalism, and the perennial question of just how the South came to lose the war.

Amid all this new scholarship, however, little has been published about the role of the Confederate governors. To be sure, the general role of the Southern states' chief executives has been mentioned in most standard histories of the war and in a number of articles and monographs dealing with specific aspects of the states' relationship with the Confederate government in Richmond. Monographs or biographies have also been written about Joseph E. Brown of Georgia (1939 and 1977), Henry W. Allen of Louisiana (1964), Zebulon B. Vance of North Carolina (1958, 1965, 2004), John Letcher of Virginia (1966), John J. Pettus of Mississippi (1975), and Francis W. Pickens of South Carolina (1986). The only work to evaluate collectively the behavior and contributions of the Confederate governors is *The Confederate Governors* (University of Georgia Press, 1985), edited by W. Buck Yearns. That book is a collection of essays by well-known Civil War scholars, each of whom discusses the war careers of the governors of one Confederate state. The essays provide important analytical glimpses of the Southern states' chief executives, without whose cooperation the Confederate campaign for independence might have come to an end much sooner than it did.[1]

The Confederate government could not have maintained itself and waged war for four long years without the support and cooperation of the state governments. As their states' commanders in chief—a status given to all governors by their state constitutions—the governors were the leaders and, to a large extent, the measure of the support that the Confederate populace gave to the war effort.

Including Kentucky and Missouri, which never seceded but had Confederate governments in exile, twenty-eight governors served in the thirteen Confederate states. Isham Harris served only nominally as governor of Tennessee after Federal troops occupied much of that state in 1862 and Lincoln appointed Andrew Johnson as military governor. With the exception of John Letcher of Virginia, all of those who were serving when their states seceded were secessionists. All but three of the original Confederate governors favored immediate secession when Lincoln was elected president in November 1860.[2]

Among the twenty-eight governors, twenty-five were Democrats prior to secession. Only three—Harris Flanagin of Arkansas, Thomas H. Watts of Alabama, and Zebulon B. Vance of North Carolina—were Whigs. Henry W. Allen of Louisiana, Charles Clark of Mississippi, and Richard Hawes of Kentucky had been Whigs at one time but converted to the Democratic Party as the sectional crisis erupted. John Letcher of Virginia was a Douglas Democrat.[3]

With the possible exception of Joseph E. Brown of Georgia, no other governor in the Confederate States of America has sparked as much historical comment and controversy as Zebulon Baird Vance of North Carolina. Some Civil War scholars and enthusiasts have portrayed and even applauded Vance as a champion of states' rights and a loyal Confederate. Others have condemned him as an antagonist to President Jefferson Davis and an obstructionist to the Confederate cause.

North Carolina writers and historians who were contemporaries of Vance tended to praise him and his performance as wartime governor. Author and friend Cornelia Phillips Spencer, who at Vance's urging published *The Last Ninety Days of the War in North Carolina* in 1866, expressed her unqualified approval of the state's Civil War governor.[4] Writer and editor Mary Bayard Devereux Clarke also portrayed Vance favorably and soon after the war asked him to write his autobiography to be included in a series of biographies and reminiscences that she planned to publish.[5] Enthused with the rhetoric of the Lost Cause movement of the late nineteenth century, historian Stephen B. Weeks, writing in the *Southern Historical Society Papers* in 1896, nominated Vance as the "War Governor of the South."[6] A year later, Vance's postwar law partner, Clement Dowd, published *Life of Zebulon B. Vance.* The book was a compilation of reprinted documents, Dowd's observations, and remembrances of Vance by such prominent North Carolinians as historian and university president Kemp P. Battle and influential educator and politician Charles D. McIver. Dowd praised Vance for his "persistence, tact, and wonderful courage" in defending civil liberties during the war.[7]

Early in the twentieth century, North Carolina's southern patriotic historian Samuel A. Ashe spoke well of all the Tar Heel State's revered leaders, including Vance, in his *History of North Carolina* (two volumes, 1908 and 1929) and his *Biographical History of North Carolina* (eight volumes, 1905 and 1917).[8] Around that same time, a number of professionally trained historians began writing about the history of their native North Carolina and its role in the Civil War. Among them were Robert D. W. Connor (the first national archivist), James G. de Roulhac Hamilton, and William E. Dodd.[9]

Among this group, the only scholar to suggest that Vance was an obstructionist to the Confederate war effort was William E. Dodd, whose complimentary biography of Jefferson Davis in 1907 depicted Vance as a foil to Davis and the North Carolina capital as a "centre of disloyalty." Dodd described Vance as a "shrewd man in conduct and character, the nearest approach to Lincoln the South had produced." According to Dodd, Vance "was the most difficult man Davis had to deal with."[10]

But the most influential of Vance's detractors was the southern historian Frank L. Owsley, who had a significant and lasting impact on how subsequent students of the Civil War would interpret Vance's performance as governor of the war-torn Tar Heel State. In his book *State Rights in the Confederacy*, published in 1925, Owsley attacked Vance with the vengeful enthusiasm of a crusader. He insisted that the South's devotion to states' rights at the expense of Confederate national unity and support was the determining factor in the defeat of the Confederate States of America. He particularly singled out Vance and Governor Joseph E. Brown of Georgia as mavericks of the Confederacy who sabotaged the South's struggle for nationhood by their commitment to state sovereignty and preoccupation with local defense and individual liberties. "There is an old saying that the seeds of death are sown at our birth," declared Owsley in his introduction. "This was true of the southern Confederacy, and the seeds of death were state rights." He maintained that Vance and Brown, as well as other obstructionists such as Alexander Stephens and Robert Toombs, "who could not see the forests for the trees," sowed the seeds of Confederate defeat. He specifically accused Vance of weakening the Confederacy by retaining troops for local defense, impeding Confederate impressment of supplies, hoarding war materials and equipment, thwarting the execution of conscription laws, and opposing laws suspending the writ of habeas corpus. When North Carolinians became discontented with the war, Owsley asserted, "Vance championed the popular discontent and fanned the flames higher."[11]

Albert Burton Moore's *Conscription and Conflict in the Confederacy* appeared a year before the publication of Owsley's book. Nevertheless, Moore too embraced the theme of destructive states' rights, and he painted Vance as a local-minded politician who helped bring down the Confederacy through his opposition to conscription. Of Vance and Brown, Moore declared:

> Controversial in character, anti-Davis in feeling, particularistic by nature and training, supinely self-confident by endowment and because of spectacular rise in life, and unbending States' rightists in principle, they were admirably equipped to torment the souls of the military strategists at Richmond. Their patriotism was essentially local. They could not think consistently in terms of the whole Confederacy. They were simply allies to other States, and often puny allies at that. They stood like divinely ordained sentinels upon the isolated peak of particularistic patriotism, flattering official prerogatives, and uncompromising personal prepossessions, and preached with equal skill two sermons for State protection: one against the devastating swords of the Federal troops, the other against the compressing tendrils of the "insatiable political octopus" at Richmond.[12]

Not every scholar, however, accepted Owsley's condemnation of Vance. In a 1927 review of *State Rights in the Confederacy*, Charles W. Ramsdell took Owsley to task for his accusations about Vance. He asserted that Owsley's evidence did not support his conclusions regarding war disaffection in the Confederacy.[13] In his own book, *Behind the Lines in the Confederacy*, Ramsdell demonstrated how difficult conditions on the home front led many Southerners to become disenchanted with the war.[14]

Although not all the historians who came after *State Rights in the Confederacy* was published embraced Owsley's views about Vance, Owsley's opinions nevertheless influenced for decades how historians interpreted the North Carolina governor's relationship with the Confederate government. As one group of historians wrote in 1986, "The Owsleian state-rights thesis crops up again and again and has had such a pervasive influence that any attempt to assess the ultimate cause for Confederate defeat must deal with Owsley's enormous impact on historiography for the last two generations."[15]

In her *Disloyalty in the Confederacy* (1934), Georgia Lee Tatum attributed the disaffection and disloyalty of many North Carolinians partly to Vance's own resistance to Confederate authority and policy. Tatum observed that the Unionism that Vance endorsed before the war continued to exist among a significant part of the Confederacy's population after the conflict began.[16]

As Thomas J. Pressly noted in *Americans Interpret Their Civil War*, Owsley's thesis also found a following in the 1920s and 1930s among the so-called Southern Vindicators and the Vanderbilt University group known as the Agrarians, of which Owsley was a member. That faction of historians and other intellectuals sought to vilify the North for the Civil War and to attribute the failure of the Confederacy to individuals such as Vance who failed to support the Southern ideal as represented by Jefferson Davis and the Confederate States of America.[17] Even the saintly embodiment of Confederate knighthood, Gen. Robert E. Lee, had to intervene to save the Confederate war effort from the uncooperative Vance. In his monumental four-volume biography of Lee, which appeared in 1934–1936, Douglas Southall Freeman noted that Vance "was on bad terms with the [Confederate] administration." So strained was that relationship on one occasion, he wrote, that the diplomatic Lee "virtually acted for the administration in dealing with the difficult and positive individual, Governor Zebulon Vance of North Carolina."[18]

At around the same time that Freeman was publishing his biography of Lee, however, historian Richard S. Yates effectively challenged Owsley's conclusions about Vance. Yates was the first professional historian to investigate Vance in depth through systematic exploration of the papers of the Civil War governor. In his 1937 article in the *Journal of Southern History* and 1940s articles in the *North Carolina Historical Review*, Yates provided a broader, more detailed perspective of Vance and his leadership during the Civil War. Unlike Owsley, he concluded that Vance was a loyal supporter of the Confederate government. Yates's findings were ultimately published in a small book, *The Confederacy and Zeb Vance*, in 1958.[19]

As a result of the contrasting conclusions of Owsley and Yates, scholars

who wrote after World War II about Vance as a Civil War governor generally walked a thin line of historical interpretation. On the one hand, they
could not separate completely from Owsley's theory about Vance as an
obstructionist. After all, the governor's frequent quarrels with Davis and
the government in Richmond gave credence to Owsley's interpretation.
But on the other hand, they had to acknowledge the support that Vance
had given to the Confederacy, as demonstrated by Yates's research. As a
result, the writings of that generation of historians painted a dual, almost
schizophrenic, portrait of the Tar Heel governor.

In his *The Confederate States of America, 1861–1865*, published in
1950, E. Merton Coulter acknowledges Vance's troubles with Davis, who
often found the North Carolina governor "difficult and ungenerous." Coulter, however, maintains that Vance "was actuated by motives quite different
from those of Brown." Although he does not elaborate on how the motives
of Brown and Vance differed, Coulter implies that Brown had an ambition
to be Confederate president that Vance did not possess. Coulter insists that
despite the Tar Heel governor's frequent resistance to Confederate policies,
"Vance was a determined Confederate, and he never let differences with
Davis obscure the ultimate purpose of all patriots." In fact, "in his own
way, he was as determined as Davis on securing independence for the Confederacy."[20]

J. G. Randall and David Donald in *The Civil War and Reconstruction*,
first published in 1961 and revised in 1969, shared Coulter's view that
Brown and Vance were "the stoutest opponents of the Southern President," but that Brown differed from Vance in that he harbored an ambition to replace Davis as president. Also like Coulter, Randall and Donald
claimed that "Vance never wavered in his loyalty to the Confederacy."[21]
Despite his portrait of Vance as a loyal Confederate, Donald could not completely divorce his own thought from that of Owsley. He continued to
cling to an element of the Owsley thesis when he contributed an essay in
Why the North Won the Civil War (1960), which he edited. In that essay,
Donald theorizes that the Confederacy "died of democracy." To his argument, he adds elements that Owsley did not include, but essentially
Donald substitutes the word "democracy" for "state rights" in his essay.[22]

Clement Eaton also defended the Confederate loyalty of Vance by insisting that the governor's opposition "to the centralized policies of the
Richmond government should be viewed in its true perspective." "Anyone," wrote Eaton in *A History of the Southern Confederacy* in 1954, "who
reads the numerous letters written to Vance, preserved in his correspondence in Raleigh, will perceive the tremendous pressure exerted on him by

the public of his state to act as he did."[23] Among historians, Eaton was perhaps the first to suggest that Vance's struggle to placate the dissatisfied citizens of his state in order keep them in the war might have contributed unfairly to his reputation as an opponent of Confederate policies.

In his biography *Jefferson Davis* (1977), Eaton defends Vance's war record as a Confederate governor. "[U]nlike Brown," Eaton writes, "he loyally supported conscription and the Confederate war effort." Undoubtedly, Eaton concedes, Vance clashed with Davis on certain issues. But "Despite Vance's obstructive tactics, motivated by a provincial concern for his state rather than for the Confederacy, he continued to be loyal to the Confederate cause in his own peculiar way."[24]

Writing from 1954 to 1989, the three most prominent chroniclers of North Carolina history, Albert R. Newsome, Hugh T. Lefler, and William S. Powell, enumerate the many conflicts that Vance had with Confederate officials. But they also agree that the governor's complaints in behalf of his state did not compromise his loyalty to the Confederacy.[25] "Though a caustic critic of Davis and the Confederate government," write Lefler and Newsome, "Governor Vance always urged the state to give support and loyalty to the Confederacy. His policy of 'fight the Yankees and fuss with the Confederates' helped to hold the confidence of the people and keep the state loyal to the unpopular policies of the Confederate government."[26]

In his comprehensive *The Civil War in North Carolina* (1963) and his essay "North Carolina" in *Confederate Governors*, John G. Barrett provides an accurate account of Vance's performance during the war. He ventures no specific opinion about Vance's loyalty to the Confederacy. But he implies that, despite controversy between Vance and Davis, Vance was supportive of the Confederacy's efforts to win its independence. On the matter of desertion, for example, Barrett declares: "Although the governor sympathized with the deserters, he realized they were jeopardizing the Confederate war effort, and he used every imaginable step to return them to their commands." Also according to Barrett, Vance's overwhelming reelection as governor in 1864 proved that "there was no danger, if there ever had been, of North Carolina leaving the Confederacy."[27]

The first and only major biography of Vance appeared in 1965, amid the fervor of the centennial celebration of the Civil War. Titled *Zeb Vance: Champion of Personal Freedom*, Glenn Tucker's book depicts Vance as a true exponent and defender of the rights of individuals but finds no conflict between a commitment to state and personal rights and a loyalty to the Confederate cause. In words reminiscent of Coulter and of Randall and Donald, Tucker writes that at the end of the sectional conflict, when most

Southerners "could observe that the death throes were at hand" for the Confederacy, Vance "was proving almost as unwilling as President Davis to abandon the conflict and acknowledge the end of the Confederacy."[28] The first volume of *The Papers of Zebulon Baird Vance* was also published in the 1960s. In his biographical sketch that prefaces the work, editor and historian Frontis W. Johnston credits Vance with a wisdom and courage that enabled him to achieve a proper balance between defending the personal freedom of his state's citizens and an undying support for Confederate independence. "His career as war governor," writes Johnston, "is more responsible than any other thing for the fact that North Carolina has loved, idolized, and rewarded no other man in her history as she has Zebulon Baird Vance."[29] Both Tucker's biography and Johnston's biographical sketch capably recount events during Vance's Civil War governorship, but at times they border on idealization and sentimentality. Published in 2004, Gordon B. McKinney's *Zeb Vance: North Carolina's Civil War Governor and Gilded Age Political Leader* is a more balanced and analytical biography.

Indeed, recent historians have taken a less emotional approach to Vance —an approach that examines his years as war governor in the context of the larger realm of Confederate political and social history. To Paul D. Escott, in his thoughtful and influential *After Secession: Jefferson Davis and the Failure of Confederate Nationalism* (1978), Vance and Davis were indeed adversaries, and their relationship worsened as the war continued. But Escott notes that Davis's rigid personality was at least partially to blame for that adversarial relationship and that Vance and Brown were not alone among politicians who had difficulties in cooperating with Davis. Like Eaton, Escott acknowledges that as governor Vance had no choice but to address complaints that North Carolinians made about Confederate laws that they considered repressive. He observes that "It was easier . . . for Davis to be stern and unyielding in Richmond than it was for Vance to follow the same course in North Carolina."[30]

In a 1979 article in the *North Carolina Historical Review*, David D. Scarboro, in a manner similar to Yates, downplays the importance of states' rights and emphasizes Vance's cooperation with the Davis government in several instances. Scarboro suggests, however, that Vance's cooperation with the Confederate government was a matter of necessity, not choice. He states that "the reason for the willingness of Governor Vance to cooperate with the Confederacy was his realization that defiance of the Richmond government was a useless exercise."[31]

Much can be learned about Vance's political behavior by examining his campaign for reelection as governor in 1864. In the election of that year, he ran against William W. Holden, who was calling for a peace convention and negotiations to end the war. A skillful analysis of Vance's actions in the election can be found in Marc W. Kruman's *Parties and Politics in North Carolina, 1836–1865* (1983). Kruman maintains that Vance defeated Holden by giving "the electorate what it desired." That is, "he defended the liberties of the state's citizens while demanding that southerners continue their armed struggle for independence."[32] William C. Harris in his *William Woods Holden: Firebrand of North Carolina Politics* (1987) also skillfully analyzes the election. He points out that against the charismatic and aggressive Vance, Holden "found himself increasingly on the defensive" regarding his peace plan. Furthermore, "Holden never understood that his capacity for leadership was also an issue in the election."[33]

The much-debated *Why the South Lost the Civil War* (1986), by Richard E. Beringer, Herman Hattaway, Archer Jones, and William N. Still Jr., continued the theme of Vance's dual approach to politics. According to these co-authors, however, Vance, as a Unionist originally opposed to secession, gave up on the idea of Confederate nationalism as the war wore on but nevertheless urged North Carolinians to fight on to the bitter end. These same writers liberate Vance and Brown from Owsley's accusations of obstruction. They write that "considerable scholarship exists which reveals fundamental flaws in Owsley's thesis." In their book, they strive to "demonstrate meticulously, as even some of Owsley's contemporaries perceived, that Owsley's work lacked good documentation and factual support."[34]

But vestiges of Owsley's thesis about states' rights and Vance have persisted. In his Pulitzer Prize–winning book *Battle Cry of Freedom: The Civil War Era* (1988), James M. McPherson accepts Albert B. Moore's conclusion about Vance's response to conscription and writes that Governors Brown and Vance "interposed state's-rights roadblocks to the southern war effort." He further observes that Vance exhibited "Machiavellian subtlety" in advising Jefferson Davis on peace negotiations.[35]

Two recent biographies of Jefferson Davis also demonstrate the extent to which historians' perceptions of the relationship between Vance and Davis have changed since Dodd's 1907 biography of the Confederate president. William C. Davis's *Jefferson Davis: The Man and His Hour* (1991) refers to the confrontations between Vance and Davis but adds that "Though strained, their relations did not impede their cooperation."[36] William J. Cooper Jr., in *Jefferson Davis, American* (2000), is even more emphatic about Vance and Davis's cooperation in a common cause. He

writes that "Although Vance is usually coupled with Brown as a gubernatorial opponent of Davis's administration, in fact, he was no such thing."
Cooper insists that "Davis took Vance seriously, and exercised considerable
judgement in his dealings with the governor." Furthermore, "The president saw Vance as a stalwart Confederate who could keep his state loyal."[37]

George C. Rable has summed up North Carolina's Civil War governor
as a skilled politician who cleverly and simultaneously straddled both sides
of the political fence—planting one foot firmly in his home state and the
other in the Confederate capital. Rable has "categorized Vance as a political
centrist who mediated between the demands for national unity and preservation of liberty." He maintains that "the governor's often brilliant ma-
neuvering through the treacherous factionalism of North Carolina politics
and his triumphant reelection in 1864 seriously weakened the peace movement and ironically strengthened the Confederate government."[38]

When he ran for federal political office after the war, Vance himself
contributed to his enigmatic reputation as wartime governor by disavow-
ing the acts he performed in support of the Confederacy. Gordon B. Mc-
Kinney, in his article "Zebulon B. Vance and His Reconstruction of the
Civil War" (1998), concludes that although Vance was committed to the
Confederacy during the war, after the conflict he attempted to disassociate
himself from the Confederacy's prolonged and costly effort to win its independence. According to McKinney, Vance later claimed that to whatever
extent he supported the Confederate war effort, "he was merely doing his
duty." Vance was particularly pressed to defend his war record when he ran
successfully against Republican gubernatorial candidate Thomas Settle Jr.
in 1876. McKinney charges that Vance faithfully supported the Davis government in many of its war policies and subsequently, like other Confederate leaders and the Nazis at the end of World War II, would "not face the
full implications of his actions."[39]

Thus, since the end of the Civil War, historians have interpreted Vance's
career as war governor in different ways. Those North Carolina contemporaries writing immediately after the sectional conflict simply praised him
as a leader, a defender of liberty, and a loyal devotee of Southern independence. But later scholars, primarily influenced by Owsley, portrayed the
governor as an old-line Whig and Unionist who reluctantly accepted secession and whose commitment to states' rights and individual liberty kept
him constantly at odds with the Confederate government. Vance's behavior, they argued, undermined the Confederacy's struggle for independence. Subsequently, other historians interpreted Vance as a more complex
figure who cooperated with the Davis government but, as circumstances

within North Carolina dictated, had to keep a watchful eye on the public's concern for states' rights, personal freedom, and peace negotiations. Today's students of the Civil War tend to view Vance as a more complex figure than has been depicted by either his contemporary proponents or his detractors of the Owsley school. Nevertheless, despite revisionism in the recent historiography of the Confederacy, the ghost of Owsley's thesis still haunts the historical image of Vance. And the debate continues over the extent to which the famous Tar Heel governor was or was not a Confederate nationalist, someone who believed unalterably in an independent and sovereign Confederate States of America. Furthermore, as difficult as it is to determine precisely *how* Vance behaved during the Civil War, it is even more difficult to ascertain *why* he behaved as he did. As a consequence, still missing from Civil War historiography is a clear explanation of the motives that led the antisecession governor of North Carolina to cast his fate with the struggle for an independent Confederate States of America. The chapters that follow strive to clarify Vance's relationship with the Confederate government and his motivation for seeking and maintaining that relationship.

The subsequent narrative is based in large part upon the papers of Vance. The largest single collection of Vance papers is found in the State Archives, North Carolina Office of Archives and History, Raleigh. That facility houses three major collections of Vance documents: the Governors Papers, the Governors Letter Books, and Vance's private papers. The State Archives holds additional collections of prominent contemporaries of Vance that contain letters to and from the governor. Other repositories throughout the United States include Vance materials. Among these are the Southern Historical Collection, University of North Carolina Library, Chapel Hill; the Special Collections Department, Duke University Library, Durham; the Manuscript Department, Harvard University Library, Cambridge; and the Manuscript Department, Library of Congress, Washington, D.C. During the Civil War centennial of the 1960s, volume 1 of the letterpress edition of *The Papers of Zebulon Baird Vance*, edited by Frontis W. Johnston, appeared. In 1987, most of the original Vance materials from all known repositories were compiled in a microfilm edition, *The Papers of Zebulon Vance* (Frederick, Md.: University Publications of America, 1987), edited by Gordon B. McKinney and Richard M. McMurry. Then the first letterpress volume was followed by my volume 2 (1995) of *The Papers of Zebulon Baird Vance*.

In this monograph, I have used both the original manuscript sources and the microfilm edition. In all but a few cases, I have worked from the original collections and thus cite documents directly from the holding institutions, most of which are conveniently located in North Carolina. When citing from the microfilm, I specify the original repository of a document and then designate that I drew upon it from McKinney and McMurry's microfilm edition.

In cases where multiple copies of the same document exist, I have used the copy of earliest origin. For example, where the same letter appears in the Governors Papers and in the Governors Letter Books, I rely upon the copy from the Governors Papers, because it is the one of earliest origin. Along these same lines, an explanation of the Governors Letter Books, located in the State Archives, is instructive. During Vance's years as governor, clerks penned into large books copies of many letters that he sent and received. Often, those letter book entries are the only known surviving copies of the correspondence. Soon after the Civil War, Federal troops confiscated the letter books, which had been removed from Raleigh to Greensboro for safekeeping. Union officers shipped the books to the War Department in Washington, D.C. North Carolina's subsequent efforts to recover them proved unsuccessful until 1886, when the federal government agreed to provide the state with certified handwritten copies of the letter books. Then in 1962 the North Carolina Department (now Office) of Archives and History applied for and received the original books.

In this volume, I strive to examine objectively Vance as governor of North Carolina, 1862–1865, and to consider him within the context of the time and place in which he lived. I contend that once he accepted secession, he became a confirmed Confederate nationalist and held that position from the time North Carolina seceded until the end of the war. As a Confederate nationalist, he accepted the expansion of national governmental power in order to achieve Confederate independence. My intention is to evaluate the effectiveness of his leadership as governor of one of the Confederate States of America, without passing personal judgment on his motivation for ultimately supporting disunion. I therefore do not dwell on the fact that his slaveholding and support for the perpetuation of a social and economic system of human bondage are generally deplored today. It is important, of course, to note that Vance believed unequivocally in the legality of slavery and in its desirability as a social and economic system. He and his family owned slaves, and he never expressed any guilt or moral ambiguity about the institution. In fact, at the core of his Confederate nationalism was his firm belief that only if the Confederate States of America survived could the institution of slavery also survive.[40]

1

"MY HAND FELL SLOWLY AND SADLY BY THE SIDE OF A SECESSIONIST"

The journey that brought Zebulon B. Vance to the governor's office in September 1862 had been a short one. At the time he took office, he was only thirty-two years old. Even so, a measure of political experience lay behind him.

Vance was born on May 13, 1830, at a Buncombe County homestead on Reems Creek, about twelve miles north of Asheville in western North Carolina. He was the third child and second son of David and Mira Baird Vance. His ancestors were a blend of Scots-Irish and German. His paternal grandfather, David Vance, had been a Revolutionary War officer, a successful farmer, and a state legislator. His maternal grandfather, Zebulon Baird, for whom he was named, was a large landowner in western North Carolina, a businessman, and a state legislator. Vance's father owned a large tract of land in what was then northern Buncombe County, where he moved with his family shortly after Vance was born.[1] "When I was thrice years old," Vance later recalled, "my father moved from the farm on Reem's Creek and settled on the turnpike road heading down the French Broad Valley, then the principal thoroughfare between the rich and thriving vallies [sic] of Kentucky and Tennessee, and the cotton region of South Carolina. Here until his death he kept an inn and country store, well known to travellers from each of these three states."[2] The site of the Vance property was near the town of Marshall (previously called Lapland) in present-day Madison County, formed in 1851 from Buncombe and Yancey Counties.[3]

David Vance ranked among the elite of Mountain society in terms of land and property. Although he could not boast of the same wealth and slaveholdings as the planter elite of the plantation regions of the South, he was well off compared to most of the inhabitants of western North Carolina and Appalachia. His estate records reveal that he owned twelve slaves at the time of his death in 1844. His landholdings on both sides of the French Broad River amounted to "near two thousand acres including the tavern & adjoining lands occupied by [him] at the time of his death & the store and tavern at the Gate of the Turnpike Road . . . & much steep land in cultivation and a large range of mountain lands only suited for wood & timber."[4]

As a son of a relatively prosperous businessman and landowner, young Zebulon Vance enjoyed certain advantages, not the least of which was a basic education. At around six years of age, he, along with his older brother, Robert Brank Vance, began attending a number of makeshift schools. Then in 1843, his father sent him to Washington College, an academy in east Tennessee, where "after a year's preparation I entered the Freshman class." Vance's father died in January 1844, and he came home to attend the burial in February. Then "in consequence of the embarrassed condition" of his father's estate, "My mother was compelled to remove me from college in February 1845." According to Vance, "I remained at home with my mother, my oldest brother, Robert, having gone into business on his own account, attended to all her business, and made a hand at all field, and house work, until 1849, when I was sent to school for two sessions in the town of Ashville [sic], to Messrs. Lee and Norwood who then had charge of the academy there. The next year my mother moved to Ashville [sic] and I began to study law."[5] Apparently Mira Vance played a large role in Vance's early education. She possessed a five-hundred-volume library left to her by her husband's brother, Dr. Robert Brank Vance, and a number of books that had once belonged to her husband's father. "Notwithstanding her own imperfect education," Vance wrote of her in 1878, "she was extremely literary in her tastes, and fostered this inclination in her children. She was the most correct and impressive reader I ever heard off the stage; and I am satisfied that whatever elocution I have came from her."[6]

Vance began his law studies with Asheville lawyer John W. Woodfin. He was not, however, conscientious in his pursuit of legal learning. Augustus Merrimon—a sober and serious young man and future United States senator and chief justice of the North Carolina Supreme Court also studying law with Woodfin—described Vance as "full of life and fun." Indeed, instead of engaging in his law apprenticeship seriously, the young Vance preferred enjoying himself among the young men who lounged about

Asheville and welcomed his company, humor, and fun-loving nature.[7] Although Asheville was a small town, it was the county seat, and compared to rural life on the French Broad, it offered enough diversion to amuse the pleasure-seeking Vance. The town boasted of two hotels, the Buck and the Eagle, and a number of barrooms. Court days brought socializing and drinking. Tourists also had begun seeking out the Mountain town. "Our village . . . excels any near us in the fashionable amusement of dancing," announced the Asheville *Messenger* in June 1850.[8]

But in 1851, when Vance reached his majority, his mind took a more serious turn, for in that year he met Harriett Newell Espy and began a courtship. Harriett Espy was born in Salisbury, North Carolina, in 1832, the daughter of Presbyterian minister Thomas Espy, formerly of Pennsylvania, and Mary Louisa Tate Espy of Hickory Grove Plantation in Burke County, North Carolina. Both of Harriett's parents died while she was a small child, and she went to live with her half-great-uncle and guardian, Capt. Charles McDowell, a prosperous farmer and legislator of Quaker Meadows in Burke County. Two of McDowell's own daughters had married into the Woodfin family, and it undoubtedly was while Harriett was visiting either John or his brother Nicholas Woodfin in Asheville that Vance made her acquaintance.

Harriett Espy's pious nature and strict upbringing as a daughter of a Presbyterian clergyman stood in marked contrast to Vance's playful outlook, raucous behavior, and risqué jokes and yarns that made him so popular among the young wags with whom he liked to cavort. As one modern student of their relationship has written, "Seldom was there a less assorted pair of lovers. She was cautious, complacent, almost entirely humorless, and religious in a way that would seem fanatical today and must even then have seemed obsessive. He was impetuous, earthy, profane of speech, and untroubled by the least shadow of mystical faith."[9]

Vance's courtship letters to Harriett Espy reveal early his ability and proclivity to choose and bend his words to suit his audience and what it might be expecting to hear from him. On March 15, 1851, he wrote his first letter to Harriett, tactfully asking permission to correspond with her. "The object of this intrusive epistle," he wrote with uncharacteristic humility,

is to beg to be allowed the favour of your correspondence, or at least the privilege of addressing a more full and expressive letter to you than this one—It is asking a considerable favour, I am aware, probably more than you would feel justified in granting, under existing circumstances, but let me say by way of apology for my presumption, that justice to my own feelings demanded that I should run the risk of incuring [sic] your displeasure by making solicitation—I have been led to hope from the candour of your disposition that you [will] deal with me promptly and justly, and therefore trusting that I shall receive an answer at your earliest convenience, and *earnestly* hoping that it will be a favourable one, I take the liberty of subscribing myself with all the Sentiments of due Respect Yours &c Zeb. B. Vance[10]

This inquiry was the first of 121 prenuptial letters that the two sweethearts would write to each other. Much of their courtship, in fact, was carried on by correspondence. In typical antebellum fashion, they began their epistolary romance with formality. Vance's initial letters began with the salutation "Miss Espy," and Harriett's to him, "Mr. Vance." But by November 1851, he was addressing her as "My dearest Harriett," which ultimately would be followed by such greetings as "My dear, dear Harriett," "My Dearest Hattie," or "My Dear Sweet Harriett." In January 1852, Harriett began referring to him as "My Beloved Zebulon," as their letters took on a more intimate nature.[11]

Possibly at least partly because of the influence of Miss Espy, Vance began to consider his future more seriously than previously, and he sought admission to the University of North Carolina at Chapel Hill in 1852. "[F]eeling the incompleteness of my education, and not having means to further it," he later remembered, "I concluded to apply to Ex. Governor [David L.] Swain, President of the University for assistance to spend a year there. Himself a Buncombe man who had risen through similar or greater difficulties, an old friend of the family, I felt confident my application would not be in vain."[12]

Swain wrote to Vance to proceed to Chapel Hill, and he arranged a loan to finance one year as a special student. According to Vance's classmates, Vance arrived at the university wearing "home-made shoes and clothes, about 3 inches between pants and shoes showing his sturdy ankles."[13]

While at the university, Vance never demonstrated brilliance as a scholar. Nor did he abandon entirely his love of jokes, pranks, and a good time. But he did take his studies with a certain amount of seriousness and made acceptable progress. He pursued a partial course of study of university courses and simultaneously studied law with professors, future legislators, and prominent jurists William H. Battle and Samuel F. Phillips. He joined the Phi Gamma Delta fraternity and sharpened his oratorical skill as a member of the student debating organization known as the Dialectic Society.

During his year at Chapel Hill, the young man from the Mountains made a number of acquaintances and friendships that served him well in the coming years. Swain became almost a father figure for Vance and during the Civil War remained a close confidant of the young governor. William H. Battle served as a justice on the North Carolina Supreme Court from 1852 to 1868, and as governor, Vance sought his counsel. At the university he formed a lasting friendship with the Battle family. Kemp P. Battle, son of William H. Battle and future president of the university, saw leadership potential in Vance. The other son, Richard H. Battle, became Vance's wartime secretary. Vance also befriended Cornelia Phillips Spencer, the daughter of his mathematics professor, James Phillips. Shortly after the war, Mrs. Spencer, at Vance's urging, wrote *The Last Ninety Days of the War in North Carolina*. Vance's favorite professor was Dr. Elisha Mitchell, who taught chemistry, geology, and mineralogy. In 1857, Vance would join the search party looking for Mitchell, after the scientist fell down a waterfall and drowned in the pool below while surveying the Black Mountain in western North Carolina. The highest peak of Black Mountain was later named Mount Mitchell in the professor's honor.[14] "I shall never forget the year which I spent at the University," Vance once declared, "and shall always covet it as the most agreeable and profitable portion of my life."[15]

Around Christmas 1852, Vance traveled to Raleigh, where he received from the state supreme court his license to practice law in the county courts of pleas and quarter sessions. He returned to Asheville, and when the office of Buncombe County solicitor became vacant in the spring, he ran for that office and won, defeating his former fellow law pupil, Augustus S. Merrimon. As solicitor, Vance prosecuted criminal cases and advised the justices of the Buncombe County Court of Pleas and Quarter Sessions. In August 1853, he married Harriett Espy at Quaker Meadows. They moved to Asheville and used her dowry to buy a five-acre lot and build a house. Two years later, Harriett gave birth to a child whom they named Espy, but the infant soon died. The couple subsequently would have four other sons. In the same year of his marriage, Vance received his license to practice in superior court, and he began riding the circuit in the Seventh Judicial District, appearing in both the lower county and superior courts.[16]

Vance's performance as a lawyer was not outstanding or heartfelt. Apparently by the mid-1850s, his real interest had turned to politics. A lack of enthusiasm for the practice of law, an impetuous nature, and a quick temper inhibited his success on the court circuit. On one occasion, he even resorted to fisticuffs with another attorney outside the Buncombe County

Courthouse. Nevertheless, he persisted in riding the circuit for five years, and the associations he made helped to fuel his political ambition. Gatherings on court days enabled him to mingle with sizable crowds and win the support of potential Mountain voters who were swayed by his rough humor, clever quips, and outgoing, down-home personality. Vance would later refer to "the rough and unpolished ways which I so early affected as stepping stones to popularity among a rude mountain people."[17]

In April 1854, Vance announced his candidacy for the state House of Commons. Although still a young man at twenty-four, he already had formed a firm loyalty to the Whig Party. "I was raised in the Whig faith, and taught to revere the names of Clay, Webster, and other great leaders of the party," he proclaimed. "My father was not only a Whig but a Federalist also, and was a life-long subscriber to the *National Intelligencer*, in whose dignified and Statesman-like columns I learned to value the Federal Union, and to admire conservatism."[18]

In southern politics prior to the 1850s, both the Whig and Democratic Parties had portrayed themselves as defenders of southern rights and protectors of slavery, as well as the Union. But when the Mexican War (1846–1848) introduced the question of the extension of slavery into the new territories acquired by the United States in the war, the national Whig Party began to disintegrate. The Compromise of 1850, spearheaded by the leading Whigs Henry Clay and Daniel Webster, temporarily settled the issue of slavery in the new territories. But in 1854, with Congress's adoption of Democrat Stephen A. Douglas's Kansas-Nebraska Bill and the concept of popular sovereignty to settle the territorial slavery question, the Whig Party dissolved in the Lower South, most of the border states, and the North. Northern Whigs joined the new Republican Party—established in 1854 to oppose the extension of slavery into the territories—or the American, or Know-Nothing, Party, which became dominated by former Whigs. But in North Carolina the Whig Party remained intact for a time. As historian Marc W. Kruman has written, "Only after it became clear that the national party had disintegrated and the new American party had become well established did most Whigs abandon their old party banner for the American party." When that change transpired, Vance became a member of the American Party, and he remained committed to the old Whig principles of Unionism and conservatism.[19]

In the legislative election of 1854, Vance announced his candidacy "as a regular built, old fashioned Whig." Opposing him for the House seat was Daniel Reynolds, also a Whig, but with a different political position on the question of slavery in the territories. Vance embraced his party's endorsement of the Compromise of 1850. But Reynolds advocated the Kansas-Nebraska Bill, supported by the Democratic slaveholders who increasingly grew more alarmed by the antislavery activities of northern abolitionists. Vance later described this disagreement that was dividing his political party and his state: "The Congressional District in which I lived had been intensely Whig and Union, but of late years so much agitation had been kept up on the question of Slavery, and so much alarm excited about Northern aggression on that institution, that my section, in common with the whole State, had begun to be Democratic on the ground that the Whig party was not friendly to the Negro system." He maintained that because he "boldly took ground against this element," he "was triumphantly elected" in 1854. "Even at that early day," he noted, "I thought I saw the downfall of Slavery in disunion, and that the Friends of the Union were the true friends of Slavery."[20]

In the 1854 legislative election, Vance carried nine of the eleven Buncombe County precincts and defeated Reynolds by an overall vote of 688 to 579. In the Democratic-controlled General Assembly, he received only minor committee appointments. The possible exception was the education committee, on which he worked unsuccessfully to help western North Carolina by instituting the distribution of common school funds according to white population in place of the existing system based on the federally designated population. He also supported a bill to promote railroad development in western North Carolina.[21]

Opposed to rhetoric or measures that might resound of disunion, Representative Vance voted to table a resolution that endorsed the Kansas-Nebraska Bill and that also called for the legislature to convene to consider secession if the United States government failed to enforce the Fugitive Slave Law or did not adequately protect the constitutional right of slavery. The motion was somehow lost, and the state lawmakers passed another motion to approve "heartily . . . the course by the Senator and Representatives from their state who supported said [Kansas-Nebraska] bill as it was finally passed." Vance voted against the motion, which nevertheless passed by a vote of 72 to 34.

When the General Assembly adjourned in 1855, the Whig Party for all practical purposes had dissolved in North Carolina. As a newly elected representative, Vance had not played a large part in the assembly's proceedings. But he—unlike some former Whigs, such as Congressman Thomas L. Clingman, also from Buncombe County—had not abandoned his old-line Whig commitment to the Union and joined the Democrats. In the 1854 legislative race, Vance had opposed Clingman's election to the United

States Senate, and Reynolds had supported Clingman. While in the legislature, Vance made clear his position regarding the growing sectional crisis over the issue of slavery in the territories. He opposed the Kansas-Nebraska Act and emphatically maintained that secession would be a fatal mistake and that only by remaining in the Union could the southern states hope to preserve slavery. He would cling to that position until the firing upon Fort Sumter and Lincoln's call for troops would force him to make perhaps the most important decision of his political career.[22]

Returning to Asheville with a burning ambition for politics, Vance set about promoting his political future. Although he had not been influential during his term in the legislature, he had made contact with a number of the state's most important politicians. He immediately purchased a half interest in the *Asheville Spectator* and, along with co-editor John D. Hyman, began attacking Democrats with the slogan "We join ourselves to no party that does not carry the flag and keep step to the music of the Union." Vance resigned as co-editor of the *Spectator* after a year, although the paper would continue to promote him and the American Party in the west.[23] In 1855, the volatile Vance narrowly avoided a duel with his cousin James S. T. Baird, after criticizing Baird for abandoning the American Party for the Democrats and presumably referring to him as "a damned liar."[24]

In 1856, Vance was again running for office, this time for the state Senate as the nominee of the American Party. Democrat David Coleman, a popular figure in Buncombe County, opposed him. The two candidates engaged in a number of debates pertaining mostly to the issue of free suffrage to allow the poorer classes to vote in the election of state senators. Vance and many western Whigs supported free suffrage, and Democrats and eastern Whigs opposed it. The popular and politically experienced Coleman defeated Vance.[25]

By the following year, however, Vance was back in the political arena, running against Democrat Thomas L. Clingman for a seat in Congress. The Eighth, or "Mountain," Congressional District had supported Clingman since he had bolted the Whig Party for the Democratic Party in 1853. The American Party was weakening, and despite the *Asheville Spectator*'s efforts to rally support for Vance, the popular Clingman won the election with a large majority. "I am completely cut off from advancement," a despondent Vance declared, as he returned to his law practice and joined the search for his old professor Elisha Mitchell.[26]

But his hiatus from politics was short-lived. When Clingman accepted an appointment to fill the unexpired term of Democrat Asa Biggs in the United States Senate in 1858, his seat in United States House became vacant. Vance immediately challenged the Democratic politician William Waightstill Avery for the congressional position. In his first really effective and well-organized campaign, Vance used his speaking and debating skill to great advantage and revived support from the old Whig faction. He learned how much his heated stump rhetoric and bawdy jokes appealed to North Carolina voters. That style of campaigning would serve him well for the rest of his political career. He debated Avery throughout the western counties and won the election with a large majority.[27]

His accomplishments as congressman, however, were not significant. He introduced no noteworthy legislation, but he did enjoy the pleasures of life in the nation's capital. He made his first speech on the floor of the House on February 9, 1859, and expressed his views on the tariff, public lands, and federal pensions. He favored raising the tariff rate to produce more revenue, opposed the Homestead Bill, and supported pensions only for the veterans of the War of 1812.[28] One congressman who served on a committee with Vance described him as "strong in integrity, wondrous in vitality" and "a strict Federalist after an intense Union pattern. His voice was never heard in Washington for disunion."[29]

Vance's reelection to Congress in 1859 almost resulted in violence between him and his Democratic opponent, David Coleman. Having lost by a margin of 1,695 votes, a resentful and sulking Coleman wrote a letter to Vance complaining about his campaign rhetoric and tactics. Vance's quick temper flared, other vitriolic letters passed, and the two candidates agreed to a duel. Fortunately, intervention by friends prevented a physical clash between the two politicians.[30]

When Vance entered his second term in Congress, the sectional conflict over slavery was intensifying. Again, as a new and the youngest representative, he did not play a large role in debates or new legislation. As one of twenty-seven members from the American Party, he generally voted with that party, although he did vote for six Democrats in the protracted struggle to elect a Speaker. He had to endure some criticism in North Carolina, however, because his ultimate refusal to support a Democrat for Speaker supposedly helped elect a Republican.[31] As he had during his congressional campaigns, Vance continued to espouse in the House his conviction that it was in the best interest of North Carolina and the other southern states to remain in the Union despite the threat posed by northern abolitionists, which to southerners grew more ominous following John Brown's raid in October 1859. Vance later insisted that "In all these canvasses, which gave me considerable State reputation with my party friends, and in my subsequent service in Congress, I took the boldest and most decided ground in favour of the Union, regarding it, not as paramount *to all* the other issues affecting the rights and institutions of the South, but as the surest *and only* means of *preserving* those rights and institutions."[32] Of course, in Vance's mind, foremost among the "institutions of the South" to which he alluded was the institution of slavery.

As the presidential election of 1860 approached, the mood of sectional discord increased in Congress and throughout the nation. "In Congress," Vance recalled, "the debates became fierce and furious; personal altercations and violence were frequent."[33] In its attempt to select a candidate, the Democratic Party divided over the issue of the future of slavery. Southern Democrats demanded that the party and its candidate resolve to protect slavery in the territories. Northern members resisted such a platform, and the proslavery delegates walked out. Northern and some moderate southern Democrats nominated Stephen A. Douglas on a "popular sovereignty" platform. Those southerners who bolted the party selected as their candidate John C. Breckinridge of Kentucky on a plank of support for slavery in the territories. The Republican Party, which opposed slavery in the territories, nominated as its candidate Abraham Lincoln. With the proslavery fire-eaters of South Carolina in the lead, a number of southern states vowed that if Lincoln were elected, they would secede from the Union. A contingent of old Whigs and members of the American Party formed the Constitutional Union Party and nominated John Bell of Tennessee. That party pledged to preserve the Union and work through compromise to resolve the issues of slavery and of threatened secession. Vance attended the Baltimore convention that formed the Constitutional Union Party, and he began to work earnestly in behalf of its nominee.[34]

During the recess of Congress in the autumn of 1860, Vance returned to North Carolina and "took the stump for the John Bell ticket." He "canvassed all of Western North Carolina, and a portion of Tennessee, distributed documents, and did every thing in my power to secure the success of Union principles."[35] Such efforts by Unionists throughout North Carolina almost carried the state's vote for Bell, who lost to Breckinridge by a small margin. Breckinridge received 48,539 votes to Bell's 44,990. Douglas won 2,701 votes. But the nation elected Lincoln to the presidency. (He had not been on the ballot in the South.) As it had promised if Lincoln were elected, South Carolina's legislature passed a bill on November 10 authorizing the election of delegates and the calling of a secession convention on December 17. By early December, six other southern states had passed bills calling for conventions to consider secession.[36]

On his way back to Washington, Vance stopped at Raleigh, where the legislature was then in session. He delivered two speeches in favor of the Union, and met with a group of legislators who assured him that "a large majority of the State were opposed to secession." Vance and the like-minded lawmakers agreed that the Tar Heel State's best interest lay in remaining a part of the United States. But they also concurred that should the Federal government attempt to coerce a southern state back into the Union by military action, "North Carolina would be forced against her judgement to take sides with the cotton States." Vance departed Raleigh with the hope that through "general consultation of all slave states, and the imposition of terms that no single state should be permitted by separation to force the others into revolution."[37]

Back in Congress, he wrote to legislator William W. Dickson on December 11 that he had met with Kentucky senator John J. Crittenden "& other friends" who were working for sectional compromise. Crittenden "is of the opinion," wrote Vance, "that the only earthly chance to save the Union is to *gain time*." Agreeing with Crittenden, he continued unfolding for Dickson his own view of the crisis facing the nation:

> The whole southern mind is inflamed to the highest pitch and the leaders in the disunion move are scorning every suggestion of compromise and rushing everything with ruinous and indecent haste that would seem to imply that they were absolute fools. . . . [T]hey are "precipitating" the people into a revolution without giving them time to think. *They fear lest the people shall think*; hence the hasty action of S. Carolina, Georgia, & the other States in calling conventions & giving so short a time for the election of delegates—But the people *must* think, and when they begin to think and hear the matter properly discussed they will consider long and soberly before they tear down this noble fabric and invite anarchy and confusion, carnage, civil war, and financial ruin with the breathless hurry of men flying from a pestilence—If we can gain time we get the Advantage of this sober second thought, and we also get the advantage of the developments in Congress which I hope may be favorable.

Vance persisted in his belief that compromise to thwart secession was still possible. Even if North Carolina and other southern states should ultimately decide to secede, "a few months" of delay would make no difference. "Fear of Lincoln when he comes into office is perfect humbuggery," he lectured Dickson, "and those that urge it know it to be so."[38]

In the meantime, the secession-minded members of the North Carolina legislature, led by Gov. John W. Ellis, had proposed a bill calling for a convention to consider secession. Despite his opposition to secession, Vance favored such a convention because he believed that Unionists would dominate it and prevent separation from the United States.[39] "A convention," he maintained, "would also have a good effect in hastening the North into such action, if any, as it intends ultimately adopting for a settlement. For when North Carolina gives away, they in the North almost look upon the sheet-anchor of conservatism as gone."[40] The Tar Heel legislature, however, did not pass until the end of January a bill authorizing a popular vote to determine whether or not to call a convention.[41]

South Carolina, on the other hand, convened its convention on December 17, and three days later its delegates unanimously voted to secede from the United States. In an effort to prevent the secession of the other southern states, Senator Crittenden brought before Congress the compromise developed by his committee. Among other measures, the compromise provided for the constitutional protection of slavery in territories south of the 36-degree 30-minute latitude line. But both houses of Congress rejected the compromise.[42] "Now what?" asked Vance. "The Union is dissolved of course. S.C. is already gone and I make not a doubt but every Gulf State will be with her by 4th March. Must N.C. and the border states go with them is our question?"[43] Vance's prediction was correct, for by the first of February 1861, five additional states from the Lower South—Mississippi, Florida, Alabama, Georgia, and Louisiana—had called conventions and seceded. Texas would become the seventh seceded state after its voters approved secession in a popular referendum at the end of February. At the urging of the Virginia legislature, a peace convention met in Washington on February 4. It included representatives from the North, the border states, and the South, but they failed to reach an agreement that would save the Union.

On the same day that the peace convention met in Washington, the delegates from the six seceded states (Texas delegates arrived later) met in Montgomery, Alabama, to establish a Confederate States of America. They worked fast to create a separate government before Lincoln was inaugurated as president of the United States in March. In a short time, this Confederate Congress adopted a provisional constitution, elected Jefferson Davis and Alexander Stephens as provisional president and vice-president, authorized a treasury, and declared the open navigation of the Mississippi River. The congress also organized the machinery of a government, made preparations for war, and adopted a national flag. In May the Confederate government would move its capital to Richmond, Virginia.[44]

But North Carolina—along with the southern states of Virginia, Tennessee, and Arkansas—remained in the United States. The slaveholding border states of Kentucky, Maryland, Delaware, and Missouri also remained and would never secede. Along with their sister states of the Upper South, many North Carolinians, including Vance, persisted in their hope for some sort of agreement or compromise that would reconcile sectional difficulties and bind the United States back together. They continued to advocate a "watch and wait" policy toward Lincoln's election. Members of North Carolina's pro-Union political party (most of whom had been supporters of the Constitutional Union Party) became known as Conservatives. Those North Carolinians who leaned toward secession (mostly former Democrats) made up the ranks of the state's Southern Rights Party. When the election for the convention took place at the end of February, North Carolinians voted against holding a convention by a slim margin of 661 votes. "But," as historian William C. Harris has noted, "because many conservative leaders, including delegate candidates, had supported the convention, the vote was not a true indicator of Unionist strength." As previously mentioned, Vance was among those Conservatives who favored the convention, because he believed that Unionists would dominate and vote down secession.

With the rejection of a secession convention, North Carolina's position in regard to the Union depended upon whether or not Lincoln would use military force to coerce the seceded Southern states back into the United States. To Vance and other Conservatives, the disagreement over slavery could, as it had in the past, still be reconciled.[45] Only military hostilities between the new Confederate States and the Federal government could tip the balance and tumble North Carolina into the secessionist camp. Such a clash would not be long in coming.

But in the interim, Vance returned to his home state from Congress to campaign for reelection. "I immediately took the stump for re-election," he remarked, "and urged every argument in favor of deliberations giving the people earnest assurances that Mr. Lincoln would not use force against the seceding states, but would exhaust every effort for conciliation." While campaigning in Madison County, Vance received word that on April 13 South Carolina troops, commanded by Confederate general P. G. T. Beauregard, had fired on Fort Sumter in Charleston. The attack was in response to Lincoln's effort to resupply the Federal fort, commanded by Maj. Robert Anderson. Two days later Fort Sumter's garrison surrendered. Lincoln then issued a call to the states for 75,000 troops to suppress the rebellion. Years after the Civil War, Vance would recall—perhaps with some characteristic dramatization—his reaction when news reached him of Fort Sumter's fall and Lincoln's call for troops:

> I was addressing a large and excited crowd, large numbers of whom were armed, and literally had my arm extended upward in pleading for peace and the union of our fathers, when the telegraphic news was announced of the firing on Sumter and [the] President's call for seventy-five thousand volunteers. When my hand came down from that impassioned gesticulation, it fell slowly and sadly by the side of a Secessionist. I immediately, with altered voice and manner, called upon the assembled multitude to volunteer, not to fight against but for South Carolina. I said: If war must come I preferred to be with my own people. If we had to shed blood I preferred to shed Northern rather than Southern blood. If we had to slay I had rather slay strangers than my own kindred and neighbors; and that it was better, whether right or wrong, that communities and States should go together and face the horrors of war in a body—sharing a common fate rather than endure the unspeakable calamities of internecine strife.[46]

With Lincoln's call for troops, Vance believed that he saw an immediate swing in the mood of North Carolinians. "The effect upon our people," he observed, "was magical; never perhaps in all time did a whole people spring to arms with swifter alacrity, with one accord and without persuasion [sic], from mountain top to tide-water. The very pressure with which the Union leaders had held back public sentiment lent double force to the fearful rebound when all their hopes and assurance were at once refuted by the President's direct requisition upon us for troops to slay Southern men and burn Southern cities."[47]

Governor Ellis responded to the United States War Department's request for troops by answering: "You can get no troops from North Carolina." He called the General Assembly in special session to authorize a state secession convention, and he ordered the seizure of Federal property, including the mint at Charlotte, the arsenal at Fayetteville, and several forts on the coast. He began preparing the state for war by providing for troops and funds. On May 1, the legislature called for an election of delegates to assemble in Raleigh to take up the matter of secession. Elected on May 13, the delegates met in the capital on May 17, and on May 20 they passed an ordinance of secession and ratified the provisional constitution of the Confederacy.[48]

Having been swept up in his state's decision to leave the Union and cast its fate with the Confederate States of America, Vance was faced with deciding his own future course of action. "What was it my duty to do?" he asked. With the call for troops by both sides, there was sure to be some further military action, although at this point no one could be sure how much fighting would occur. Yet, men were rushing to join volunteer companies to win Southern independence and perhaps to secure a share of glory before the war ended. Furthermore, a war record was always an asset to an ambitious politician's career. Some friends and associates urged Vance to campaign for the new Confederate Congress.[49]

But Vance decided to join the many volunteers who were forming military companies throughout the Tar Heel State. He joined a Buncombe County company known as the Rough and Ready Guards and was soon elected captain. In June 1861 he and his company traveled to Virginia, where they became Company F, Fourteenth Regiment North Carolina Troops. Although he had no military training and had experienced no combat, Vance soon was appointed colonel of the Twenty-sixth Regiment, and he returned to North Carolina in August to take command. As one authority on that regiment, Rod Gragg, has written, "so unsoldierly did he appear when he joined the Twenty-sixth—attired in civilian garb and sporting shoulder-length hair—that he was at first mistaken for a chaplain."[50] Despite his exposure to politics and society in Raleigh and Washington, Vance still had a rough, unkempt appearance in 1861. A photograph made of him in the following year shows a dark, almost sinister countenance, with untrimmed hair and mustache. As a boy, Vance had broken his leg, which did not heal properly. As a result, one leg was shorter than the other, which gave him an ambling gait that was only partially rectified by wearing a thick heel on the shorter leg. But the colonel stood straight and erect at a height of six feet. He weighed well over two hundred pounds, and his love of food and drink would mean a continued weight gain. In later years, a more flattering and shorter hairstyle, a trimmed mustache, and more attention to his appearance in general gave Vance a dignified, statesman-like look.[51]

The Twenty-sixth Regiment was organized on August 27, 1861, at Camp Carolina, just west of Raleigh. The troops of the Mountain and Piedmont counties who formed the regiment had been training under the demanding young drillmaster Maj. Henry K. Burgwyn Jr., who recently had been a student at Virginia Military Institute. Upon being organized into a regiment, the men of the Twenty-sixth elected Burgwyn as their lieutenant colonel, second in command to Vance. Because the young Burgwyn was a strict disciplinarian who worked hard at drilling his men, the soldiers preferred the more fun-loving and less martial Vance. Although Vance commanded the regiment officially, in reality Burgwyn bore most of the burden in preparing and leading the troops.

On the day after the Twenty-sixth was organized, it received orders to move to the North Carolina coast. A Federal expedition, led by Gen. Benjamin F. Butler, had recently captured Cape Hatteras on the Outer Banks. The Federals posed a threat to the port of Beaufort, near Morehead City. Vance's regiment camped at Fort Macon, which stood across the inlet from the village of Beaufort and had been among the United States forts earlier seized by North Carolina. At Fort Macon, Vance joined his regiment for the first time and took command.[52]

In February 1862, a Federal amphibious expedition led by Gen. Ambrose E. Burnside captured Roanoke Island and began using it as a base for operations to seize other North Carolina ports. In March, Burnside's troops crossed Pamlico Sound and launched an attack on New Bern, an important railroad junction and river port on the mainland. Vance's regiment received orders to move to New Bern to join the rest of a Confederate force under the command of Gen. Lawrence O'Bryan Branch in defense of that town. On March 13, Burnside landed his troops on the banks of the Neuse River below New Bern and began moving on its defenses. The Twenty-sixth Regiment was on the extreme right of the Confederate line. In the ensuing battle, the Federals quickly breached a weak point between Vance's left flank and a brick kiln located along the Atlantic and North Carolina Railroad. Forced to retreat along with other regiments, the Twenty-sixth, under the calm direction of Burgwyn, fought a successful withdrawal for almost an hour. In order to escape capture, however, the regiment had to retreat across Brice Creek in its rear. While attempting to cross the creek, Vance tumbled from his horse and almost drowned. Only the quick action of some of his men on the bank saved him. Resourcefully procuring boats and exercising discipline over the men clambering into them, Burgwyn was largely responsible for getting the Twenty-sixth across the creek. He was the last man to cross. Once on the other side, the regiment fled inland to the town of Kinston, where it rendezvoused with other regiments to form a defense in the event the Union troops attempted to pursue beyond New Bern.[53]

At Kinston Vance's regiment came under the command of Gen. Samuel G. French, who had replaced Branch. French soon was transferred to Virginia, and command of the brigade fell to Gen. Robert Ransom Jr. While his men drilled, Vance made a public appeal for uniforms and equipment for his troops. He also called for volunteers to replace those men lost at New Bern. A number of recruits answered his call, including one undetected female, Malinda (alias Sam) Blalock. She served until she announced her gender in order to be released from duty along with her husband, Mc-Kesson Blalock, who had received a discharge by deceiving medical officers with a poison ivy rash. The Twenty-sixth Regiment reorganized to include only volunteers who enlisted to serve until the end of the war. The reorganized regiment reelected Vance and Burgwyn as colonel and lieutenant colonel. The Confederate War Department, however, rejected Vance's ambitious plans to form a legion under his command.

In June 1862, Ransom's brigade departed North Carolina to join Robert E. Lee's Army of Northern Virginia defending Richmond against assault by Gen. George B. McClellan's Army of the Potomac in the Seven Days campaign. On July 1, 1862, Ransom's brigade, including the Twenty-sixth Regiment, participated in the bloody Battle of Malvern Hill, in which McClellan's defenders repelled Lee's assault with devastating effect. As at New Bern, it was Burgwyn, not Vance, who displayed the most ability and leadership. The Twenty-sixth suffered six dead, forty wounded, and twenty-five missing. Vance reported that his troops "acted gloriously," although he considered the Confederate attack "murderous and ill-advised." Within weeks after Malvern Hill and the conclusion of the Seven Days campaign, Vance left his regiment. He had been elected governor of North Carolina.[54]

While Vance was serving in the army, political dissension had grown in North Carolina. Many North Carolinians had become increasingly dissatisfied with the Davis administration's conduct of the war. The Federal army's invasion and occupation of much of the coastal region and the constant threat of raids into the interior of the state from that area resulted in much criticism of the Confederate War Department. Governor Ellis had died in July 1861, and the successor to serve out his term, Henry T. Clark, also suffered blame for the Union invasion. The Conscription Act of April 16, 1862, which drafted into military service men of ages eighteen to thirty-five, also rankled Tar Heels. The lower class particularly resented the law's provision allowing the hiring of substitutes, which favored the wealthy. By the summer of 1862, the initial patriotic fervor that had impelled men to rush to join the army had begun to diminish, and the pinch of home-front shortages was starting to be felt.[55]

As the state divided over the extent to which its citizens should support or resist the Confederate government, the prosecessionists and members of the 1860 Southern Rights Party, mostly prewar Democrats, formed the Confederate Party and rallied behind their gubernatorial candidate, William Johnston. Johnston was a railroad executive and former state commissary general from Mecklenburg County (born in Lincoln County). The

Conservative Party, mostly former Whigs and Constitutional Unionists—led by William W. Holden, editor of the Raleigh *North Carolina Standard*—looked about for a candidate to oppose Johnston. At the urging of Holden and the influential editor of the *Fayetteville Observer*, Edward J. Hale, the Conservatives ultimately selected Vance as their candidate. With his stump-speaking style of campaigning and colorful personality, he had proven himself popular with the voters before the war and then with the North Carolina troops. In general, the Confederate Party supported the Davis government and such Confederate policies as conscription that might help win the war and independence. On the other side, the Conservatives, for the most part, questioned the effectiveness of the Davis administration and the legality of its policies, which seemed to them to defy the concept of state and individual rights.[56]

During the election for governor, Vance remained with his regiment, and neither he nor Johnston openly campaigned. The debate over their qualifications and their position on the issues facing the voters was waged in the state's newspapers, which were about evenly divided in the numbers that supported each candidate. The major charge levied against Vance by the Confederate Party newspapers was that he was not supportive of the Confederate cause, including the Conscription Act. The Conservatives denounced Johnston as an original secessionist, claiming that such secessionists in the Confederate and state governments were responsible for poor progress in winning or ending the war, growing inflation, lack of support for soldiers and their families, and conscription.[57]

As it awaited the final election returns, the *Spirit of the Age* in Raleigh announced that "Either Colonel Vance or Col. Johnston would make a worthy, competent patriotic governor—and those who have vilified either, for party purposes, will now admit the fact." The newspaper implied that Vance, despite his Unionism, would defend the Confederate cause with the same vigor as Johnston. "Let whomever be returned as Governor and legislators, if our common enemy believe that their election is any evidence of sympathy for the old Union, or indication of disposition to cease the struggle for Southern independence and Southern nationality, the sequel will prove how egregiously they have been deceived: North Carolina is as true to the Southern Confederacy as the needle to the pole, and she will never give up the struggle till victory is ours, final and complete."[58] A Caswell County editor also defended Vance against charges of Union sympathy. He lectured his readers that the press opposing Vance's election was not the voice of the majority of the population, and that "the Yankees . . . are most outrageously mistaken if they infer from the tone of the press in opposition to Colonel Vance that his supporters are Union sympathizers,

1. Zebulon B. Vance at the time of his inauguration as governor of North Carolina in 1862. North Carolina Office of Archives and History, Raleigh.

or that one of his supporters would not shoot a live Yankee as quick as the quickest of Mr. Johnston's supporters."[59]

In Vance's home county of Buncombe, however, the *Asheville News* supported Johnston and denounced Vance's supporters for attempting to discredit the Confederate Party candidate. "We are informed on good authority," asserted the editor, "that the report is industriously circulated in the various military camps, by Mr. Vance's friends and the Standard's special strickers [sic], that Mr. Johnston is a native of South Carolina. Numerous other false statements are made concerning him—all for party purposes." The *News* particularly vented its anger at the *Standard*: "This venal sheet says we have charged all the old Union men of this State with being traitors. This is a falsehood, and we defy the Standard . . . to produce the proof, or stand convicted before the public as the basest caluminator [sic] and most infamous liar in the state!"[60] The Charlotte *Daily Bulletin* also noted the preference of the Queen City's voters for Johnston over Vance.[61]

North Carolina troops cast their votes on July 28 and civilians on August 4. Vance won the election by a large majority, receiving 72.7 percent

2. Vance delivered his first inaugural address from the west side of the State Capitol in Raleigh. North Carolina Office of Archives and History, Raleigh.

of the combined vote. He received 65.8 percent of the army vote and carried all but twelve of the state's counties. According to Marc Kruman, "By far the largest margin of victory in any gubernatorial election to that date, it represented a dramatic popular repudiation of the Democratic leadership that had controlled the state for more than a decade." In the election, Conservatives also secured a large majority of seats in the General Assembly and replaced Democratic officeholders, including judges and solicitors, with members of their own party. They elected former Whig governor and United States secretary of the navy William A. Graham to the Confederate Senate and former Whig politician Jonathan Worth as state treasurer. They rewarded Holden with the position of state printer.[62]

Vance was inaugurated as governor of North Carolina on September 8, 1862. For the morning ceremony, a crowd gathered on the square at the State Capitol. The Johnny Reb Band from Vance's own Twenty-sixth Regiment North Carolina Troops had arrived in Raleigh two days earlier and serenaded the capital city with martial airs and other tunes. On inauguration day, the band marched from the Yarborough House Hotel to Capitol Square, where it played for the first time publicly "Governor Vance's Inauguration March," composed for the event by Edward Leinbach, brother of Julius Augustus Leinbach, regimental band musician and diarist.[63]

Vance spoke to the crowd from a platform on the west side of the Capitol. He delivered a brief history of the events that led to North Carolina's reluctant secession from the Union. He reminded those gathered below that "our separation from the government of the United States . . . was not a whim or sudden freak but the deliberate judgement of our people. Any other course would have involved the deepest degradation, the vilest dishonor, and the direst calamity." He professed that he was under no illusions about the terrible conflict that secession had wrought. "We also accepted with the act," he told his listeners, "all of its inevitable consequences, a long and bloody war. We were not deceived by the idea of a 'peaceable secession' or by vain and unmanly hopes of foreign protection." But having joined the other Confederate states, "we have but the one, great and all absorbing theme. The war which we are fighting for our liberties and independence, is indeed the sea which will receive our every stream of thought." To secure Confederate independence would require, he insisted, the loyalty and support of all North Carolinians, united in a common cause. "One of the most vital elements of our success is harmony," he continued. "On this great issue of existence itself, let there, I pray you, be no dissenting voice in our borders. Let the names and watchwords which divide us, divide us no more forever. Let a new order of things take place, and while the contest lasts, at least, let us see nothing, hear nothing, know nothing but our country and its suffering." If anyone had reservations about fighting against the Yankees' invasion of his homeland, "let him see the burning homes and desolated fields which mark the track of their armies; the murder of unarmed citizens, and in some instances of little boys; the threats against the chastity of our sisters in New Orleans; the well authenticated murder of prisoners taken in battle; and lastly the attempt to arm brigades of African slaves against us, in whose hands our mothers and sisters would find murder indeed a message of relief."[64]

Although Vance used his powerful oratory to excite the crowd and exhort the people of his state to support the Confederate war effort, he also was astute enough to recognize that many of his citizens were becoming disgruntled with the laws and policies coming from the administration of Jefferson Davis in Richmond. He knew that many North Carolinians considered the Confederate conscription law of April 1862 to be a repressive violation of their civil rights, and he was careful to pander to this faction of his constituency. Regarding the conscript law, he told the inaugural crowd: "Many of you thought it harsh and unconstitutional; it was harsh, and *may have* been unconstitutional, though many of our ablest statesmen thought it not." The governor-elect urged North Carolinians to accept the provisions of the conscription law despite their concerns and, when called to the army, to serve faithfully in the cause of Southern independence. "To stop now to argue it," he cautioned, "could only produce the greatest mischief, for the reason that it has already been executed upon at least four-fifths of those subject to it, however objectionable in its execution. But I am sure that if every man who has his country's good at heart but knew of the necessity which existed at the time, he would render it a cheerful obedience."[65]

But lest his call for adherence to the conscription law leave the impression that he was forsaking the rights of North Carolinians in order to bolster the Davis government, Vance reminded everyone that he would not allow the Tar Heel State to suffer from too much Confederate authority, especially military rule. Nor would he forsake local interests and autonomy. "Fellow citizens," he proclaimed,

> There are other dangers which beset us, besides those which come from the foe. Bloody revolutions have necessarily a chaotic tendency. Yielding ourselves up gradually to martial law—accustoming ourselves by slow degrees to submit to the execution of arbitrary power in our military leaders and looking with less and less concern upon the disordered morals which a state of war must produce, we may endanger both civil liberty and the frame work of society. This time-honored principle in the charter of our liberties, "that the military should be subordinate to the civil authorities," should still be honored and maintained. It should never be departed from except in cases of most obvious and undeniable public necessity, when the safety of the State would otherwise be imperiled. . . . Exorbitant grants of power to any man or set of men, are dangerous to the extreme. . . . The Judge, the Magistrate and the Sheriff should travel regularly the path of their accustomed duties, and all respect and obedience be yielded them—a custom for which the good name of North Carolina has become proverbial. Let all the complicated machinery of the law, with the numberless auxiliary organizations of society be kept in unremitting action. Beware of infringements thereon under the plea of *necessity*; none has ever been found so plausible and specious by which to rob the people of their liberties. It is the complacent excuse of the despot the world over. The *people* must keep watch at this pass. Their officers are responsible to them, and must be held to a strict account. So far as I am concerned, next to the preservation of the State itself, I shall regard it my sacred, paramount duty to protect the citizen in the enjoyment of his rights and liberties.[66]

3. The Governor's Palace in Raleigh stood at the opposite end of Fayetteville Street from the State Capitol. North Carolina Office of Archives and History, Raleigh.

Thus, in his inaugural address, Vance set the paradoxical tone that would characterize his terms as governor. As he would on so many occasions during the war, he strove to keep North Carolina united and under control by proclaiming himself a defender of individual and states' rights and simultaneously urging North Carolinians to bend to the will of the Confederate government. Once his election was certain, most of the state rallied behind him as a champion of the war effort and the establishment of a Confederate nation. "It is evident," concluded the Charlotte *Daily Bulletin*, "that Col. Vance is determined not to relax efforts that be deemed necessary to prosecute the war vigorously, looking to a distinct nationality and total independence of the Yankee nation."[67]

After being sworn in as North Carolina's chief executive, Vance, along with his family, took up residence in the Governor's Palace at the opposite end of Fayetteville Street from the Capitol. When he first sat down at his desk in his Capitol office, the young governor—despite his inspirational oratory and political acumen and instinct—could not have foreseen the many trials that awaited him as war leader of the Tar Heel State.

2

"LET EVERY PATRIOT IN THE LAND ASSIST"

The first conundrum that Vance had to face when he assumed office as North Carolina's chief executive was the realization that his influence and authority as governor did not extend over the entire state. After General Burnside's expedition of early 1862, much of coastal North Carolina lay under the control of the Federal army. With its headquarters at New Bern, the U.S. Army staged raids into the interior of North Carolina. Such raids engendered fear among the population of the interior.[1] The Federal presence in the east also made it possible for many of the state's slaves to flee to freedom and Union protection at New Bern, Roanoke Island, and other occupied sites, where refugee camps were established for them. Eventually a significant number of the escaped slaves joined black regiments in the U.S. Army.[2] Also in the eastern region of the state, a number of white North Carolinians remained loyal to the Union, and some of them— known as "Buffaloes"—were organized into U.S. regiments and fought in several operations in the state.[3] To the president of the United States, eastern North Carolina seemed ripe for reconstruction and a possible return to the Union. As he did in other occupied areas of the Confederacy, Abraham Lincoln attempted to establish a military government for the area of eastern North Carolina held by the Union army. He hoped that the governor whom he appointed for occupied North Carolina—Edward Stanly of New Bern, a former Whig and Unionist—would be able to take advantage of Union and peace sentiment in the state and lead North Carolina in a program of reconstruction and readmission to the Federal Republic.[4] Although Lincoln's plan failed, and Union raids into the interior were largely ineffective, the Federal presence and threat in the east plagued Vance throughout his governorship.

When he first became governor, Vance worried about the possibility of a Federal raid penetrating into the interior and actually seizing the state capital. In January 1863, for example, Northern troops raided toward Goldsboro, and an excited Vance telegraphed Secretary of War James A. Seddon for assistance to thwart the Yankee advance. "Let me beg you to send every available man, as I am sure the crisis is upon us in North Carolina," he implored the secretary of war.[5] In response to Vance's concern, the War Department assigned Gen. Daniel H. Hill to command a detachment of troops in a campaign against the Union army in eastern North Carolina. Hill arrived in the eastern part of the Tar Heel State from Virginia in early 1863. But Seddon agreed with Gen. Robert E. Lee, who cautioned the secretary against being swayed too heavily by Vance's apparent panic over reports from civilians about Federal strength in coastal North Carolina.[6] As Lee pointed out, his Army of Northern Virginia was facing the main Union offensive in the East. In fact, in July 1862 Burnside and 7,000 of his troops in eastern North Carolina had been summoned to reinforce Gen. George B. McClellan's Army of the Potomac in its campaign to capture Richmond. Gen. John G. Foster then replaced Burnside in North Carolina.[7]

On January 5, 1863, Lee wrote Seddon that "I have always believed that Genl. Foster's force has been much overrated. The reports from citizens, however intelligent and honest, cannot be relied on. Had Genl. Foster received all the reinforcements that have been reported . . . , he ought to have the largest Federal army now in the field. I am not certain that he will attempt any expedition, except those of a predatory character." Lee stressed that to avoid overreacting to rumors of the Union threat in North Carolina, "Information should be obtained by our own scouts, men accustomed to see things as they are, and not liable to excitement or exaggeration."[8] Despite his worries about the military threat in eastern North Carolina, which never entirely left him, Vance eventually came to realize that the major challenge to the Confederacy in the East was being faced in Virginia by Lee's army. He began to see that, as troubling as Federal raids from the coast could be for his citizens, the real threat to North Carolina's survival as a Confederate state was the Federal campaign against the Army of Northern Virginia. As time went on, he made requests for troops from Lee's army, especially to hunt deserters, but the alarm that he initially felt over possible Federal conquest of his state from the coast diminished, and he acquiesced to General Lee's military acumen.

Vance also faced difficulties of Confederate loyalty and violence in the western part of the state, where conflict between Unionists and pro-Confederates frequently resulted in bitter violence that included robbery, torture, and even murder. The situation was exacerbated by the Unionists who infiltrated into the North Carolina Mountains from eastern Tennessee, where Unionists constituted a significant portion of the population. Federal troops also raided in western North Carolina from Tennessee.[9] At the core of the inner Civil War between pro-Confederates and Unionists in North Carolina was the large-scale desertion among Tar Heel troops. The western part of North Carolina had probably the largest number of deserters in the state. As historians John C. Inscoe and Gordon B. McKinney have noted about the analysis of historical sociologist Peter Beauman, "the rate of desertion in the mountains was just over 24 percent of all men who enlisted from the region, as compared with a mere 12 percent for the state as a whole."[10] In the area, a guerrilla war raged between Unionists and Confederates. Militant Unionists—sometimes called "bushwackers," "tories," or "Yankees"—often raided Confederate troops and supplies and brutalized pro-Confederate families. Confederate troops and sympathizers—sometimes called "destructives" or "secessionists"—committed equal violence against the Unionists.

Perhaps the worst incident of violence occurred in the community of Shelton Laurel in January 1863, when a group of Union men, including some deserters from the Confederate army's Sixty-fourth North Carolina Infantry, raided Marshall, the seat of Madison County. The raiders, led by Confederate deserter and guerrilla John Kirk, were in pursuit of salt, which was sorely needed, and they terrorized and plundered the businesses, homes, and families of Confederate sympathizers in the area. In response to such guerrilla raids, Vance requested the assistance of Confederate troops under Gen. Henry Heth, who commanded the Department of East Tennessee, with headquarters in Knoxville. Heth ordered that such guerrilla activity be ended once and for all, and he assigned the task to Col. Lawrence M. Allen and Lt. Col. James A. Keith of the Sixty-fourth North Carolina. Both men were residents of Marshall, and their regiment was under the provisional command of Gen. William George M. Davis.

The regiment attacked the homes of several suspected Unionists in Shelton Laurel. The troops sacked the homes of the tories and tortured or whipped a number them, including women and children. They took fifteen men and boys prisoner. Two of the captives escaped, but a detachment commanded by Keith assembled the others in a ravine on January 18 and shot them, leaving their bodies buried in a shallow grave. North Carolinians were alarmed by the news of the massacre, and Vance demanded an investigation. The subsequent inquiry by Confederate authorities brought little resolution or justice. Keith and four of his officers resigned, and Keith served a short time in jail after the war. But Allen remained in the army, with only a six-month suspension, and Heth transferred to the East, where he continued to command troops.[11]

Evidently the first official news that Vance received of the Shelton Laurel massacre was in a letter of January 31 from Augustus S. Merrimon, solicitor of the Eighth District in Asheville. Merrimon was responsible for prosecuting the Unionists and deserters who had raided Marshall prior to the massacre at Shelton Laurel. "I learn that the Laurel expedition is about over," Merrimon wrote the governor. "I can't give you any of the details of the affair. I suppose the proper officers will report to you. I learn that a number of *prisoners* were *shot* without any trial or hearing whatever. I hope this is not true, but if so, the parties guilty of so dark a crime should be punished. Humanity revolts at so savage a crime. Our Militia had nothing to do with what was done in Laurel. I am glad of this."[12]

On January 21, Heth had informed Vance of the raid on Marshall and that thirteen tories had subsequently been killed, but he did not relate the circumstances of their execution at Shelton Laurel. The marauding tories numbered about sixty, of whom twenty had been captured, Heth said. "Should this estimation of their force be True," he told Vance, "I do not think it advisable to alter our plans." There is no evidence that Vance would ever have approved of an unlawful execution of prisoners or that, once he knew about it, he attempted to cover it up. Certainly, once he had confirmation of the massacre, he demanded an investigation by the War Department. He also took care to put himself on record as opposing any violent and illegal retaliation against the men suspected of raiding Marshall. In fact, he might have backdated a memo in order to ensure that, although he supported action against marauding Unionists and deserters in the west, there was a record that he never condoned summary execution. Sometime after receiving Heth's telegram of January 21, Vance wrote the following "answer" directly at the bottom of Heth's message: "Yours recd. I hope you will not relax until the tories are crushed, but do not let our excited people deal too harshly with these misguided men. Please have the captured delivered to the proper authorities." Vance made a point of instructing his private secretary, Richard H. Battle, to make a copy of his response to Heth. That Vance alludes to a possible massacre not mentioned by Heth and that he took care to order his secretary to make the copy perhaps indicate that the governor wrote his response on Heth's telegram sometime after receiving official news of the massacre.[13]

In any event, by February 2, Vance was aware that an execution had taken place at Shelton Laurel. On that date he wrote to Gen. William George

M. Davis, who had led the expedition into western North Carolina from Tennessee and then had replaced Heth in command of the Department of East Tennessee.[14] "I was fearful," Vance informed General Davis, "in the great excitement prevailing among our people, that the misguided people of Laurel might be dealt too harshly with, and warned the officers to be cool & just." He had just learned that some of the prisoners *had* been executed by Confederate troops. "I hope this is not true, as it would be much better to have them dealt with by the law." Vance also told Davis that he approved of the plan to move some of western Carolina's Union sympathizers to Kentucky, "provided they desire to go. I would not wish however to excite the women & children or old men, if they desire to remain. As the law ought to be strong enough to keep them in subjection." In general Vance praised the performance of Davis's troops in the Mountain region. "The result is quite satisfactory," he declared, "and I am especially pleased to learn that there appears to be no regular organization of enemies to the Government in that country. I was loath to believe so, and from the first was of the opinion that the raid [on Marshall prior to Shelton Laurel] was only for plunder and that the whole matter was probably exaggerated. I hope now that quiet and order are restored in that region, and have to return you my thanks for the very prompt and energetic aid offered by your command in producing this state of things."[15]

No matter how much Vance may have approved in general of the Confederate army's campaign in western North Carolina, he was not willing to have the Shelton Laurel massacre go uninvestigated. On February 9, he asked Merrimon "to take such steps as may be necessary to secure and prosecute all the prisoners on Laurel taken by the recent expedition." But he also instructed Merrimon "to make an investigation officially into the reported shooting of a number of these prisoners, with all the circumstances, as I intend to look into the matter myself."[16] Armed with the facts of the killing, he dispatched another letter to General Davis. "I fear that it is even worse than was first reported," he expounded. "Whilst expressing again my thanks for the prompt aid rendered by your command in quieting the troubles of the region, I cannot reconcile it to my sense of duty to pass by in silence such cruel & barbarous conduct as is alleged to have characterized a portion of them."[17] He also wrote to Secretary of War Seddon asking to have "proceedings instituted at once" against Lieutenant Colonel Keith, "who seems to have been in command and to have acted in this respect without orders from his superiors, so far as I can learn."[18]

Rumors soon reached the governor that Keith had been tried by a court-martial and "honorably acquitted" by claiming that he was merely obeying the orders of his superiors when he ordered the shooting of the prisoners. Vance also received official notification that the War Department had accepted Keith's resignation from the army. Vance maintained that justice had not been served by Keith's resignation, and he requested a copy of the court-martial proceedings. "Murder is a crime against the *common law* in this state," he told Seddon, "and [Keith] is now subject to that law."[19] Merrimon had alerted Vance that Keith had been allowed to resign and that he was apt to "decamp to a point beyond the reach of the *civil* or any other arm in this country [North Carolina]. If no action has been taken against him for the alleged crime, it is important that he be arrested *at once* and held to answer for his crimes according to law."[20]

Seddon responded to Vance that no court-martial had been convened to hear charges against Keith and that the Confederate inspector general had accepted Keith's resignation. His resignation was accepted on the recommendation of Gen. Dabney H. Maury, who had replaced Davis in command of the Department of East Tennessee.

According to Seddon, Keith's explanation for his actions was that he had received verbal orders from Heth that he did "not want to be troubled with any prisoners & the last one of them should be killed." Keith supported this testimony with a deposition by a certain Dr. Thompson and vowed that he could produce another witness to verify the instructions given him by Heth. Seddon informed Vance that Heth admitted "he told Keith that those found in arms ought not to be treated as enemies & in the event of an engagement with them to take no prisoners, as he considered that they have forfeited all such claims. But he denies in strong terms the making up of any remarks which would authorize maltreatment of prisoners who had been accepted as such, or to women & children."[21] With that response by Seddon, Vance apparently dropped the matter of the Shelton Laurel massacre—an early indication of his willingness to bend to the decisions of the Confederate government. Heth and Keith went virtually unpunished.

Conflict and violence between loyal Confederates and Unionists also were rampant in the region of the Carolina Piedmont known as the Quaker Belt. Vance initiated a number of campaigns to quell the inner Civil War raging between Confederates on one side and militant Unionists, deserters, draft dodgers, and peace advocates on the other.

The Quaker Belt had a long tradition of pacifist and antislavery sentiment and activity, due in large part to the number of Quakers, Dunkards, Moravians, German Reformed, Lutheran, and antislavery Wesleyan Methodists who settled in the area. Among the antiwar leaders in the region were the Guilford County Quakers Levi and Vestal Coffin, who founded and operated the underground railroad for the liberation of slaves. The area also spawned Hinton Rowan Helper of Davie County, author of the antislavery tract *The Impending Crisis*, and Benjamin S. Hedrick of Davidson County, who was fired from his professorship at the University of North Carolina and forced to flee the state for publicly proclaiming his antislavery views.[22]

The Quaker Belt was the headquarters for North Carolina's Heroes of America, also known as the Red Strings. That secret society, organized in the state by John Hilton, pledged allegiance to the United States flag and vowed to fight "in support of the Lincoln government." The organization employed various tactics to undermine the Confederate war effort, including aiding "outliers" (deserters and draft dodgers) and escaped Federal prisoners, and operating the underground railroad. It utilized sabotage and clashed with the militia, the Home Guard, and Confederate troops, who were attempting to arrest deserters and enforce conscription in the Piedmont.

The Heroes began agitating against the Confederacy in the summer of 1861, and Hilton and the other leaders were soon arrested in March 1862 for "using incendiary language and making many violent threats." Militant Unionists again mobilized in retaliation against Gov. Henry T. Clark's draft of the militia to oppose the Federal invasion of coastal North Carolina. The protestors held peace meetings at which they called for an end to hostilities, resistance to conscription, and peace negotiations. In response, Clark ordered troops into the Quaker Belt to suppress the peace movement. A number of peace advocates were arrested or pressed into the Confederate army. Hilton escaped to Union lines and joined the Federal army.[23]

By the time Vance took office, the opposition to the war was growing as each side terrorized the other. Murder, arson, torture, robbery, and violence of all kinds were on the rise. Outliers raided and plundered the homes and farms of pro-Confederates for provisions and supplies. They attacked the militia and regular troops—known as "hunters"—who were sent to find and capture them. The militia and Confederate troops retaliated against the families of the outliers and militants. According to historian William T. Auman, "homes and barns were burned, crops were destroyed or stolen from the field, and men, women, and children and the elderly often were tortured and abused."[24]

Chief among the militant Unionists leaders was William Owens, a farmer and a Confederate deserter from Moore County. Owens and a band of Unionist guerrillas responded to the Conscription Act of April 1862 with an attack upon pro-Confederates in Moore County. Rumors circulated that

Owens and his men intended to attack the Confederate arsenal at Fayetteville to procure weapons to arm themselves and those anti-Confederate supporters who joined their ranks.

In response to the growing violence and number of deserters and draft dodgers in the Piedmont, Vance in September 1862—almost immediately upon taking office—ordered militia and two companies of North Carolina troops into the Quaker Belt to arrest deserters and recusant conscripts and to campaign against the outliers. The militia campaigned for two months but with few results. Then, beginning again in January 1863, several units of Confederate troops hunted down deserters and draft dodgers in Randolph, Chatham, Moore, and Montgomery Counties. They were joined in February by militia, and the two forces campaigned for about six weeks. But despite the efforts of the combined forces, assisted by a unit of cavalry, the outliers and militant Unionists largely eluded capture and maintained their attacks on pro-Confederates.

Vance continued to receive letters about the atrocities committed against loyal Confederates. He also received many reports about acts of violence and impressment committed by the militia and the army on families suspected of being pro-Union or having relatives who were deserters.[25]

In April 1863, Vance asked Gen. Daniel H. Hill, commanding in eastern North Carolina, to send troops into Moore County to hunt deserters and draft evaders and quell antiwar violence. Hill answered that because of the threat of invasion by Federal troops in the east, "This . . . is a bad time to weaken my force." He would, however, "send 25 horsemen and 50 infantry." Hill remarked that Gen. James Longstreet, then commanding the Department of North Carolina and Southern Virginia, thought Vance should call out the militia to help repel the anticipated Federal attack in the North Carolina interior. But, said Hill, "I don't know that any good would result from it except the Exposure of skulkers. The men staying at home are consumers and non producers. They ought to be kicked into ranks by some means." Hill urged the governor to issue a public proclamation denouncing desertion and appealing to the Confederate patriotism of North Carolinians. "Your scathing rebuke of deserters and skulkers makes even cowards blush," the general declared, alluding to a January proclamation issued by Vance. Hill maintained that much of North Carolinians' dissatisfaction with the war was caused by the state's newspapers. "I fear that the discontent and demoralization of the troops have been mainly caused by unwise ebillitions [sic] of temper on the part of our local press," he insisted. "Would to God that our Editors could fight the common enemy and let their private quarrels lie over."[26]

Displaying his characteristic willingness to cooperate with Confederate generals in the field, Vance responded to Hill that "In view of the alarming information" that the general conveyed "of this probable invasion of the State, I will not press for the troops to be sent to Moore County at present." He did not, however, think that calling out the militia to repel a Federal attack from the coast was a good idea, because "Their help would be little, their consumption of rations great, and beyond any sort of doubt, their removal now from their crops would be followed by the most disastrous consequences." Nevertheless, "If you think it necessary, when the enemy's movement is fully developed I will call out the *Militia Officers* of whom there are some two or three thousand, which will be a larger number, I fear[,] than we can arm and make available—I can bring them to Raleigh at once by *An Order*." In response to Hill's complaint about the press, Vance "addressed a note to the City Editors urging them to avoid exciting panic among the people, and to be cautious not to speak of the movement of troops &c."[27]

As Hill suggested, Vance on May 11 issued a strong and dramatic public proclamation denouncing deserters and those who encouraged and harbored them. He had "learned with great pain," he proclaimed, "that there have been latterly numerous desertions from the ranks of our gallant army and that there are many persons in the country who incite and encourage these desertions and harbor and conceal these misguided men at home, instead of Encouraging Them to return to duty." He continued with his passionate admonishment of the disloyal: "Certainly no crime could be greater, no cowardice more abject, no treason more base, than for a citizen of the State, enjoying its privileges and protection without sharing its dangers, to persuade those who have had the courage to go forth in defence of their country, vilely to desert the colors which they have sworn to uphold, when a miserable death or a vile, skulking and ignominious existence must be the inevitable consequence: no plea can excuse it." Vance observed that many deserters had "rejected the pardon" that he had offered in his January 26 proclamation if they would return to their companies by February 10. But although "I am not authorized to promise it, yet I am assured no man will be shot who shall voluntarily return to duty" now. In the end, however, Vance's proclamations, which both threatened retaliation and shame and offered forgiveness to deserters, did little to correct the increasing problem of desertion.[28]

Nevertheless, Vance continued to offer pardons unofficially to some deserters, even after the terms of his proclamations had expired. In October 1863, he wrote to Col. Shubal G. Worth, commanding a battalion of Home Guard hunting deserters in Randolph County:

You may in all cases where you think proper, promise a pardon to all men who will voluntarily come in, except such as have been concerned in crimes or outrages upon the community and provided they have never deserted before. Those guilty of the 2d. offense I can not entercede for.

Make no publication of this, but use it privately whenever you think it judicious.[29]

Secretary of War Seddon, having received accounts from various generals about the large number of desertions among North Carolina troops—including a report from North Carolina's own Gen. William D. Pender—urged Vance to "aid in arresting the progress of desertion among North Carolina troops, which unless promptly checked will be destructive of the discipline and morale of our Army." The secretary promised that he would instruct General Hill to provide Vance with a regiment if the governor needed it to hunt down deserters and conscripts.[30]

Gen. Robert E. Lee became so concerned about the number of North Carolinians deserting from the ranks of the Army of Northern Virginia that he complained directly to Secretary Seddon. "The desertion of the No. Caro. troops from this Army is becoming so serious an evil, that unless it can be promptly arrested I fear the troops from that state will become greatly reduced," Lee wrote. "I need not enlarge upon the extent to which that evil will grow if not at once stopped. I hope that you will represent the matter to his Excy. the Gov. of No. Caro. so as to induce him to take active measures in the case, and to enlist all the good men in the State to reprobate and discountenance it. I must also request that you do everything in your power to remedy the evil." Seddon forwarded Lee's letter to Vance with the request that he take immediate measures "to arrest the evil" of desertion.[31]

Several circumstances induced North Carolina soldiers to desert in large numbers. The devastation and hardships of war and army life, the impoverishment and suffering of families back home, and the influence of the peace advocates and press all contributed to the disaffection and dissatisfaction of the soldiers with the Confederacy's struggle. But, as Vance and the War Department realized, the immediate cause of desertion among Tar Heel soldiers was a state supreme court decision made by Chief Justice Richmond M. Pearson.

When the North Carolina militia arrested deserters in Yadkin County in early 1863, the deserters killed two of the militiamen. The deserters escaped punishment when Pearson issued writs of habeas corpus and ordered the release of all the deserters arrested by the militia, on the ground

4. Richmond M. Pearson, chief justice of the North Carolina Supreme
Court, clashed with Vance over the issues of conscription, desertion,
and habeas corpus. North Carolina Office of Archives and History, Raleigh.

that the state militia had no authority to arrest Confederate deserters or
recusant conscripts. Such action, Pearson argued, was the responsibility of
the Confederate government. Pearson's ruling led many North Carolina
soldiers to believe that he had declared the Confederate conscription law to
be unconstitutional. Therefore enrolled conscripts would be justified in
resisting the law, and those men conscripted into the service would not be
arrested if they deserted.[32]

To add to the conflict over conscription, when the War Department began drafting men who had previously hired substitutes, Pearson ruled that
substitutes were not liable for conscription according the Conscription Act
of September 1862. Moreover, the men for whom they had substituted
could not be legally drafted either. Pearson issued writs of habeas corpus
and ordered the discharge of a number of men who had previously hired
substitutes. This led more North Carolinians to the conclusion that conscription was unconstitutional and that they could apply to Pearson for
relief from its strictures.[33]

Alarmed by the impact that Pearson's ruling could have on the Confederate war effort, Vance appealed to the state legislature for authority to arrest deserters and asked for a law against harboring them. But the state lawmakers denied his request "on much the grounds as those assigned by the Chief Justice, to wit, that it was the business of Congress to provide for the execution of its own laws." Vance then ordered the militia just to "aid the Confederate officers as a *posse* when requested" in the apprehension of deserters. "In the meantime," Vance wrote Jefferson Davis on May 13, 1863, "news of Judge Pearson's decision went abroad in the Army in a very exaggerated and ridiculous form, soldiers were induced to believe that it declared the conscript law unconstitutional and that they were entitled if they came home to the protection of their civil authorities—Desertion . . . broke out again worse than before."[34] When the Home Guard, composed of men not eligible for the draft, supplanted much of the militia in July 1863 and attempted to make arrests, the state's chief justice ruled that the Home Guard also had no authority to apprehend Confederate deserters and recusant conscripts. Not until December 1863 did the state legislature heed Vance's advice and pass a law that authorized the governor to use the Home Guard to arrest deserters and conscripts.[35]

By that time, however, desertion and resistance to the draft had reached epidemic proportions. The number of deserters and draft dodgers, as well as the violence between militant Unionists and loyal Confederates, swelled following the Confederate defeat at Gettysburg, when hundreds of North Carolina soldiers abandoned the army and returned home. Worried that a large-scale revolt might result in the Tar Heel State if this activity went unchecked, Vance asked General Lee to send Confederate troops into North Carolina. In response, the War Department in the fall of 1863 dispatched the brigade of North Carolina general Robert F. Hoke to Piedmont and western North Carolina. Hoke, who found the counties of the Quaker Belt to be particularly troublesome, combed the countryside in search of outliers. The Home Guard cooperated with the troops, and together they ambushed, captured, and killed a number of deserters and draft dodgers. But Hoke's troops made only marginal progress in solving the problem. Deserters continued to elude capture. Militant Unionists and deserters continued to terrorize, rob, and destroy the property of pro-Confederates, who committed the same atrocities on the families of outliers. After a few months, Hoke returned to Virginia, claiming that his expedition had been a success. But actually he had accomplished little in arresting deserters or halting the problem of desertion and draft-dodging.[36] In February 1864, Clement Dowd, the commander of the Moore County Home Guard and Vance's postwar law partner, informed the governor that when Hoke departed, "the deserters and skulkers . . . resumed their acts of violence and robbery. Not a week and scarcely a night passes without . . . some act of violence done to families and property of loyal people."[37]

As desertion and attacks on loyal Confederates continued, Vance ordered eleven battalions of the Home Guard into Moore, Chatham, Montgomery, and Randolph Counties in the Piedmont in the summer of 1864. Part of his motivation was his concern that the anti-Confederate sentiment and opposition to the war would lead to support for his opponent, William W. Holden, the peace candidate in the upcoming gubernatorial election. The Heroes of America had gained support, and deserters and militant Unionists might vote for Holden or intimidate Vance supporters. This new expedition by the Home Guard proved as ineffective as previous campaigns. In Randolph and Wilkes Counties, centers of peace sentiment in the Quaker Belt, Holden carried the vote for election as governor. Outliers "rampaged throughout" the region when they learned that Vance had won the election.[38]

The problems of desertion, conscription resistance, and the associated terror continued to plague North Carolina until the very end of the war. The fear of violence perpetuated by deserters was compounded by the dread that the deserters would arm the slaves to overthrow state and Confederate authority. In 1864 Vance received reports that deserters intended to enlist and arm escaped slaves. In Montgomery County, authorities arrested a free woman of color for assisting deserters. When Federal cavalry general George Stoneman invaded western and Piedmont North Carolina in 1865, George Clark, a free black carpenter of Davidson County, served as a guide.[39]

In the winter and spring of 1865, as each day Confederate defeat became more certain, desertion among North Carolina troops continued to grow. General Lee, distraught over the number of Tar Heels who were leaving their posts around Petersburg and Richmond and going home, called upon Vance to help stem the tide of their flight. Lee blamed the extent of desertion on the expressed dissatisfaction and war weariness conveyed by the home-front populace to the soldiers in the field. "The state of despondency that now prevails among our people," Lee wrote to Vance on February 24, "is producing a bad effect upon the troops. Deserters [sic] are becoming very frequent, and there is good reason to believe that they are occasioned to considerable extent by letters written to the soldiers by their friends at home." North Carolinians, Lee maintained, made up the largest number of deserters. According to the general, "despondent persons represent to their friends in the army that our cause is hopeless, and they had better provide for themselves. They state that the number of deserters is so large in the several counties that there is no danger to be apprehended from the home guards. The deserters generally take their arms with them. The greater number are from regiments from the western part of the State." The situation could be improved, Lee felt, if Vance would make a public effort "to change public sentiment, and cheer the spirits of the people" and "explain to the people that the cause is not hopeless." Lee thought that with encouragement by Vance and other prominent North Carolinians, "our sorely tried people would be induced to make one more effort, to bear their sufferings a little longer, and regain some of the spirit that marked the first two years of the war."[40]

Only days before Lee's letter, Vance had made a public appeal to the citizens of the state asking them to remain steadfast and not to forsake the Confederate cause, even in the face of great hardship and despondency over the progress of the war. He told North Carolinians that only through continued fighting in the hope of victory could North Carolina and the other Southern states preserve their social and economic system. Defeat, he asserted, would sound the death knell of slavery, bring on a race war, and impose a harsh Federal reconstruction that would devastate the South and hold it in subservience.[41]

Vance assured General Lee that he was well aware of "the increase of desertions from our armies," and he agreed that "the cause of it was to be found in the general public despondency." By means of his proclamations and public meetings, he was doing all he could to win the support of the people for the army. "[Y]et the near and triumphant approach of the enemy has so alarmed the timid and so engrossed the loyal in preparation for his coming that I fear they will hardly have their proper effect. I have myself been so busy in trying to organize my Militia and secure my vast public stores that [I] have only been able to address the people at two or three points. Rest assured however General that I am fully alive to the importance of the crisis and whatever man can do in my situation, shall be done. I shall now order out in every County that class of Home Guard not subject to duty in the field and put them to work arresting deserters. In many counties however they are necessarily inefficient from the great number of the deserters and the natural fear of the destruction of their property &c." Vance requested that the general send him "as many as two regiments of Cavalry." He recommended that they quarter the cavalry in the "disaffected districts" and allow them to forage "upon the friends of the deserters." Thus they could not only sustain themselves and their horses but "restore confidence and inspire with courage the local forces."[42]

Lee thanked the governor for his "zealous efforts in behalf of the army and cause." He had read Vance's proclamations, and "I trust that you will infuse into your fellow citizens the spirit of resolution and patriotism which inspires your own action." Lee had no cavalry to detail to North Carolina, but he dispatched a unit of infantry, under the command of Gen. Richard D. Johnston, to guard the line along the Roanoke River. He also ordered a detachment of 500 men, commanded by Lt. Col. Alexander C. McAllister, into Chatham and Moore Counties, "in which the bands of deserters were represented to be very numerous." They could also operate in other counties as needed. Lee ordered these troops "to take no prisoners among those deserters who resist with arms the civil or military authorities." He told Vance that "I hope you will raise as large a force of local troops to cooperate with them as you can, and think that the sternest course is the best with the class I have referred to. The immunity which these lawless organizations afford is a great cause of desertions, and they cannot be too sternly dealt with."[43]

The Confederate troops assigned to North Carolina campaigned for several weeks against the deserters, capturing, wounding, and killing a number of them. In the meantime, Sherman's army had entered the state on March 8, 1865. Sherman's troops moved into the interior of the state, fighting and winning the Battle of Bentonville and joining with Union troops pressing inland from the coast. By the time Lee surrendered at Appomattox on April 9 and Sherman pressed Gen. Joseph E. Johnston's army toward an ultimate surrender at Bennett Place, in Durham County, in late April, massive numbers of North Carolina troops had abandoned their regiments in both Virginia and their home state.

Although it is not known precisely how many troops from North Carolina deserted from the Confederate army, it is generally believed that North Carolina had the highest number of desertions of any Confederate state. Whether or not North Carolina can claim that dubious distinction, it can be said with certainty that the state suffered large-scale desertion. It is equally certain that Vance, despite his best efforts to keep Tar Heels in Confederate ranks, was never able to deal effectively with the problem.[44]

Vance grasped that the major cause of desertion among troops from North Carolina was the Confederate Conscription Acts. The first act met immediate opposition from a populace that had not known a military draft before and was beginning to feel the hard reality of war, which was creating a dread and despondency that were fast replacing the initial enthusiasm and Southern patriotism that had greeted the outbreak of hostilities in 1861. Many North Carolinians considered compulsory military service to be an infringement on their liberty and individual rights. Still others feared that it gave the military too much power and violated the doctrine of states' rights.[45] Some conscripts bitterly complained of being forced to suffer the hardships of service in the Confederate army. Prior to his desertion from his Confederate unit in Chowan County, conscript Norm Harrold, from Ashe County, wrote a letter to President Davis blaming the chief executive for the circumstances that he was involuntarily forced to endure. Every conscript, Harrold wrote Davis, will "sink under the calamity of an exquisite joy when you shall have reached that eminent meridian whence all progress is perpendicular. And now, bastard President of a political abortion, farewell."[46]

One provision of the First Conscription Act particularly rankled the ordinary folk. The provision of substitution allowed a man with sufficient wealth to avoid the draft by paying someone to serve in the army in his place. Widespread protest by the poor that this measure unfairly favored the rich led the Confederate Congress in late December 1863 to pass a bill abolishing substitution. Another bill, passed on January 5, 1864, made all those persons who had furnished substitutes now liable for service.[47] Nevertheless, by the time substitution was finally abolished, it had created much resentment and disaffection among the poorer classes.

Many North Carolinians also resented the large number of exemptions from army service allowed by the Conscription Acts. Soon after the First Conscription Act was passed, the Confederate Congress established the classes that could be exempt from the draft. Those exempt persons who theoretically were essential to state operations or more useful at home than on the battlefield included "Confederate and state officers, and the clerks allowed them by law; mail carriers and ferrymen on post roads; pilots and persons engaged in the marine service; employees on railroads and river routes of transportation; telegraph operators; ministers in the regular discharge of their duties; employees in mines, furnaces, and foundries; printers; presidents and professors in colleges and academies; teachers of the deaf, dumb, and blind; teachers having 20 pupils or more; superintendents, nurses, and attendants in public hospitals and lunatic asylums; and one druggist in each drug-store. Superintendents and operatives in wool and cotton factories would be exempted at the discretion of the Secretary of War." The granting of exemptions led to many abuses of the system by persons who scrambled to establish or occupy an exempt position in order to avoid the draft.[48]

The Second Conscription Act, which was passed in September 1862, raised the draft age to forty-five years. An amendment passed in October increased the classes of exemptions. The new classes included a variety of mechanics, artisans, professionals, and railroad and navigation company employees, as well as physicians who had practiced for five years, salt workers who produced twenty bushels of salt per day, certain religious pacifists who paid a tax or hired a substitute, and "other persons whom the President might designate because of justice or equity." The Confederate Congress passed its third and final conscription act on February 17, 1864. That act lowered the draft age limit to seventeen and raised it to fifty. Those men conscripted who were younger than eighteen or older than forty-five (the age limits specified by the Second Conscription Act) were to be reserves utilized to defend their respective states and for special details.[49]

The provision of the Second Conscription Act that raised the greatest ire and discontent among the common people of North Carolina was the so-called Twenty-Negro Law. The provision was intended to ensure that every plantation with twenty or more slaves had at least one white man who remained on the plantation to keep watch on those slaves. It stipulated that either the planter or his overseer on such a plantation would be exempt from conscription.[50] Many North Carolinians contended that this exemption favored the planter class, and it led to much class resentment and the frequent refrain that the conflict was "a rich man's war and a poor man's fight." A number of Tar Heels complained to Vance of the exemption. "The poor soldiers is fiting for the rich man's Negroes," L. K. Walker, a farmer, wrote to the governor on January 16, 1863.[51] Gen. Daniel H. Hill denounced the law as a shield for slackers. "Some exempts claim to own twenty negroes," he told his troops, "and with justice might claim to be masters of an infinite amount of cowardice."[52]

In May 1863 and February 1864, the Confederate Congress modified the Twenty-Negro Law to make it more restrictive in granting exemptions and, it was hoped, less offensive to the poor.[53] Although only 120 exemptions were granted under it in North Carolina during the war,[54] the common people of the state, until the conflict's bitter end, objected to the law as beneficial only to the rich. Even the state legislature asked Congress to repeal an exemption that "made unjust discrimination between such persons and their less fortunate fellow citizens."[55] Vance himself deplored the Twenty-Negro exemption. "This Govr. does not feel justified in following this feature of the Conspt. Law, believing it to be unjust & unfair," he wrote to Jesse G. Shepherd, a prominent jurist and legislator who had asked Vance's assistance in getting the army to discharge a friend who owned twenty slaves.[56]

Many Tar Heel soldiers, such as Private Ollin Goddin, complained to the governor about how the Twenty-Negro Law and substitution had exempted the "rich man" from his share of the burden of waging the war. In the view of these troops, destitution at home combined with the poor pay for soldiers had placed the hardships and responsibility of defending the Southern right to independence solely and unjustly upon the backs of the poor.[57]

Although during the war Vance realized that the Confederacy's conscription policies were the chief cause of desertion and dwindling popular support for Southern independence, not until after the conflict did he publicly acknowledge the devastating impact that conscription had on Southern morale and commitment to the war effort. "It was," he declared in a speech in Boston in 1886, "perhaps the severest blow the Confederacy ever received, as it did more than anything else to alienate the affections of the common people, without whose support it could not live for a day. It was only regarded as a confession that the new government was not able to depend upon the voluntary support of the people, with which it so triumphantly started out . . . but it opened a wide door to demagogues to appeal to the non-slaveholding class, and make them believe that the only issue was the protection of slavery, in which they were to be sacrificed for the sole benefit of the masters."[58] As the conflict raged, however, Vance made every effort to cooperate with the Davis government in enforcing the draft and keeping men in the ranks of the army.

He did complain frequently to the Davis government about what he considered the injustice and illegality of the War Department's actions in enforcing the conscription laws. His ire was particularly raised when the officer in charge of conscription in North Carolina attempted to draft state officials into the army. Vance contended that these officials—including local officers such as magistrates, constables, and policemen—were essential and exempted according to the conscription acts. Therefore, "The ground I shall assume," he wrote to Col. Thomas P. August, commandant of conscripts in North Carolina in March 1863, "is that all state officers and employees necessary to the operation of this government—of which necessity I must judge—Shall not be interferred with by the enrolling officers and any attempt to arrest such men will be resisted."[59]

The War Department had attempted to circumvent the exemption of state officials by claiming that, according to the Second Conscription Act, state officials who were subject to militia duty were not exempt from Confederate conscription. Gen. Gabriel J. Rains, superintendent of the Confederate Bureau of Conscription, informed Vance that "The law exempts Judicial and Executive officers of State Governments, except those liable to militia duty. This you will readily perceive must be the rule of guidance for the agents of this Bureau, and there are no means, short of supernatural power, for them to know, outside the law, of such employees your Excellency wishes to be exempt."[60]

An angry Vance responded that in North Carolina "*No body*" was exempt from militia duty and consequently, according to the War Department's interpretation of the conscription law, "*every body* is liable to conscription." Despite a long diatribe about the bureau's usurpation of his authority and the sovereignty of the state of North Carolina, Vance reminded Rains of his commitment to keeping a sufficient army at the front. "The fact," he wrote, "that the conscript law has been more faithfully executed in North Carolina than any other state in the Confederacy, and that no other Southern executive (So far as I am aware) has used the whole power of the State Militia to execute it, might be taken as an earnest [indication] of my intention to sustain the government, so far as it be rightfully done." He boasted to Rains that he did not "belong to that class of politicians who made the 'night (and day) hideous with cries for *State rights*,'" and, in fact, because of his cooperation with the Confederate government, he had been "accused of Consolidationism."[61]

Vance also reminded President Davis that the drafting of state officers on the ground that they were subject to militia duty "would render every able bodied man in the State liable to conscription. . . . If this construction should prevail you will perceive that it is in the power of the War Dept. to abolish the State government by a very simple process." The governor went on to explain why the magistrates, or justices of the county courts of pleas and quarter sessions, were essential to the operation of county government. In addition to convening and holding county courts, the magistrates also served as the administrative officers of the counties—levying taxes, assisting the poor, and performing other duties essential to maintaining county government. He also pointed out the necessity of retaining mayors, sheriffs, constables, and policemen on duty to keep local governments functioning and ensure law and order. He continued to plead with Davis:

> With the magistrates, the Militia, and the municipal officers of our incorporated towns, constables & such like officers of the State swept into a camp of instruction, I am at a loss to know what would be left of the power or sovereignty of this State or any other? So obvious is the great damage and disparagement which this lattitudenous con-

struction of the law could work against the States, that I can not believe its framers so intended it. And with all due respect I doubt the wisdom and the policy of the War Department in urging it so far. Having made no question of its constitutionality, and interposed no obstacles to its faithful execution, but on the contrary, acquiesced in it as a great measure of necessity and assisted with zeal in its enforcement, I am content now to state my opinions simply upon a fair construction of its terms. And I am quite confident, that your sense of justice will not fail to perceive the weighty reasons of comity, policy and respect for States rights—the great democratic doctrine of our revolution—which admonish you of the impropriety of alarming the jealousy of the States, exciting the murmurs of the people and crippling the security of their government, by seizing a few officers who could do little toward increasing the ranks, or officering of the army; but who as a part of the government are deemed necessary at home.[62]

North Carolina Confederate congressman Thomas S. Ashe, who became a postwar state supreme court justice, supported Vance's opposition to drafting state officials. "I think you are right," he wrote the governor from Richmond, "and for me, I will sustain your course as much as I should deprecate any collision between State and Confederate authorities upon a vital question like this. I am on the side of my native State[.] I am clearly of the opinion that Congress has no power to conscript any officer of a State, unless the State Legislature shall declare him to be liable to service in the Confederate army."[63]

Vance also raised objections with the War Department when generals in North Carolina arbitrarily drafted citizens into the army without going through the commandant of conscripts and the standard procedure for conscription. In April 1863 he complained to Seddon that Gen. Daniel H. Hill had enrolled some men whose exemptions had been approved by the commandant. Hill also had "seized" and "conscribed" several soldiers "who were members of a State battalion raised under an act of Congress, by volunteers from counties within or near the enemy's line, where the enrolling officers could not go to do their duty." He asked that those volunteers be returned to their battalion, "and as for other regulations . . . I am clearly of opinion and so request, that the best way would be to comply with the law *strictly in all respects*—that all conscripts should pass through the hands of the proper enrolling officers alone."[64]

As was the case with the Confederate disregard of state officers' exemption and Hill's unilateral and unauthorized conscriptions, Vance's quarrel with the War Department was not over the issue of the Confederate government's right and authority to impose conscription, but rather over the War Department's failure (as he saw it) to carry out conscription as specifically prescribed by Confederate law. Despite his complaints to the Richmond government about conscription, Vance, on the whole, cooperated with the Confederate War Department in enforcing the draft and apprehending deserters. In his inaugural speech, he had appealed to North Carolinians to abide by the conscription laws, even though they might consider them objectionable and a usurpation of their rights. The greater cause, Southern independence, depended upon the people's willingness to make sacrifices and serve in the army until that cause was won.[65]

He was equally diligent in ensuring that men who were subject to service in the militia or Home Guard also did their duty. In August 1863, Frederick J. Lord, the vice-consul for Spain with an office in Wilmington, asked Vance to excuse two consuls, the banker and railroad executive James G. Burr and the lumber dealer and railroad promoter P. K. Dickinson, from duty in the Home Guard. Lord pointed out that the Confederate government, desiring to keep consulates open, had "exempted all foreign Consuls from [Confederate] military service, and I have now the honor to ask from your hands exemption from the Home Guards for the same reason." Irritated by such a request, Vance declined to grant it. "Whenever it is well established," he told Lord, "that Spain has any right to a consul in the port of a government she does not recognize and having authority under an exequatur from Abraham Lincoln I will cheerfully comply."[66]

After Chief Justice Pearson prohibited the use of militia to arrest deserters and the legislature failed to pass a law requested by Vance allowing him to use the militia for that purpose, the governor appealed to President Davis and North Carolina's Senator William Dortch for aid. Vance asked Dortch to sponsor a helpful bill in the Confederate Congress, but Dortch "informed me that Congress had also declined to take action in the matter, for what reason I do not know." Vance suggested to Davis that he call out the militia in all the Confederate states for service in capturing deserters. "Inasmuch as you have the power to call the Militia of the Confederacy for certain purposes," he wrote the president, "and as no one denies your right to arrest deserters from the armies of which you are Commander in Chief, would it not give validity to my action if I proceeded under your request or requisition." The governor felt, though, that Davis should make his requisition to all the states, as "it would seem invidious to make a requisition alone upon North Carolina for the militia for this purpose, as implying that there were more desertions from this State than any other, which I hope and believe is not true, except in so far as our troops are nearer to their homes and therefore more tempted than those further South."[67]

When Secretary of War Seddon complained to Vance of the extent to which Pearson's rulings on conscription had fueled desertion in the army, he urged Vance to "restrain" the judiciary in North Carolina. Vance snapped back "that every thing which is possible for me to do had been already done." He was utilizing the militia to the extent that he could legally—"to guard all fords and ferries and public highways"—and he had written to Davis for an executive call-up of the state militias. He reminded Seddon that habeas corpus was a fundamental tenet of democracy and democratic law, and as governor he was obligated to abide by and uphold such law. He also pointed out to Seddon that because the Confederate Congress had never created a Confederate supreme court, "no appeal lies from the Supreme Court of a State to that of the Confederate states and the decision of the Supreme Court of No. Ca. when formerly [sic] rendered will be binding upon all parties." He told Seddon that while "it is my intention to make every possible effort to sustain the common cause, it is my firm intention to sustain the Judicial Authority of the land, the rights and privileges of the citizens, to the utmost of my power."[68] He then instructed the state adjutant general to issue an order forbidding the militia to arrest any deserter or conscript who had been released by a writ of habeas corpus.

The clash between the War Department and the governor had recently intensified as a result of a substitution case that had come before Pearson on a writ of habeas corpus. Pearson ruled that John N. Irvin, who had been drafted under the First Conscription Act and hired a substitute, was not subject again to conscription just because the second act had removed his substitute's age-based ineligibility. Pearson ordered Irvin's release.[69] Upon receiving word of Pearson's order, Superintendent of Conscription George W. Long (who had replaced Rains) instructed the North Carolina commandant of conscripts, Col. Peter Mallett, that "The opinion of Mr. Ch. Justice Pearson is not regarded by the Department as a sound exposition of the act of Congress, and you will not regard it in your official action as such."[70] Nevertheless, Pearson and the state superior court judges at chambers continued to hear cases involving habeas corpus and to discharge from military service a number of draftees who applied to the courts.[71]

Although Vance had defended Pearson's decisions regarding habeas corpus and the arrests of deserters and conscripts, he hoped that when the state supreme court met in June 1863, it would overrule Pearson. "I was highly gratified . . . to hear you had hopes of over ruling Judge Pearson," General Hill wrote to him. "He is injuring the noble old State incalculably.

The whole Confederacy now admits it to be the best of all fighting States and I have been as much surprised as gratified at the frankness with which this is admitted. The Yankees declared the same thing."[72]

When the supreme court convened in June, one of the three justices, Matthias E. Manly, was ill. So Pearson and Justice William H. Battle held court. Vance informed them that the War Department objected to the discharge of Confederate conscripts and deserters following writs of habeas corpus issued by the state courts. The department, he said, maintained that state courts had no jurisdiction over Confederate conscription laws. Pearson invited the Confederate attorney general to argue the question in the case of one J. C. Bryan, who had petitioned the chief justice for a writ of habeas corpus after being arrested as a conscript. When conscripted the first time in June 1862, Bryan had hired a substitute. But a year later he was arrested as a recusant conscript under the Conscription Act of September 1862. The Confederate district attorney argued before Pearson and Battle that the North Carolina judiciary had no jurisdiction over Confederate conscription. Attorneys for the state, Bartholomew F. Moore and Patrick H. Winston, argued that North Carolina supreme and superior court judges did have jurisdiction to order writs of habeas corpus and hear cases involving Confederate conscription. Pearson and Battle decided in favor of Moore and Winston and ruled that North Carolina judges had such jurisdiction and that the secretary of war had no judiciary standing and therefore no authority to overrule state courts. In Bryan's case, they decreed that he could not be held for army service. Any conscript, they declared, who furnished a substitute under the First Conscription Act could not be drafted again under the provisions of the second act.[73]

Pearson continued to issue writs of habeas corpus to conscripts and to discharge those who qualified under the June decision of the state court. But he never ruled that Confederate conscription was unconstitutional. His actions brought much anger from the Davis government, which complained frequently to Vance but did not authorize the suspension of habeas corpus in 1863 as it had done for a time in 1862. For his part, the governor continued to defend the right of the North Carolina judiciary to order writs and discharge draftees. In the absence of a Confederate supreme court to overrule North Carolina's justices, state law prevailed, and as chief executive, he was responsible for executing that law. Vance also had to face the fact that many North Carolinians supported Pearson and wanted the principles of states' rights and habeas corpus protected.[74]

But Vance also saw that Pearson's issuing of writs and discharging conscripts was encouraging draft evasion and desertion and undermining the

Confederate army. He therefore continued to attempt to arrest deserters and recusant conscripts. Those attempts led to animosity between him and the chief justice. The conflict between the two men erupted in September 1863 when Vance ordered the Home Guard in Davie County to arrest deserters and recusant conscripts. One guardsman, Richard M. Austin, refused to obey Vance's order. He was jailed, and he petitioned Pearson for a writ of habeas corpus. The chief justice issued the writ and scheduled a hearing at Salisbury. Judges Manly and Battle were absent from the hearing, and Pearson alone heard the case. He ruled that Vance had exceeded his authority in ordering the Home Guard to arrest Confederate deserters and conscripts. He ordered Austin discharged.[75]

Pearson continued to deny Vance's authority to use the Home Guard to arrest deserters and conscripts, and he released a number of them on writs of habeas corpus. The correspondence between the governor and the chief justice grew increasingly heated. On September 26, Vance protested Pearson's dismissal of two deserters—Edwards and Bailey—who had killed two members of the Yancey County Home Guard attempting to arrest them. Pearson held the hearing in Morganton in Burke County and discharged the two deserters on the ground that the Home Guard had no authority to arrest them. Vance was particularly enraged that Pearson had heard the case without notifying Col. John W. McElroy, commander of the Yancey County Home Guard, or hearing the testimony of other witnesses. Pearson responded to the governor:

> As the matter had been passed on by *justices of the peace* & no witnesses were in attendance, I felt it to be my duty to prepare the case, to be heard at Morganton, the following week.
>
> I make it a rule when the warrant of commitment is made by one *having jurisdiction* not to dispose of the case unless the prosecutor, if there be one or the committing magistrate, has been notified. If however the matter had stood upon the order of Col. McElroy alone, I should have felt it my duty to discharge the prisoners forthwith—for when the imprisonment is against law & in violation of the constitution, the party must be discharged without going into the evidence.

Miffed that Vance would have the audacity to question his decision, he sarcastically told the governor:

> I know that you & all other good citizens of the state, feel assured, that I will at all times, discharge the duties of my office, to the best of my judgment. For this reason, I understand, that by the expression "I

protest against their being tried . . . without due notification of Col. McElroy" you mean only to *suggest the propriety* of a postpone-ment—otherwise I should have felt called on, to demand, on what ground, the Governor, or anyone else, has a right to attempt by "pro-test" or in any other way, to interfere with the independent action of a judge in the discharge of his official duties?[76]

Vance responded with equal resentment and sarcasm:

You are correct in supposing that I meant no interference "with the independent action of a judge in the discharge of his official duties" by protesting against the discharge of these men without the evi-dence. . . . I was of the opinion (and am yet) that they were purposely taken before you, that the witnesses could not be present: & that two men alleged to have been found with arms in their hands in open resistance to the authority of the State, and accused of being *particeps criminis* to the murder of two of my militia, might be turned loose.
. . .

First it is declared incompetent for me to use my militia to arrest deserters and to execute the laws of Congress: next, when the militia have been absorbed by conscription, and the exemption Bill, the mili-tary given me in place of the militia [the Home Guard] is decided out of my hands by the same process: and lastly, the Chief Justice of the State goes outside of the case in question to pronounce a portion of my order against law, which was not called in question by the case! And yet I have been *patient* under it all, & shall submit to it quietly without even by implication, impeaching the motives of the Judge, rendering the decision.[77]

But Vance had no intention of submitting to Pearson's decisions. Be-cause the chief justice had rendered his verdicts in the cases of Austin and Bailey and Edwards alone without the opinion of the other two justices, Battle and Manly, Vance hoped to have Pearson's rulings overturned by the full court. He began to prepare a case to be presented in a petition for a writ of habeas corpus before the full court, which he intended to invite to hold a special sitting in Raleigh. At that hearing "out of term time" he anticipated and hoped that the court—with Battle and Manly present—would, in the new case before it, rule that using the Home Guard to arrest deserters was legal. "The consequences to the country," he wrote Battle, "of withdrawing all the forces of the State from the arresting of deserters, who are numerous in the State, and in many places have overawed and almost silenced the civil authorities, would be so great and alarming, that I am unwilling to assume the responsibility of so doing upon the decision of one judge." He needed the "benefit of their council [sic]," he told Battle, "if they will have the kindness to come to this place and set [sic] upon" the new case.[78] Battle wrote to Pearson and Manly asking them to name a convenient day on which they could hold a special session of court to hear the case Vance had selected. The case involved a petition for writ of habeas corpus by W. W. Woodell of the Wake County Home Guard, who, like Austin, had refused to participate in the arrest of deserters and conscripts. The petition was made to Battle.[79]

Vance also wrote to Pearson of his intention to call the court into special session:

> Desiring very much to get a decision of the Supreme Court in the matter of my power to order out the "Home Guard" to arrest deserters, I have been heretofore prevented by the continued absence of the Attorney General on his circuit, and even now, had to have a case prepared without him. The petition for the writ has been sent to Judge Battle instead of yourself for the reason . . . that your decision in the matter of Austin would prevent you from doing more than to discharge the man upon the return, but that you would sit on this case by my invitation and Judge Battle [sic].

Vance hoped that Pearson would agree to hear the petition with the other two justices and "relieve me and the public service from the embarrassing situation in which I stand." Otherwise, he might be forced to appeal to the legislature for a state law specifically allowing him to use the Home Guard to arrest deserters and conscripts.[80]

Although Vance prepared the case for presentation to the court without the assistance of the state attorney general, who was traveling the state circuit, he did not leave that official out of the procedure. He asked Sion H. Rogers, the attorney general, for an opinion on the question "Does the opinion of a single judge in such a case bind the Executive, the other judges and settle the law of the land as an 'adjudicated case' by the Supreme Court or does it simply operate in the individual case[?]" Rogers equivocated by saying that the question should be decided by the supreme court. "It is important," he told the governor, "to have uniformity in the decisions of our Judges; especially where the liberties of the citizens are involved. . . . [T]he Supreme Court I suppose upon invitation will meet and express an opinion which I have no doubt will be followed, emenating [sic] as it will from the members of the Supreme Court. Certainly no case of greater importance to the Citizen or Country has ever arisen for this unusual method of procedure." But he did tell Vance that he believed that the act creating the Home Guard implied that the governor had the authority to call upon the Home Guard to arrest deserters. He also declared that in an *individual* case involving habeas corpus, a single judge's decision was "final . . . until reversed by the Supreme Court."[81]

Pearson let Vance know in no uncertain terms that he would not attend a special meeting of the supreme court, if the governor called one. He claimed that the ruling he made in the Austin case was binding, because the decision of a "single judge in vacation" "settles the law" until such time as it might be overruled by the supreme court meeting at the scheduled date. He further insisted that "a decision of the court cannot be obtained until its next [regular] term."[82]

Pearson also informed Battle that he would not sit at the special session as Battle had requested. In light of that response, Battle suggested to Vance that "it would be better to have the application for the [Woodell] writ withdrawn upon the release of the petitioners," because "it is manifest that a decision of the question, having the effect of settling it cannot now be made, until the meeting of the Supreme Court." Battle observed that "this is a strong argument in favour of having the winter term of that court restored."[83]

Without the assistance of Battle and Manly, Vance realized that he had little chance of having Pearson's decisions overturned. He therefore carried out his secondary plan to request from the General Assembly an amendment to the Home Guard Act of July 1863 to allow the use of the Home Guard to arrest deserters and conscripts. The legislators complied with his request and approved the amendment in December.[84]

In the meantime, Vance fired off a letter to Pearson asserting that "in this case, where the consequences were bound to be of so serious a character, when the withdrawal of the Home Guards from this Service would have been accepted as an invitation to desertion from the Army, and a license to the outrages perpetrated by those absconding soldiers, I felt clear [*sic*] that it was my duty to give law and order and the Confederate cause the benefit of the doubt." But to the chief justice's implication that he was "prostrating the judiciary by disregarding its *decisions*," he responded: "I yield to no living man in respect for the courts of my country."[85]

Pearson replied with a long legal justification for his decisions regarding habeas corpus and the arrests of deserters and conscripts. "I will not pursue the subject further," he finally concluded in his letter of December 7. "I fear there is a radical difference of opinion between us, as to the powers conferred on the Executive by the Constitution, but hope we will each discharge the duties of his position without any unkind feeling toward each other."[86]

The wounded and annoyed Vance, however, was not willing to let the matter rest. On December 26 he wrote again to Pearson. He had withdrawn the Woodell case "from before Judge Battle at his request," he said. And the state lawmakers had given him the power he sought to arrest deserters and conscripts. But "there was no power in them to decide the issue between you and me and I am still left to bear the imputation of prostrating the Judiciary of my country with all who are so uncharitable as to believe it." He upbraided Pearson for not according him the proper respect as governor or recognizing the difficulties under which he had to labor. "I submit that you did not treat me with equal forbearance and consideration," he lamented, "surrounded as I was and am with a thousand difficulties, embarrassments and dangers, new to the Executive office and which none of my predecessors have felt." He had the double burden of supporting both the cause of Confederate independence and the civil liberties of the citizens of his state. "I know that it is almost impossible," he explained, "to bend every energy of the State for national independence, and to maintain intact all the rights and majesty of the civil law, without offending both. Yet I told the people of North Carolina this when they unsolicited, called me to this position, and I intend to keep this promise or perish in the attempt."[87]

Determined to have the last word, Pearson answered the governor again on January 11. He condescendingly implied that Vance was motivated by lowly political ambition, while he—with no political aspirations—occupied the Olympus of impartial constitutional justice. "I am satisfied you possess the talents and qualities of a politician," he lectured Vance, "& having long since withdrawn from the arena, I can see no useful purpose that will be effected by a continuation of our correspondence—but a few remarks are called for, in reply to your last letter." The "few remarks" swelled into another long legalistic—but not always relevant—defense of his decisions. In a catty tone, Pearson continued to patronize the governor as if Vance's reservations about his rulings and cooperation were not really worthy of consideration. "I should be exceedingly sorry," he feigned concern, "to think myself obnoxious to the charge of a want of forbearance towards a young and inexperienced governor, who *had* [italics added] my support." He particularly resented that Vance had the audacity to think he, as chief justice, should be at "'the beck & call' of the executive in violation of the constitutional provision, that the judiciary shall be independent of the executive."[88]

Although the legislature had authorized Vance to use the Home Guard to arrest deserters and conscripts, Pearson continued his defiance of Confederate authority in connection with applications for writs of habeas corpus. The Confederate Congress abolished the practice of substitution in late December 1863 and on January 5, 1864, passed a law that all conscripts who had provided substitutes were now liable to conscription.[89] Within a few weeks, Pearson ruled against that law. In a case involving conscript Edward S. Walton, who applied for a writ of habeas corpus, the chief justice declared that the law was invalid because the previous Conscription Act, allowing substitution, was a binding contract, which the Confederate Congress could not repudiate with a later law. Pearson held that the January 5 law making principal conscripts liable for the draft was unconstitutional, and he ordered Walton's discharge.[90]

This latest decision by Pearson led President Davis, growing ever more impatient with North Carolina and its chief justice, to ask Congress to authorize him again to suspend the writ of habeas corpus. In February 1864 Congress passed a new act permitting the president to suspend the writ in thirteen categories, including desertion and defiance of the draft. The eleventh clause was directed at peace advocates. It suspended the writ of habeas corpus for anyone arrested for "advising or inciting others to abandon the Confederate cause, or to resist the Confederate States, or to adhere to the enemy."[91]

By this time, Vance had decided to run for reelection for governor on a platform of support for continuing the war until Confederate independence was achieved. He cautioned Davis that the suspension of habeas corpus might lead to further public discontent with the war effort. He urged the president to be "chary of exercising the powers of the new habeas corpus law." Such actions, Vance warned, would play right into the hands of the dissenters. His reelection, he implied, was vital to keeping North Carolina on a pro-Confederate course, and a suspension of habeas corpus by the president might hurt Vance's chances in the upcoming gubernatorial election. But "If our citizens are left untouched by the army of military violence," the governor wrote Davis, "I do not despair of an appeal to the reason and patriotism of the people at the ballot box."[92] Davis angrily responded that he had no intention of suspending the writ of habeas corpus without just cause, "but should the occasion unhappily arise when the public safety demands their employment, I would be derelict in duty if I hesitated to use" such powers.[93] Despite his sharp retort to Vance, Davis was not quick to revoke the writ of habeas corpus, and he performed that act in only a few cases in the Confederate states.[94] Nevertheless, fearful that he might resort to such usurpation of states' rights, the North Carolina legislature in May passed a resolution against the suspension of the writ of habeas corpus and a bill making it a high misdemeanor to ignore a writ issued by a state judge. But in almost the same breath, the legislators also passed a resolution that any peace negotiations should be made only on the basis of Confederate independence.[95]

Vance warned Secretary of War Seddon not to resist Pearson's orders regarding the discharge of the principal conscripts who had hired substitutes. He cautioned the War Department that "if a man is discharged, I am bound to protect him and if the process of the court is resisted I am forced by my oath of office to summon the military power of the state to enforce it." He implied that he did not agree with Pearson's decision in declaring the January 5 law unconstitutional. "I have taken the ground," he told Seddon, "that the decision of a single judge at Chambers, does not possess the binding force of an 'adjudicated case' but it only operates to discharge the individual." But until it was overruled by the state supreme court, "it is final and absolute, made so expressly by the Statutes of this State." Vance, however, intimated that if Seddon would refrain from defying Pearson's decisions until the full supreme court met in June, then the other two justices would overturn the chief justice's rulings regarding the drafting of principal conscripts. "I therefore earnestly request," he wrote Seddon, "that you will order a suspension of the enrollment of the principals of substitutes in No. Ca., at least until time sufficient be allowed to exhaust all efforts at an amicable arrangement." Such a response by the War Department, although it "would deprive the Govt. of the services of these men until June, would yet give still greater advantages by preserving that peace and harmony between the respective governments, without which all our labors will be in vain." Vance reiterated that much of the legal difficulty between the states and the Confederate government could be attributed to the lack of a Confederate supreme court. "[H]owever unfortunate it may be," he opined, "to the efficient and equal working of the Government the laws of Congress are at the mercy, so to speak, of the various Judges of the various states. I submit that it is not possible to avoid it in the absence of a Supreme Court of the Confederacy to give harmony and uniformity of construction."[96]

The willingness of Davis and Seddon to heed Vance's advice and back away from suspending the writ of habeas corpus in North Carolina paid off for Confederate conscription. For when the full supreme court met at its regular term in June and reviewed the Walton case, Battle and Manly overturned Pearson's ruling that laws abolishing substitution and declaring principals subject to the draft were unconstitutional.[97] Over time thereafter, Pearson's influence "waned" and "Battle and Manly took over" the court.[98] But the chief justice continued to make some rulings "in vacation" that were not reversed by the full court.[99]

One such case involved Daniel L. Russell Jr., the son of a wealthy former Whig planter and large slaveholder of Brunswick County. After the war, Russell would become a U.S. congressman, a judge, and Republican governor of North Carolina. The young man left the University of North Carolina in 1862 and organized at his own expense a company of artillery from his home county. He was elected captain, and his company saw service at the mouth of the Cape Fear River below Wilmington. Russell's several attempts to have his company transferred to Virginia failed, and, exasperated, he finally moved his men to Wilmington in an effort to have them sent by train to Virginia. Confederate officers arrested him for acting without orders, but his "family connections enabled him to get off with only a reprimand."[100]

By 1863, however, Russell and his father became disaffected and antagonistic to President Davis and the War Department's policies. Daniel Russell Sr. spoke out publicly against the conscription laws. Aware of the Russells' views, the Confederate enrolling officer at Wilmington, Capt. William W. Swann, ordered Captain Russell to surrender four men in his company to be conscripted. Swann claimed that the men had volunteered for Russell's company—presumably to avoid serving away from home—after the new conscription law had become operative. Russell refused to give over the men and, according to Swann, used abusive language to the conscription officer. Swann informed his superiors that Russell and his father had publicly denounced the conscription laws and interfered with his duties. He pressed charges against young Russell for disobedience of orders and improper conduct.

The eighteen-year-old Russell responded by marching into Swann's office and beating the officer with a hickory stick. He was on the verge of shooting Swann when his aim was averted by bystanders, who restrained him. A court-martial in late February 1864 found Russell guilty of Swann's charges but because of his youth recommended him "to the clemency of the Commanding General." Gen. William H. C. Whiting, commanding at Wilmington, concluded that Russell would be permitted to enroll as a soldier in a new company of his choice. Russell and his father refused to comply with that order, and the young captain demanded that Whiting revoke it. But the general stood fast and advised Russell to "go quietly to your company without *for the present* making any attempt to have your sentence changed."[101]

But with the assistance of Vance, Russell and his father managed to influence the Brunswick County magistrates to appoint Russell as commissioner for poor relief in the county, even though the young man was probably not eligible for the office because he was not twenty-one years old. Vance then claimed "the exemption of Daniel L Russell Jr., the county commissioner of Brunswick as an officer necessary to the Civil administration of the State Government." The Russells further strengthened their case by convincing the voters of Brunswick County to elect Russell Jr. to his position as commissioner. The Conscription Act of 1863 allowed each county one commissioner to distribute aid to destitute soldiers' families.[102]

The War Department, however, ordered Russell to report for duty, over Vance's protest that Russell had been "duly elected to an office which I deemed necessary" before he was enrolled as a conscript and was therefore exempt from military service.[103] Vance cautioned Whiting that an attempt "to arrest Mr. Russell or to disturb him in the discharge of his official duties will be taken as a deliberate and unwarranted usurpation of authority & will be resisted accordingly."[104]

Russell also applied to Pearson for a writ of habeas corpus, and on July 25, 1864, the chief justice ruled the young man discharged on the ground that as a state official he was exempt from conscription. The War Department challenged Pearson's decision. Ultimately the Confederate attorney general, George Davis, a native of Wilmington and apparently an acquaintance of the Russells, informed them that President Davis had reviewed Russell's case and revoked the sentence against him, thereby releasing him from conscription.[105] Evidently, the other two members of the state supreme court concurred with Pearson's ruling in the Russell case, because Battle "released a prisoner on habeas corpus citing the Russell decision as precedent later that summer."[106]

Vance's role in the Russell affair did him no credit. His official papers are filled with examples in which he turned down appeals from poor, noninfluential men who asked for his help in getting appointments that would earn them exemptions. Many of these men had dependent families and presumably were killed or wounded while serving in the army. Vance's usual response to such petitioners was that they were subject to Confederate conscription laws, and that he could provide them no assistance. That he went considerably out of his way to help Russell contradicted his public stance on the legitimacy of Confederate authority regarding conscription.

The difficulties of conscription, desertion, and legal jurisdiction weighed upon Vance. Also vexing to the governor and the people of the state was the Confederacy's impressment of food supplies, equipment, and slaves. The impressment act passed by the Congress in March 1863 allowed the

Confederate Commissary Department to impress, with compensation to owners, food, forage, livestock, wagons, and other private property, as well as blacks (enslaved and free) to support and aid the army. The Quartermaster Department was responsible for collecting the supplies and equipment and transporting them to their destinations. The governor appointed the state impressment commissioner, or agent. A price schedule plus arbitration by two "disinterested" parties—one appointed by the commissioner and the other by the property owner—determined the amount of compensation. The system often created dissatisfaction and resentment throughout the South. Many North Carolinians considered such a policy to be a usurpation of states' rights. Commissioners, or "pressmen," sometimes took items with only promises to pay, and some engaged in speculation with the impressed goods. Popular animosity grew in the late months of the war when an amendment to the law replaced the price schedule with the phrase a "just price," which did not take into consideration the inflation of Confederate currency.[107]

Vance usually supported official Confederate impressment performed under the provisions of Confederate law. He protested impressment by Confederate army officers prior to the law of March 1863, which legally authorized compensated confiscation by the Commissary Department.[108] But after the law was passed, he made every effort to cooperate with the War Department in securing supplies, equipment, and labor. "The call for aid to the Army has met with a liberal response from a generous people," he wrote Seddon one month after the law went into effect, "and I trust all fears may be dismissed."[109]

Vance's cooperation included providing slaves to build fortifications in the state. Before the impressment law, he had refused Seddon's call for slaves to work on the railroad connection from Greensboro to Danville, Virginia. He pointed out that planters were already volunteering their slaves to work on the Wilmington-to-Petersburg railroad. Slaveholders were complaining about the absence of their slaves; "the very existence of the people required them to labor on their farms."[110] But subsequently the governor assisted in providing slaves for working on the fortifications at the port of Wilmington. On April 23, 1863, he informed General Whiting that the "second lot" of slave laborers was ready to depart to the coast. But he asked Whiting if perhaps there was a "chance of dispensing" with the second group: "They are so greatly needed in the fields," he implored the general, "and the matter of provisions is one of such immense importance to us all, that I beg you to do without them, if the safety of the Country will at all permit. Of course this must depend upon your judgment, and I know I need not argue the matter with you. They shall be sent promptly if you deem it indispensable."[111]

A month later, as slaveholders complained about the impressment of their slaves, he asked Whiting again if he would release those "at work under your command" to their owners. "It would almost prove ruinous to keep them after the wheat harvest, which will be early in June," he told the general. Vance also noted that he had received rumors that slaves were being used for purposes other than those for which they were impressed. He heard that some were being "employed in cleaning out the town and waiting on the officers." He did not know for sure if this was true, but he reminded Whiting "that negroes could not be taken from the fields for such purposes."[112]

Vance always maintained that free blacks could be a vital labor supply for work on railroads, fortifications, and other Confederate facilities. He encouraged Seddon to recruit them to work on the Danville rail line. Under the provisions of the March 1863 act, the impressment of free blacks was to operate as a draft administered by Confederate conscription officers. In July 1863 Vance wrote to Seddon that Col. (soon Gen.) Jeremy F. Gilmer, Confederate military engineer, had written to him about enrolling 50 percent of North Carolina's free blacks to work on the Danville line connection at Greensboro. At first Vance thought 50 percent was too great a number, but after a conference with Gilmer, "he satisfied me that the needs of the road would demand that proportion." He encouraged Seddon to order the enrollment of the black laborers.[113] However, in the final days of the war, when some Confederate leaders favored enlisting slaves into the Confederate army to help save the failing war effort, Vance remained opposed to the idea. The state legislature and most white North Carolinians joined the governor in opposition to the arming of slaves. "The proposition to conscript negroes for soldiers may do to talk about but it will not answer to practice," the *Milton Chronicle* concluded in November 1864. "We are satisfied of two things. 1st, that white troops would not companionship [*sic*] with them, and 2ndly, they could not be trusted if left to manage themselves. We regard the proposition as one to augment the Yankee army."[114]

Although Vance cooperated with Confederate authorities in the lawful impressment of supplies, material, and labor, the cooperation did not extend to arbitrary impressment by military officers in the state. He registered angry protest with the War Department when Confederate officers on their own authority confiscated forage or other supplies from the populace.[115] Vance remained adamant that all impressment must be made through the Commissary Department according to the Impressment Act of 1863. He also insisted on that principle in the enrollment of free blacks. Daniel Locklar of Richmond County complained to the governor that he and other free blacks were being impressed to labor at the state salt works. The agent from the works, he told the governor, "Comes at the dead hours of night and carries us off wherever he thinks proper, gives us one dollar and fifty cents per day." Locklar asked if there was a law permitting a state salt agent to impress free blacks. "I am perfectly willing to do for our country whatever the law requires of me," wrote Locklar, "but if there be no such law and this Agent taking this power within himself perhaps speculating on the labor of the free colored men and our families suffering for bread, I am not willing to submit to such, please let me know if this Agent [has] *the power to use me as he does.*" Vance responded that the salt agent "has no such authority."[116]

Vance maintained that the claims of General Lee and others about the desertion and disloyalty of North Carolinians were unfounded and unfair. And he quickly expressed his displeasure to authorities in Richmond when he and his constituents felt that North Carolina's soldiers were not receiving the recognition that they deserved from the War Department and the Virginia press. "There has been much complaint among our people," he wrote Seddon on July 3, 1863, "that the participation of our troops, has not been noticed, with that commendation to which they are supposed to be entitled." He suggested that, because there were no news reporters from North Carolina with the Army of Northern Virginia, his friend journalist Murdock J. McSween be assigned to Lee's command to report on the performance of North Carolina troops.[117] The secretary of war forwarded the request to Lee. The general responded to Seddon that "I cannot recommend" that the governor's proposal "be adopted." If it were, then the same privilege would have to "be extended to all the states and it can readily be seen what would be the result." Lee insisted that official reports of troops in battle were accurate and sufficient. "If the officers commanding do not tell the truth they should be removed," he argued.[118]

Thus denied his request, the piqued Vance responded that he did not question the army's official reports. Rather, "I only desired Sir," he told Seddon, "that newspaper correspondents from N.C. should be allowed to attend an army, with the same protection, and the same access to information as I learn is given to others. But as Genl Lee objects to it and has seen proper to think that I object to official reports, which have never yet been published, I beg leave to withdraw the request." Miffed that his request had been summarily dismissed, Vance petulantly informed Seddon that

"The troops from N.C. can afford to appeal to history: I am confident that they have little to expect from their associates."[119]

On several occasions, the Tar Heel chief executive protested to President Davis about "the appointment of citizens of other states to offices and positions here that should of right be filled by our own people."[120] Confederate senator George Davis, who became the Confederacy's last attorney general in January 1864, was the only North Carolinian to hold a cabinet position in the Davis government. North Carolina could claim no full generals in the Confederate army. Of the nineteen lieutenant generals, only two were from North Carolina.[121] Vance accused Davis of denying general officer rank to North Carolinians because he considered them antisecessionists. "It is of course impossible for me to prove," the governor told the president, "that any other than military considerations have governed your army appointments; but I desire to call your attention to the fact that out of twenty-five or thirty generals appointed from North Carolina only three were anti-secessionists."[122] Vance raised a heated objection when the Virginian Col. Thomas P. August was appointed commandant of conscripts after North Carolinian Col. Peter Mallett was wounded and temporarily absent from his duties as commandant. Vance did not approve of a Virginian's conscripting North Carolinians, and he requested that the recovered Mallett be returned to the position of commandant.[123] On another occasion, he complained to President Davis that Col. Edmund Bradford, a native of Pennsylvania who had settled in Virginia, had received from the quartermaster general an appointment as the chief collector of the tax-in-kind in North Carolina.[124]

Except for this complaint about the collector, Vance accepted the imposition of a tax-in-kind as a necessary measure to support the Confederate war effort. He lent his support to the collection of the tax despite considerable protest from North Carolinians who objected to giving 10 percent of their crops and livestock to Confederate agents. Tar Heels' resentment of the tax-in-kind led many, who were already facing hard times, to hope for an end to hostilities, even if it meant peace negotiations. "The Confederate Tax in Kind will produce dissatisfaction if not oppersition from the people," Philip Hodnett, a Caswell County farmer, wrote to the governor in July 1863. "There seems to be no escape for us from these sore troubles but to make peace with the North on the best terms we can, and I solemnly beleave that three fourths of the people of Caswell desire peace now, while we have power enough to assure our constitutional rights."[125]

Desiring to placate Vance and thereby retain his support, Davis and Seddon appeased him by removing August and reappointing Mallett.[126]

But, beginning to show some irritation about Vance's complaints over Confederate appointments of North Carolinians, Davis implied that part of the governor's motivation in protesting the lack of appointments was to promote his own political career at home. On July 18, 1863, the president wrote the governor that he and Seddon had discussed the Bradford affair and decided "that not only this but every impediment to your successful career should be removed." Nevertheless, he recognized the difficulties that Vance faced in keeping North Carolinians committed to the Confederate war effort. "I am aware," he told the governor, "of the embarrassments you may have in carrying out your patriotic efforts to aid the Confederate government in this struggle and relying on your capacity and energy to overcome them would be far from willingly allowing any additional obstruction to be thrown in your way."[127]

Davis also attempted to soothe Vance's bruised feelings over the lack of recognition that North Carolina troops were receiving from the Confederate government and the Richmond press. The president seized upon an opportunity provided by Lt. Frank M. Harney of the Fourteenth Regiment North Carolina Troops. At the recent Battle of Gettysburg, Harney had been killed while capturing the colors of a Pennsylvania regiment. His last request reportedly was that the flag be "presented in his name to the President." Stroking the ego of Vance and North Carolinians in the hope of encouraging their continued support, Davis wrote the governor:

> The wish of the dying hero has been complied with. The flag is in my possession and will be treasured by me as an honorable memento of the valor and patriotic devotion which the soldiers of North Carolina have displayed on many hard fought fields.
>
> I have thought it due to the lamented officer, with whose family I have not the advantage of being acquainted, to communicate these circumstances to you as the Chief Magistrate of his State, and to express through you to his State, his comrades and his family the sincere sympathy I feel with them for the loss of one so worthy of their admiration and esteem.[128]

Davis's effort to praise Tar Heels for their important contributions to the war was partly undone by the irony that Harney was not a North Carolinian. He was a native of Kentucky who had been working as a carpenter in Asheville when he enlisted in the Fourteenth Regiment. Still, Vance acknowledged Davis's attempt to commend North Carolina's soldiers. "I do not know Sir, that he has any relatives whatever in N.C.," he informed the president. "Though without kindred in this his adopted State, I assure you

She will be proud to see his name placed on the long list of her heroic dead, and all will welcome his memory among their bravest sons, and mourn him as a noble brother slain for her defence."[129]

As the war continued and turned against the Confederacy, the strain of the conflict led to growing dissension between Vance and Davis. Much of Vance's testiness over Confederate authority and policies stemmed from his personal sensitivity to slight and a conviction that neither he nor North Carolina was receiving the proper deference, respect, and credit due a sovereign state and its chief executive. The extent of his temper and his insecurity about the respect he deserved as governor was demonstrated by a volatile encounter that he had with Lt. Col. Charles E. Thorburn, who was in charge of defenses at the port of Wilmington. In late June 1863, Vance traveled to Wilmington to inspect the cargo aboard the state-owned blockade-runner *Advance*, which had just arrived through the blockade. According to usual policy, blockade-runners were quarantined for a time in order to thwart an outbreak of yellow fever. Vance, however, received permission from the Wilmington Commissioners of Navigation, who supervised the quarantine, to board the *Advance*. But when the governor attempted to disembark, he was met by Thorburn, who refused to let him leave the vessel. An angry confrontation ensued between the two men.[130]

According to Vance, after showing "the permission of the Commissioner and assuring him [Thorburn] of the assent of Genl Whiting and remonstrating with him in person, he replied that he 'did not care for Gov. Vance nor Gov. Jesus Christ,' that I 'should not come off that boat for fifteen days'—and accordingly placed a guard on the wharf with orders to shoot any one attempting to get off." Ultimately the chairman of the board of commissioners arrived on the scene and ordered the governor's release, but not before the fuming Vance had missed the train back to Raleigh.[131]

When he heard of the incident, General Whiting immediately dispatched a letter of apology to Vance. He admitted that he had given the governor permission to board the *Advance* "On ascertaining that she was from Bermuda with a clear bill of health." Thorburn confessed that he "was disrespectful in language," and Whiting, who had been absent from Wilmington when the confrontation occurred, relieved him from command at Wilmington. "I regret exceedingly that any disrespect to the Governor should have occurred in my command and I present as the Chief Confederate officer here my apology," the general wrote Vance.[132]

But Vance continued to seethe and was not content to let the matter rest with Whiting's apology and reassignment of Thorburn. His sensitivity and temper, which in earlier days had resulted in fisticuffs and challenges to duels, flared again. He wrote to President Davis expressing his outrage at the insult he had suffered. He demanded Thorburn's departure from the state: "Having thus deliberately, wilfully and without excuse, inflicted a gross insult upon the people of North Carolina through her Chief Magistrate, in their name I demand his removal from the State, and that he be no more placed in command of her troops. If it be deemed indispensable that North Carolina soldiers should be commanded by Virginians, I should regret to see the old Dominion retain all her gentlemen for her own use, and furnish us only her blackguards."[133]

The relationship between Davis and Vance remained strained and sometimes antagonistic, and their correspondence often disintegrated into petulant quarreling. But historians should be cautious about inferring from the disagreements between Davis and Vance that the governor was anything less than totally committed to the Confederacy and its efforts to win its independence. One must consider the relationship between Davis and Vance in light of Davis's stubborn, proud, and inflexible personality and the youth and impetuous temper of Vance, who throughout both his terms was quick to take offense at any perceived slight to him or his state, or any implication that North Carolina was not doing all it could for the Confederate cause. Despite their quarrels, Vance made conscientious efforts to cooperate and compromise with the Davis government. On two occasions he visited Richmond in order to talk personally with Davis to smooth out difficulties between the state and the government in Richmond. Shortly after taking office in 1862, he traveled to the Confederate capital to discuss with the president how the two governments could best operate together to prosecute the war. Again in August 1863, he called on Davis to talk over the dissatisfaction in North Carolina about certain Confederate policies and appointments. He came away encouraged by Davis's response. "I trust things will be better now that we are understood in Richmond," he reported after the meeting.[134]

To be sure, Davis frequently quarreled with Vance, but then the obstinate and proud president had difficulties in dealing with many officials and army officers.[135] Vance, on the other hand, had a temper that displayed a certain insecurity and immaturity and that sometimes led him to fire off to Davis or the secretary of war angry missives about alleged Confederate injustices, before he took time to reflect on his comments or to verify facts about reported outrages, such as impressment or other abuses of North Carolina soldiers or civilians. But neither Davis nor Vance ever denounced the other as a demagogue, and Davis never openly questioned Vance's loyalty to the cause of a free and independent Confederate States of America.

Nonetheless, such problems as conscription, desertion, tax-in-kind, impressment, and disaffection plagued Vance throughout the war. But not all the *official* policies that taxed his leadership among his citizens originated with the Confederate government. One Federal mandate—issued by none other than President Abraham Lincoln—came close to generating an internal crisis in North Carolina that called upon all Vance's skills as governor to prevent.

3

"HUMANITY SHUDDERS
AT WHAT MAY TAKE PLACE"

Vance feared that the Emancipation Proclamation might excite panic in North Carolina. He worried that Abraham Lincoln's edict for African American freedom would create—among slaveholders and nonslaveholders alike—a chilling and widespread fear that slaves would be incited by news of the proclamation to rise up and murder their white masters and then turn upon the white population throughout the state. Vance and the Tar Heel lawmakers therefore took new and extraordinary measures to combat potential trouble from slaves who might be inspired by news of Lincoln's document. Vance and his supporters also struggled to prevent the fear of slave violence and revolt engendered by the Emancipation Proclamation from instilling disillusionment and weakening war support among the common people in North Carolina.

So fearful was the state legislature that the Emancipation Proclamation would lead to slave insurrection that it passed—shortly after the proclamation was issued in its final form in January 1863—a law that provided for the speedy trial and execution of African Americans who were accused of capital crimes. Titled "Courts of Oyer and Terminer," the act of February 1863 authorized the governor to call special terms of county superior courts "to indict and try all white persons, slaves, and free persons of color, and persons charged with capital felonies, crimes, misdemeanors, or any violation or offense whatever of the criminal law of which the superior courts of their regular terms have jurisdiction."[1]

A prior law of 1854, titled "Slaves and Free Negroes," already empowered the governor to call for courts of oyer and terminer to try African Americans charged with conspiracy or insurrection immediately.[2] Since the colonial period, the governor had had the authority to call such courts. But the laws of 1854 and 1863 further specified the governor's power and broadened the jurisdiction of the tribunals. The 1854 statute had been a response to the ever-increasing fear among North Carolinians that growing abolitionist activity in the United States might lead to violent slave uprisings. The courts of oyer and terminer specified in that law enabled authorities to try and execute with dispatch blacks accused of plotting or participating in insurrection. As an emergency power given to the governor, the convening of such courts eliminated the potentially long wait for district superior courts to hear the cases at their regularly scheduled terms. State officials feared that during such intervals, news and rumors of violent crimes allegedly committed by slaves would create panic among the white populace and possibly inspire further revolt among other slaves.

Past events seemed to justify their fears. A nervous dread and anticipation of slave revolt had haunted North Carolinians for decades. In North Carolina in 1802, a white panic over rumors of a slave insurrection in the counties around Albemarle Sound resulted in the execution of two dozen slaves and the whipping and cropping of a large number of others. North Carolina slaveholders were also alarmed by the alleged Denmark Vesey conspiracy, which occurred in South Carolina in 1822. Then in 1829, a widely circulated pamphlet calling for slave rebellion appeared in North Carolina. Titled *An Appeal to the Coloured Citizens of the World*, the publication was written by David Walker, a free black and native North Carolinian who had settled in Boston. To prevent slaves from reading such subversive and incendiary literature, the state legislature in the following year passed a law forbidding any North Carolinian to teach a slave to read or write. Slave patrollers became increasingly diligent as white anxiety about slave discontent increased.[3] Slaves traveling off their plantations were required to have a pass from their owners. "If you were out without a pass," Wake County slave Andrew Boone recalled, "they would sure git you. . . . If you was out of place, they would wear you out."[4] White fears intensified even further in 1831 when the white abolitionist William Lloyd Garrison published, in Boston, the newspaper the *Liberator*. Garrison's newspaper called for moral thinkers everywhere to unite to eliminate the evil of slavery through any means possible, including inciting African Americans to violence. The newspaper infuriated southern slaveholders, including North Carolinians, who increasingly became paranoid about their slaves and hostile toward the abolitionists.

The year 1831 brought a bloody slave revolt in Southampton County, Virginia, not far from the North Carolina border. The leader of the revolt, a literate and deeply spiritual slave named Nat Turner, organized a group of enslaved African Americans that brutally murdered fifty-seven white men, women, and children. Although Virginia authorities quickly crushed Turner's insurrection, the uprising nevertheless excited panic in North Carolina. Rumors circulated throughout the state, especially in the large slaveholding counties in the east, that slaves were conspiring to rise up and kill whites. Responding to the hysteria, militia and local officials unjustly arrested and tortured a number of innocent slaves whom they suspected of conspiring to revolt. County superior courts executed several slaves said to be involved in an armed conspiracy.[5]

Fear of African American resistance or revolt led white North Carolinians to petition the state legislature to pass a law making it mandatory for all free blacks to leave the state. The lawmakers took no action on this request, perhaps because of the value of the state's relatively large number of skilled blacks and their contributions. But a state constitutional convention in 1835 revoked the voting privileges of free blacks. Subsequent state legislation also prohibited free African Americans from possessing any seditious publications (such as Walker's *Appeal*), teaching slaves to read or write, gambling with slaves, selling outside their county of residence without a license, and leaving the state for more than ninety days and then returning. Other laws eventually denied free blacks the right to preach in public, to possess a gun without a license, to buy or sell liquor, and to attend public meetings. As the conflict over slavery progressed, whites increasingly looked upon free blacks, who generally were more skilled, educated, economically secure, and autonomous than their slave counterparts, as potential leaders and instigators of slave revolts.[6]

The debate over the expansion of slavery into the territories acquired during the Mexican War in 1846–1848, the Kansas-Nebraska Act of 1854, the subsequent violence in Kansas, and other instances in the 1850s intensified the conflict between slaveholders and abolitionists.[7] Amid the growing anticipation that abolitionist activity would inspire slave violence within its borders, North Carolina passed the 1854 law giving the governor the power to move swiftly to quash slave insurrection by the speedy trial and conviction of African Americans accused of conspiracy or insurrection.

With the outbreak of the Civil War, whites became increasingly apprehensive about the flight of slaves to Union lines and also the impressment of blacks to work on Confederate fortifications, where they were away from their masters' close supervision. The propensity of impressed slaves to run away led Pitt County slaveholder E. J. Blount to complain to Governor Vance in 1864 that

There is an order in this c[oun]ty for inroling [*sic*] the Slaves . . . to work on breastworks or fortifications. From a thorough knowledge of the disposition of our slaves & the ease with which they can make their escape to the enemy, making an attempt to carry them off or even enrolling them will have a very bad influence. The last draft for that purpose caused several to run off & will certainly make more do so if there is an attempt made to carry them off now. At the request of a great many citizens of the county I respectfully wish you to intercede with Col [Peter] Mallett [conscription officer for N.C.] and have the order for this county countermanded, at least so far as to carry them off is concerned, as you cannot receive this in time to prevent their inrolment [*sic*]. This is not asking any thing more than justice of him, when he is made acquainted with our exposed condition & the ease with which our slaves can make their escape to the enemy.[8]

When Lincoln issued his preliminary Emancipation Proclamation in September 1862, members of the Confederate Congress expressed their outrage, denouncing the document as a call for slave uprising and uncivilized warfare. They vowed to retaliate in kind. Some congressmen from the Deep South proposed that the Confederacy abandon the rules of civilized war and fight under the black flag. The Judiciary Committee submitted a resolution stating that if Lincoln did not revoke the proclamation, all captured United States officers and noncommissioned officers "shall be imprisoned at hard labor or other wise put at hard labor until the termination of the war." The committee's resolution further stipulated that all white commanders of black troops or Union soldiers who incited slaves to revolt should be put to death when captured. The Confederate Senate, however, did not adopt either proposal, although such discussions continued. President Davis informed the Congress that in response to the Emancipation Proclamation, he would deliver all captured Federal officers to the Confederate states to be tried and sentenced as "criminals engaged in exciting servile insurrection." The president, however, never carried out his threat, apparently because he anticipated that the Federals would retaliate with similar acts against captured Confederate officers.[9]

News of the preliminary Emancipation Proclamation infuriated white North Carolinians. The Tar Heel State's newspaper editors denounced the document with venomous anger. In the *North Carolina Standard*, William W. Holden referred to the preliminary proclamation as

one of the most monstrously wicked documents that ever emanated from human authority. . . . If this proclamation could be carried out,

it would consign the whites and blacks of the North American conti-
nent to one common ruin. . . . Emancipation once effected, a struggle
would commence between the two races for the mastery. Every one
knows how that struggle would terminate. Four millions of blacks
would soon be reduced to a handful—they would be slaughtered by
the whites until every hill and valley in the South would be stained
with blood. They would disappear like the mist of the morning, even
before any well-directed attempt could be made to colonize them. . . .
Here is an edict, by the head of a so-called Christian people, which not
only violates palpably and grossly the Constitution of his country,
but which if successful in its operation would make four millions of
innocent creatures parties to a bloody struggle, and, by arraigning
them against their masters, who are their best friends, would inevitably lead to their destruction as the only means left for preserving the
white race.[10]

If the Emancipation Proclamation engendered slave uprising, Holden continued, it "would utterly desolate the South" and record the North "down
in history as worthy of the most eminence among fiends." The bloodshed
caused by such a document would make the "deified *Union* . . . stand out as
the greatest moral and political monster ever known in the history of man-
kind." Holden, however, opposed the Confederacy's fighting under the
black flag as proposed by some Confederates. "We profess to be Christians,
not savages," he declared.[11]

Some citizens of the Old North State asserted that instead of creating
panic and helping the Federal cause, the Union president's proclamation
would only unify and strengthen the Confederacy and its efforts for independence. John W. Syme, editor of the *Raleigh Register*, insisted that "Lincoln's proclamation and its bid for servile insurrection" would even bring
into the war the "Border states on the side of the Southern Confederacy"
and convince foreign countries of the Confederacy's resolve. Unlike Holden
of the *Standard*, Syme supported the severe retaliatory measures proposed
by the Judiciary Committee and other members of the Confederate Congress. He maintained that "far too much leniency has already been shown
to the accursed Yankees." Their "devillish mission," he proclaimed, "is
either to cut our throats or manacle our limbs." Other newspapers, such
as the Wilmington *Journal* and Raleigh's *Spirit of the Age*, agreed with
Syme that the proclamation would "strengthen the unity of the South and
embitter its hostility to the whole vile Yankee nation."[12] Despite such
rhetoric, however, the prevailing feeling among North Carolinians about

the Emancipation Proclamation was one of fear that the edict would inspire slave violence and social upheaval, perhaps centered at first in the east, where Federal forces occupied an extensive area along the rivers and sounds.

Nowhere was that fear more prevalent than among the common people of North Carolina, who did not own slaves or owned only one or two. After all, without the physical protection that wealth and influence with public officials could bring, they were just as vulnerable to slave violence as were slaveowners. In fact, planters and local authorities worried that the lower classes would wreak social havoc if they armed themselves and banded together to inflict retribution on slaves accused of murder or rape. Furthermore, many soldiers might desert the army in order to come home to protect their families from feared slave disorders. State leaders therefore implored Vance to avoid vigilantism and social unrest from poor whites by dealing swiftly with slaves charged with capital crimes.

Many yeoman North Carolinians were already discontented and disillusioned with the war. By 1863, they were becoming weary of the battlefield deaths, Federal raids, Confederate conscription and impressment, tax-in-kind, violence among deserters and lawless bands, and shortages and deprivations.[13] Lincoln's proclamation added to their worries by instilling anxiety that slaves would be inspired to revolt by news of the document. That the Emancipation Proclamation provided for the arming of escaped slaves as Union soldiers further intensified white nightmares about defiant and unruly bondsmen. White anxiety had been growing in North Carolina since the Union army began occupying much of the state's coastal region following the capture of Roanoke Island in February 1862 and New Bern in March. Thousands of North Carolina slaves seized the opportunity to flee to Union lines, where Northern officers assigned them the status of contraband of war and refused to return them to their masters in Confederate territory.[14]

The final Emancipation Proclamation of January 1, 1863, provided for the enlistment and arming of escapees in black regiments in eastern North Carolina and throughout the occupied South. In April 1863, Federal secretary of war Edwin M. Stanton authorized Col. (later Gen.) Edward A. Wild of Boston to organize a brigade of black troops in coastal North Carolina.[15] Even before the proclamation officially called for the formation of black units, Union generals, on their own initiative, had begun organizing escaped slaves into United States regiments. These generals included James H. ("Big Jim") Lane in Kansas, David Hunter in South Carolina, and John W. Phelps in Louisiana. In the Militia Act of July 17, 1862, Congress authorized Lincoln to organize African Americans and use them "for any military or naval services for which they may be found competent." But before the Emancipation Proclamation, Lincoln moved cautiously in *officially* authorizing the use of black soldiers and declined to endorse Hunter's First South Carolina Infantry (later formed and commanded by Col. Thomas Wentworth Higginson).[16]

Rumors that Yankee invaders were enlisting blacks in North Carolina alarmed and infuriated slaveholders and other whites in the state. Halifax County plantation mistress Catherine Ann Devereux Edmondston angrily recorded in her diary on July 30, 1862: "Throughout the North Negro Regts are being raised, equipped, & drilled as soldiers, Lincoln in this having yeilded [*sic*] to the popular cry. Hunter in S C has a Regt of them which he styles the 1st S C Volunteers. Amo writes me that he has seen two men who were taken prisoners at Port Royal guarded by negroes in the US uniform. Cuffee did not do his duty, as they escaped! In this State they are doing the same thing. Some of them marched from Washington [N.C.] to Plymouth last week. [Confederate] Col Williams hung two sent out as emissaries to induce others to run away & enlist. They had U S money & enlistment papers with them."

Following the issuance of the proclamation in its final form, Mrs. Edmondston expressed further outrage at the enlistment of former slaves. On February 10, 1863, she declared: "Think of it, armed negroes! Think of what it means! And this is the nineteenth century! and the proposers of this infernal act call themselves Christians."[17] The Emancipation Proclamation and the recruiting of former slaves as Federal soldiers also alarmed Gen. James Johnston Pettigrew, commanding a brigade of North Carolina troops in the eastern part of the state. "Bad times are coming here," he wrote to Governor Vance on February 5, 1863, "for the Yankees seem to have selected this State and Louisiana for the practical experiment of arming the negroes in the midst of the white population. From all appearances the 'blag [black] flag' is imm[inent]. . . . In view of this enforcement of Lincoln's proclamation, among the negroes, I think that the Legislature should take some step calculated to encourage our people and add to the confusion of the enemy, and [increase] the dissatisfaction [against blacks in the Union army], which we know to exist, by adding thereto the powerful notion of the fear of consequences."[18]

A number of the state's politicians worried that existing North Carolina laws did not go far enough in dealing with armed blacks. William T. Dortch, a former legislator and a Confederate senator, expressed his concern to Vance on January 7, 1863:

My object in writing is to call your attention to our laws in regard to the punishment of armed slaves & Yankees who may be found with them. My books have been sent up the country, but according to my recollection our statutes are not sufficient to embrace cases which may occur under the proclamation of Lincoln & our President.

The mere fact of finding a colored person armed ought to be made a capital offence, & the presence of a Yankee with an armed negro ought also to be made capital.

After examination if you think necessary, I hope you will bring the subject to the attention of the Legislature.[19]

Slaveholders and law enforcement officials agreed that speed was of the essence in bringing rebellious slaves to justice. They feared that the news that slaves were plotting and murdering their masters might incite hysteria among an already nervous population and compound disillusionment with the war. Such news might inspire other slaves to revolt and might even result in the panicked killing of a large number of innocent African Americans, as had occurred during the Nat Turner uprising. The 1854 law specified that courts of oyer and terminer were to be convened only in cases of revolt or insurrection. In the minds of many prominent North Carolinians, this provision did not allow the governor to convene such courts for the immediate trials of *individual* slaves—those not members of an organized uprising—who might be inspired by the Emancipation Proclamation and Yankee encouragement to kill their masters and bolt for freedom. Furthermore, worried authorities and slaveholders wanted the governor to have the authority to order courts of oyer and terminer for slaves accused of other capital crimes, such as burglary and rape.

The wording of the 1854 law also posed an ironic problem for state officials. The irony lay in the fact that in order for Governor Vance to thwart widespread slave insurrection by calling for courts of oyer and terminer under that law, he and law enforcement authorities had to acknowledge that indeed a conspiracy or revolt had taken place. Vance and other officials would be reluctant to make that acknowledgment because they feared the impact that such an admission might have on both the white and black populations. In the 1863 act, state lawmakers thus changed the reference to conspiracy and insurrection to read "capital crimes." By this maneuver, they hoped to convict and execute with haste slaves who murdered or threatened to attack whites, but without alarming whites or inspiring other slaves to revolt.

In addition, the 1863 law provided for the quick trials of free blacks and

whites who committed such crimes as murder, burglary, and rape. As noted
earlier, white North Carolinians had always been suspicious of free blacks
as potential leaders of slave revolt. And the Tar Heel State had a significant
number of white Unionists and antiwar proponents, particularly in the
western region and in the Quaker Belt of the Piedmont. Deserters, draft
dodgers, and poor whites disaffected with the war could also turn violent
and even conspire to revolt. They, too, would have to be dealt with summarily if and when they posed a threat to law and order, especially if they
were cooperating with incendiary slaves.[20]

That North Carolina's political leaders and slaveholders harbored fears
about slave violence is evident in events that occurred in Orange County
only weeks after the final Emancipation Proclamation was issued. In two
separate incidents in February 1863, slaves suddenly killed their masters.
In the southwestern part of the county near the Chatham County line,
two slaves belonging to Isaac Stroud killed him. Almost simultaneously,
three slaves murdered their master, John Lockheart, near Hillsborough.
The county's prominent citizens immediately petitioned Vance to deal
with the murders by ordering courts of oyer and terminer. Paul C. Cameron, probably North Carolina's largest slaveholder, wrote to the governor
on February 19: "As you might suppose the community is much excited
and I am told a strong disposition prevails to take the matter in hand &
execute the slaves without waiting the action of a court. I hope no such step
will be taken—but I think in times like this it is very desirable that a trial
should be had at the earliest day and the punishment should be prompt."
Two days later, Cameron made a special point to caution Vance that the two
murders were not part of an insurrection among slaves. "There is *no* pre-
tence whatever," he wrote, "that there exist in this Community or County
any conspiracy or plot for rebellion and murder in any part of the slave
population." He insisted that "The killing of poor Stroud and Lockheart . . .
is to be regarded as far as I can learn—as just a singular coincidence[.] Yet
nevertheless our entire population desires an early and prompt punishment if to be had."[21]

Henry K. Nash, the attorney for Orange County, also implored Vance to
convene a court of oyer and terminer quickly to try the five blacks accused
of murder. "I have taken the liberty," Nash informed the governor,

> as the County Attorney for Orange in the absence of the Solicitor for
> Circuit, and at the request of many of our citizens, to address you
> upon the state of affairs in our County; and urge you . . . to hold a
> Court of Oyer & Terminer here without delay—Within the last ten
> days two most atrocious murders have been committed by slaves

upon their masters, both highly respectable citizens of the county, &
the excitement among our people is necessarily very great—Seven
are now in jail, and three more will be brought up today—Nothing
but the hope & expectation of their having a speedy trial prevented
their instant execution . . . & I fear if this expectation of immediate
trial is disappointed summary justice will be executed upon them,
without regard to law—This should by all means be avoided if possible, but cannot, I fear, unless the course suggested can be adopted.[22]

William A. Graham, former North Carolina governor and a Confederate senator-elect from Hillsborough, also wrote to Vance encouraging him
to call for a court of oyer and terminer and suggesting that the governor
appoint superior court judge Robert B. Gilliam to preside over the trial.
Graham urged Vance to invoke if necessary both the law of 1854 and the
recent law of 1863, "because it is imperative there shall be no mistake in
the holding of the court—For the public excitement against the criminals
can with difficulty be controlled."[23]

Vance heeded the pleas and advice of Cameron, Nash, and Graham and
issued a commission to Judge Gilliam "to hold a Court of Oyer and Terminer in said County of Orange, at such Early time as you may be pleased
to designate."[24] Upon receiving the commission, Gilliam convened the
court at the March term of the Orange County Superior Court. A jury
found four of the five slave defendants guilty of murder and the fifth
guilty of accessory to murder after the fact. The four were hanged at
Hillsborough on April 10. The fifth defendant received a new trial in September, was found guilty, and then was hanged on October 16.[25]

Within weeks of the murders by slaves in Orange County, an almost
identical incident occurred in Lincoln County. On March 16, the justices of
the peace petitioned Vance to convene a court of oyer and terminer to try
two slaves accused of murdering their master. "Your petitioners," their letter stated,

represent to Your Excellency that one of the most diabolical outrages
on record has been perpetrated on the body of Hugh Lyttle [or Little]
one of the good citizens of Our County, by two of his Slaves (Bill &
Frank) by the murder of their own master in the most brutal manner,
and the Culprits now confined in the Jail of Our County. The evidence is conclusive against them besides their own volintary [sic]
confession corresponding with the testimony, all of which appears
without the slightest provocation, the friends and relatives of the
deceased is very much incensed against the negroes, so much so that

there is reason to believe that they may seek an opportunity to rescue the culprits and dispose of them in a most summary manner. And according to the present arrangements of the courts having jurisdiction of such cases, and that the defenders may have meeted [sic] out to them at as early a day as possible the reward which they so justly merit, we pray therefore that Your Excellency will . . . issue Your Commission of Oyer and Terminer to some one of the Judges of the Superior Courts of Law to hold said court forthwith according to the provisions of said act.[26]

On March 23, Vance commissioned Judge Robert R. Heath to convene a court for the trial of the two slaves who murdered Lyttle. A jury convicted the two. On the day of their sentencing, according to superior court records, Frank and Bill were "brought into court and placed at the bar, and it being demanded of them what they have to say why Sentence of death shall not be passed on them," neither the slaves nor their attorney made any reply. So the court ordered the accused men "taken from the jail . . . to a place of public execution in the County of Lincoln and there . . . by the Sheriff be hanged by the neck until they be dead."[27]

Officials throughout the state continued to report capital crimes committed by slaves. On April 4, 1863, Augustus S. Merrimon, solicitor of North Carolina's Eighth District, reported to Vance that a number of capital crimes—mostly committed by whites—were pending court adjudication in the western part of the state. Among the accused were a number of "slaves indicted for arson." Merrimon noted, however, that the accused slaves were out of jail on bail, and he did not mention any outrage or any heated passion for revenge on the part of whites. Merrimon informed Vance that he had received word of the new 1863 law. "It is probably my duty to report to you," he wrote the governor, "whether there are any capital crimes in this circuit to be tried and I hereby do so." But apparently Merrimon initially left the decision of whether or not to convene courts of oyer and terminer to the chief executive. In the case of the Shelton Laurel massacre by Confederate troops of tories, or Unionists, in Madison County in January 1863, Merrimon advised Vance not to call for a court of oyer and terminer if the men accused of the crime were to be indicted and tried in North Carolina courts.[28]

Most of the capital crimes with which Merrimon had to contend in the west involved whites and the internal civil war raging in that area. Murder, burglary, arson, and other crimes frequently occurred among Confederate and Union sympathizers, deserters, draft dodgers, and guerrillas. On occasion, western courts of pleas and quarter sessions asked Vance to convene courts of oyer and terminer to try whites for capital crimes. In March 1863, for example, the justices of Rutherford County petitioned the governor for a court "to try George Suttles, Nancy Floyd, Sally Huggins alias Sally Floyd and Thomas Falls, who are confined in the jail of this county charged with murder."[29] Although Solicitor Merrimon initially did not call for courts of oyer and terminer, by December 1864 he had begun requesting such tribunals in order to deal with increasing violence in the west and "high crimes such as murder, Burglary, Larceny &c &c."[30] But the only capital crimes by slaves that Merrimon reported were those of arson.

The incidents of slaves' being accused of murder or other capital crimes occurred primarily in the large slaveholding areas of the Coastal Plain and the Piedmont, and it was from those districts that Vance received the most requests for speedy trials by courts of oyer and terminer. Historians John C. Inscoe and Gordon B. McKinney have observed that during the war, slaves in the North Carolina Mountains—where slaveholdings were generally small—did at times prove troublesome to white owners and increased concern and vigilance among local officials and other whites. African Americans in the west provided assistance to Union sympathizers and refugees and to Federal soldiers who invaded the area. But Inscoe and McKinney record no wartime slave revolt or conspiracy in the Mountains. They note that the "Emancipation Proclamation . . . caused less of a stir among highlanders than residents elsewhere in the state or South." Yet "no doubt many highlanders were alarmed by the possible scenarios its enactment could generate." According to the two scholars, "slaves in western North Carolina seem to have responded to the war's disruptive forces in much the same manner as slaves throughout the war-torn South. It was only that such situations came later and with less frequency than was the case in other parts of the Confederacy."[31]

The slaves of North Carolina, especially in the east, quickly learned of the Emancipation Proclamation, and they clearly grasped its significance. More than ever before, when a chance of a successful escape to Union lines presented itself, they immediately seized the opportunity. As news of the proclamation traveled from plantation to plantation and village to village, the numbers of slaves bolting for freedom continued to swell. By January 1864, the number of escaped slaves who were residing in Union territory in North Carolina totaled 17,419.[32] One Union soldier, George Winston, noted in February 1863 how well the escapees understood what the Emancipation Proclamation meant for them. "We visited one family in particular," he wrote home to Massachusetts, where several times we enjoyed breakfasts of which the principal portion was corn cake. They were very intelligent and although they could neither read nor write yet had ideas upon matters pertaining to themselves & very correct ones too. They are quite well informed upon the President's proclamation at least the portion relating to their immediate change of condition, viz freedom. There is no use in repeating that they are not capable of taking care of themselves, and that they do not desire their freedom, for it is wholly false. Necessity alone would soon teach them the former invention. The fact that all of them who can run away from their masters is a sufficient answer to the latter assertion.[33]

Although intended primarily as a response to the Emancipation Proclamation and the black violence it might inspire, the 1863 law, as noted earlier, also provided for the trial of whites who were accused of capital crimes. In at least one case, the courts invoked the law for the trial of a white man accused of killing a slave. In May 1857 Robeson County officers arrested Benjamin A. Howell for the murder of a slave, Pompey, who belonged to Alvin G. Lewis. Upon his arraignment, Howell was moved to neighboring Cumberland County for trial. But prior to the regular superior court session, he escaped from jail and remained at large until arrested in Wilmington in 1863. On April 11, 1863, Ralph P. Buxton, solicitor of the Fifth District, wrote to Vance that the Robeson County Court of Pleas and Quarter Sessions had asked the "County Court of Cumberland to petition for a Special Term of the Superior Court, (under the recent Act of Ass.) for the trial of Howell." Cumberland County agreed to the Robeson petition and requested Buxton, "as the prosecuting officer," to ask for a special term of the superior court. "In compliance with that request," wrote Buxton to Vance, "I ask your excellency to issue a special commission to some Judge to hold a Court of Oyer and Terminer for the County of Cumberland in order that Howell may be tried. I have not seen the Act authorizing the holding of such courts but have been told that you are applied to for that purpose." Buxton and Howell's defense attorney, Jesse G. Shepherd, requested the second Monday in May for the defendant's trial. Buxton also requested that Vance intervene to help secure the furlough of an important witness, William Bass, who was then serving in the Confederate army, to testify at Howell's trial.[34] The Cumberland County Superior Court heard the case at a May 1863 session and acquitted Howell of the murder of Pompey.[35]

The specification that whites accused of capital crimes could also be tried quickly in courts of oyer and terminer made it possible for the state to move with speed to deal with whites who, through violent activity, might undermine support for the war and morale among the population. Nowhere was disaffection with the war more prevalent than in Randolph County, located in the heart of the Piedmont's Quaker Belt. In that region, war dissatisfaction reigned, and such peace societies as the Heroes of America defied conscription, concealed deserters, and clamored for a return to the Union. Violence between Confederate sympathizers and deserters, conscription violators, and antiwar exponents was epidemic. On June 16, 1864, Randolph county attorney B. B. Bulla wrote to Vance:

> The citizens of Randolph County direct me to apply to you for a court of Oyer and Terminer for Randolph County and for cause shown that there are now confined three prisoners charged by indictment with Capital crimes to wit two white men Indicted for three or four different cases of Burglary and one Negro indicted for a rape on a white woman (the wife of a soldier).
> And it is deemed necessary to have a Guard of about ten men to Guard the jail[.] [S]aid Guard has been kept up here, ever since the first of last winter, and according [to] our custom the Guard is changed every week, so that ten men usually farmers are required every Monday to leave their business & stay at our jail, the loss is enormous to our community, both in point of time and money.
> I make this application at the instance of many of our most worthy citizens[.] Indeed we fear violence if something is not done shortly.[36]

Vance also received petitions for courts of oyer and terminer for cases involving free blacks accused of capital crimes. On April 29, 1863, the justices of Duplin County petitioned the governor to call a special term of superior court to try Sam Rouse and Leonard Mathis, "free persons of color now detained in prison for capital felonies said to have been committed within the body of this county." Also charged with capital crimes and held in the Duplin County jail along with Rouse and Mathis were slaves Joe of Brunswick County and Scott of New Hanover County.[37]

On at least one occasion, Vance himself sounded the alarm to Confederate authorities about suspected slave revolt. On May 21, 1863, the governor informed President Davis:

> Captain [John T.] Elliot[t] Comdg. a Company of State Troops, captured last Saturday two Steamers in the Albemarle and Chesapeake Canal, one of them carrying a large mail. Upon overlooking the mail, in addition to various items of intelligence, we found a letter from a man by the name of Montgomery in Washington City to [U.S.] Genl.

[John G.] Foster at New Berne proposing a general negro insurrection and distruction [*sic*] of all rail road bridges &c in the South. I enclose you a copy of the letter [not extant] giving all the minutia of the damnable scheme. You can of course make such use of it as you may think best. The necessity for increased dillegence [*sic*] in guarding our bridges &c is apparent. This letter has not been made public.[38]

Without seeming overly concerned, Davis thanked Vance for the information and informed the governor that "The matter has been referred to the special attention of the Secretary of War, who will communicate a warning to Generals commanding armies in the field."[39] As he did with the evidence uncovered by Captain Elliott, Vance refrained from making public the information that he received about other suspected insurrections or conspiracies by blacks. Although he received a significant number of notifications about such suspected plots and issued orders for courts of oyer and terminer to try capital crimes, the governor attempted to prevent anxiety and panic among white North Carolinians by not publicizing violence supposedly planned or committed by slaves or free blacks.

As the war entered a critical phase during the summer of 1863, white fears of slave insurrection and the warnings and petitions to Vance increased. Rumors of slave revolts multiplied following Confederate battlefield defeats, after news that Union troops were on the move from the coast, and after the war turned decidedly against the Confederacy. Following the defeat of the Army of Northern Virginia at Gettysburg in July 1863, Gen. Daniel H. Hill wrote to Vance from near Richmond of a suspected insurrection planned by North Carolina slaves to take place in August. "I spoke to Mr. Davis," Hill wrote on July 10, "about notifying our people of the contemplated insurrection on the first of August. I told him that the negroes would know it and silence only kept their masters in ignorance. I hope you will inform our people either publicly or by circulars to the colonels of militia. Humanity shudders at what may take place, should our people be unprepared."[40] But as was his custom, Vance strove to prevent panic among the state's populace by declining to publicize through the press or circulars the rumored plot reported by Hill. Despite his restraint, however, rumors of slave conspiracies sometimes reached the population.

A number of slaveholders in eastern North Carolina suspected that the August insurrection of which Hill spoke was planned to coincide with a raid into the interior by Federal troops from the coastal region of the state. Rumors spread that the Federal raid would include black troops from Gen.

Edward A. Wild's African Brigade, and that the African American soldiers would lead slaves in an armed uprising. On July 25, John Pool—a Bertie County planter, lawyer, legislator, former Unionist, and postwar United States senator—wrote from the town of Windsor about the Federal raid and pending insurrection. "I have been requested to write to you," he informed Vance, "by several of the most prominent citizens of this county, who assembled in this place today. Information has just reached us from several distinct sources, that it is arranged to land a negro regiment, or perhaps two regiments, for the purpose of inciting & sustaining a servile insurrection in this county & in Hertford." Pool went on to state that Union troops were currently along the Chowan and Roanoke Rivers. "Yesterday," he reported,

> the Yankees landed at Mr. Wm Sutton's on Salmon Creek, burned several of his buildings, destroyed property, & carried off his overseer—the only white person on the premises. They held communication with his negroes, but went off without carrying any of the negroes. Yesterday morning, when the only white man on my plantation went out, very early, he found the Yankees there in conversation with my negroes. They went off without carrying any of them— In the afternoon, they went to Coleraine & held communication with the negroes there & carried none away. Last night, the barn, stables, &c on the farm of Dr. [Turner] Wilson, of this village were burned— They were several miles from town. Threats & warnings against other loyal citizens, have been reported to me, today. All con[cur], in regard to the movement of the slaves, that it is to occur between the 29th. inst. & the 2nd. of August. I have carefully weighed the circumstances surrounding these reports, & listened to the opinions & suggestions of intelligent gentlemen, today—& I really think, the matter ought to claim your prompt attention.[41]

Apparently Vance did not share Pool's alarm, because there is no indication that he requested or ordered additional troops to the area. In any event, the August insurrection that Hill, Pool, and other slaveholders feared in eastern North Carolina did not take place as they anticipated.

But in December 1863, General Wild did lead two regiments of black troops into northeastern North Carolina. The mission of the raid was to reopen navigation on the Dismal Swamp Canal, to protect Union inhabitants plundered by Confederate guerrillas, and to entice as many slaves as possible away from their owners and procure recruits among the escapees. The African American troops freed about 2,500 slaves, burned four guerrilla camps, captured more than fifty guns along with much ammunition and equipment, took a number of prisoners, hanged one guerrilla, captured four large boats engaged in the transportation of war contraband, and seized many horses.[42]

Vance was outraged by the attack. He claimed that Wild's men had refused to treat Confederate soldiers as prisoners of war. He was particularly indignant that the black soldiers held two white women as hostages in exchange for two African American soldiers who had been captured by Col. James H. Hinton's Sixty-eighth Regiment North Carolina State Troops. On December 29, the angry governor wrote to Robert Ould, Confederate commissioner for exchange of prisoners of war:

> I beg to call your attention to the condition of the troops of this State on the Chowan river under the command of Col. Hinton. As you will see by the letters from a Yankee General by the name of Wild, which Col. H. will show you, they refuse to treat them as prisoners of War, although regularly commissioned by law. They have also murdered several soldiers, and have arrested two respectable ladies whom they keep handcuffed for two negro soldiers and declare their purpose to hang them in case the negroes are hung. I must ask you to see if some arrangement cannot be made to include these troops within the cartel of exchange and repress if possible this horrible, cowardly and damnable disposition on the part of [the] enemy to put women in irons as hostages for negro soldiers! Such men as this Wild are a disgrace to the manhood of the age, not being able to capture soldiers they war upon defenceless women! Great God! What an outrage. There is no reason why those men are not entitled to be treated as prisoners of war. If it is not done and these outrages upon defenceless females continue, I shall retaliate upon Yankee soldiers to the full extent of my ability, and let the consequences rest with the damnable barbarians who begun it.[43]

In January 1864, Gen. George E. Pickett, then commanding Confederate troops in eastern North Carolina, ordered the hanging of one of the African American infantrymen, Private Samuel Jordan. The Confederates left Jordan's body hanging from a tree near South Mills in Camden County as a warning to Wild's black soldiers about the price they might pay for taking up arms against their former masters.[44]

So effective were the raids of Wild's black troops that 523 Pasquotank County citizens petitioned Vance in December 1863 to remove Hinton's "partisan rangers" from northeastern North Carolina. They informed the governor that "we have been lately visited . . . by such force and under such circumstances as to cause panic and distress." They assured Vance that Wild had convinced them that as long as the rangers and guerrillas under Hinton's command continued to operate in the region and smuggling or blockade-running persisted, his troops would wreak havoc in the area. The petitioners therefore "earnestly petition the Governor and Legislature of North Carolina, satisfied that you cannot protect us with any force at your command, to remove or disband these few rangers."[45] But Vance himself had organized the regiment of partisan rangers to help ensure the commitment of the northeastern counties to the Confederate war effort. He formed the state regiment to combat Unionist activity in the region and to respond to pressure from the War Department in Richmond to arrest and conscript into Confederate service all eligible males not specifically exempted. In an effort not to alienate those inhabitants who had reservations about the prosecution of the war, Vance initially had asked former Unionist John Pool to command the unit. Pool, however, declined, and command of the rangers had been given to Hinton.[46] Ultimately, Vance satisfied the petitioners by transferring Hinton's rangers out of the area. In the summer of 1864, the Sixty-eighth would be operating against Confederate deserters in the western part of the state.[47]

So outraged at and fearful of armed blacks were North Carolina troops that they gave no quarter to African American soldiers on the battlefield. They considered black troops fugitives and insurrectionists, not legitimate combatants or prisoners of war. North Carolina troops usually killed black soldiers on sight, even those who threw down their arms and attempted to surrender. At the Battle of Plymouth in April 1864, for example, the North Carolina troops commanded by Gen. Robert F. Hoke massacred large numbers of African American soldiers, summarily executing those who tried to surrender and chasing others into the swamps, where they shot them down in cold blood. Black women and children captured at Plymouth were remanded into slavery.[48]

Throughout the last year of the war, Vance continued to receive reports of capital crimes and suspected insurrections by slaves, as well as requests for courts of oyer and terminer to deal with these accused offenders. On May 28, 1864, Sion H. Rogers, attorney general of North Carolina, asked Vance to "issue a commission to some judge to hold a court of Oyer and Terminer for Franklin Co. There are two capital felonies in the court. The persons charged are slaves." Both were named Sam, and they were charged with rape. One of them belonged to a Captain Edman [sic] Sykes and the other to the widow Amanda M. Moses. A jury found them guilty, and the court sentenced them to hang.[49] On January 2, 1865, Rogers reported that there were "four negroes" in Wake County charged with "capital felonies," and he requested from Vance a court of oyer and terminer to try the cases. A grand jury, however, indicted only one of the slaves, Ben, owned by T. C. Robertson. A jury acquitted Ben of murder but found him "guilty of felonious slaying &c," and the court sentenced him to be branded on the left hand—a relatively light sentence in view of the verdict.[50]

On December 9, 1864, the justices of the peace for Richmond County wrote to Vance that they had "at this time confined in our Jail two negro slaves, namely Jack, belonging to Dan'l D. McRae and Asa belonging to Mary Bostick." The officials maintained that the slaves were "committed upon a Magistrate's warrant upon a charge of conspiracy & plotting, & persuading other slaves to Insurrection." The justices requested "your excellency to issue a Commission of Oyer and Terminer to some one of the judges at as early a day as practicable, for the trial of the said slaves—and, if allowable, all others that may be alike implicated by the time."[51] Five days later, Fifth District solicitor Ralph P. Buxton also asked Vance to move immediately to convene a court to try the slaves accused of plotting insurrection in Richmond County. "I also learn," he wrote to the governor, "that one negro supposed to be the ringleader of the movement has been hung by the citizens."[52] The grand jury for the January 2 court of oyer and terminer heard evidence against eight slaves: Jack, Asa, Aaron, Bob, Milton, Daniel, Peter, and Willis. But it found "a true bill" against only Peter and Willis. The court discharged the other accused slaves. Apparently a trial for Peter and Willis never took place either, because the Richmond County superior court records do not record their subsequent appearance as the war drew toward an end.[53]

On at least two occasions, Vance pardoned African Americans who were tried and convicted of capital crimes under the 1863 law. One of the pardons involved the aforementioned Sam, the eighteen-year-old slave of Amanda M. Moses in Franklin County. As noted previously, a court of oyer and terminer held in June 1864 had convicted Sam of raping Malitia Pullen, "a free woman of color." The court found Sam guilty and sentenced him to be hanged. Immediately after the court passed sentence, however, a number of Franklin County citizens, with the urging of Judge Robert R. Heath, petitioned Vance to pardon Sam.[54] Apparently the evidence against the accused had not been conclusive, and Malitia Pullen's past reputation and her race made the crime—in the eyes of white residents—less heinous than if Sam had been charged with raping a white woman. In the petition to the governor, Judge Heath described the circumstantial evidence surrounding the defendant's conviction:

The offence, as sworn to, was committed on *the Road*—within 300 yards of a dwelling—about 11:00 o'clock in the day, and was done forcibly, without any solicitation to voluntary intercourse. The person on whom the offence was alleged to have been committed, was a free woman of color—had lived with two slaves, as the wife of each at different times; & at the commission of the alleged offence, she was living with a white man by whom she had several children. Aside from this, her character was shown to be good. She was collaborated only by evidence of a conflict [a struggle] near where she said the offence was perpetrated. If pardoned it ought to be on condition the costs [of court] be paid, & the convict removed from the state *permanently*.[55]

Vance pardoned Sam on the condition that his mistress, Amanda Moses, pay the costs of court before his release and that Sam "immediately thereafter be removed from the State not to return or be brought back." In March 1865, the governor also pardoned the slave Aleck, "property of Benjamin Thorp," of Montgomery County. The court had sentenced Aleck to hang for killing the slave Cornelius, "property of Peterson Thorp of said county."[56]

In September 1864, Vance pardoned a free black youth, Wesley McDaniel of Montgomery County. The court had convicted McDaniel of burglary and "an assault with intent to commit a rape on the person of Mary Boyd, a white female of said county." Judge Robert B. Gilliam sentenced the defendant to be hanged. But Solicitor Ralph P. Buxton, who "prosecuted the case with great reluctance," implored Vance to pardon the youth, "as I was by no means satisfied that the facts alleged by the prosecutrix made out the crime charged. Under this impression," Buxton explained to Vance,

I had sent a Bill to the Grand Jury charging a simple assault & Battery, but afterwards was induced by the importunity of the girl's friends to send the Bill, upon which he was convicted. Immediately after the trial, I volunteered to sign a petition to your Excellency in the prisoner's behalf—before making application for Executive Clemency, his counsel thought it their duty to have the judgment of the court ... reviewed by the Supreme Court, which was done at the June term last, when the Supreme Court affirmed the Judgment of his Honor Judge [Robert S.] French, who tried the case.

Last week, at Montgomery Court, it became the duty of Judge Gilliam, who is riding that Circuit, to sentence the prisoners, which he did, appointing the 21st. October as the day of his execution.[57]

A number of local residents signed a petition to the governor to pardon McDaniel, and Buxton affixed his signature. But still apprehensive that the young free black might not receive executive clemency, the solicitor made a personal appeal to Vance. "Being more fully persuaded in my own mind by subsequent reflection," Buxton wrote to the governor,

> that McDaniel's case is one calling for the interposition of the pardoning power, not only on account of the youth of the prisoner (he was barely 16.) but also for the reason that he desisted voluntarily from the consummation of [the] offence, and on account of the singular and unsatisfactory statement of his conduct on the occasion, as made by the witness and as correctly set forth in the petition, I have thought it right not to content myself with barely endorsing the application for Executive Pardon, but to make your Excellency a representation of the circumstances of the case, and in a distinct communication, *earnestly* to *ask* and to *urge* your Excellency, to pardon this boy.[58]

Vance pardoned McDaniel, but "on Condition that he shall receive at the Hands of the Sheriff of Montgomery County on two separate occasions with one weeks intermission between them, thirty nine lashes on his bare back & that all costs in his case incurred be paid by him or his master."[59]

In such cases as those of the slave Sam and the free black Wesley McDaniel, Vance may have conceded that the state possibly was going too far in acting without sufficient evidence in its efforts to suppress violence by African Americans. Nevertheless, when called upon to order courts of oyer and terminer, he complied swiftly, when he thought the request warranted his intervention. Apparently he exercised his executive privilege to grant clemency in only one case—that of McDaniel—involving black crime against whites. And then he intervened only when petitioned by the prominent white jurist Buxton. Furthermore, in the pardoning of McDaniel, Vance took care to make an example of the accused by ordering that he suffer a severe flogging.

It cannot be determined with absolute certainty how many courts of oyer and terminer Vance ordered following the law of February 1863. But a close examination of the governor's papers for the period 1863–1865 reveals that he did not automatically convene such courts simply because they were requested. According to his official papers of 1863, for example, he received twelve requests to convene courts of oyer and terminer, but he ordered only three such courts in that year.[60] Vance realized the panic that rumors of slave violence could create in the state, and he attempted to keep such news quiet by being circumspect in how he reacted to reports of slave violence or crime. During his tenure as governor, he never issued public proclamations of alarm or called out the militia or Home Guard to control blacks. His reports to the Confederate government of suspected plots— such as the one to President Davis on May 21, 1863—were confined to his official correspondence and not made public. Even when Vance became outraged at the raid in northeastern North Carolina by General Wild's black troops, he limited his angry vows to "retaliate" to Confederate authorities. He did not publicly alarm white North Carolinians that African American soldiers might be leading slaves in violence or revolt against their owners.

Vance learned firsthand how paranoid, volatile, and prone to vigilante justice the white people of his state could be against their own servants. Within the eleven months following the enactment of the Emancipation Proclamation in January 1863, he received eight reports of slave killings by whites in the state. Seven of those reports crossed his desk within five months of the proclamation. The last of the year reached him in November.[61] In the face of such evidence of white alarm and vengeance, Vance managed to maintain calm and possibly avoided a bloodbath against blacks by not overreacting to reports of slave violence. When called upon—as in the incidents of slave violence in Orange and Lincoln Counties in 1863—to convene courts of oyer and terminer in order to keep vengeful white populations subdued, he quickly did so. He also recognized the importance of preventing further slave crime or insurrection by imposing swift punishment through special superior court sessions. But he reserved such courts for cases that seemed truly volatile and refrained from publicizing reports of slaves accused of committing capital crimes.

In May 1861, the abolitionist Joshua Giddings remarked that nothing else would "strike terror in the whole south" as an emancipation proclamation would.[62] In North Carolina, Giddings's prophecy came close to fulfillment. In large part because of Vance's efforts to maintain calm, a reign of terror between whites and blacks did not occur. But far from becoming a realization of Lincoln's worst fear that it would be ineffective, "like the Pope's Bull against the comet,"[63] the Emancipation Proclamation had a significant impact on the Tar Heel State. It instilled among whites a demoralizing fear that their slaves could be motivated to rise up and murder them. A psychological uneasiness prevailed among North Carolinians that they must remain constantly vigilant, lest their servants —inspired by news of Federal liberation and protection—try to slaughter them in their beds. The number of courts of oyer and terminer requested in response to the alleged capital crimes by blacks is evidence of the anxiety that whites felt.

Lincoln's proclamation also encouraged thousands of North Carolina slaves to flee to Federal lines, and that flight denied their labor to the Confederate war effort. The proclamation, furthermore, made it possible to enlist many of those escaped slaves into black regiments. These new African American Union soldiers then leveled their weapons at the state's slaveholders in northeastern North Carolina and at the Confederate troops who fought to keep their brethren in chains throughout the South. In the summer of 1863, Lincoln himself publicly proclaimed that "the emancipation policy, and the use of colored troops constitute the heaviest blow yet dealt to the rebellion."[64] Thus, given the impact of the proclamation and the panic that it might have excited, it is perhaps a testimony to Vance's political skill and commitment to the Confederate cause that he managed to maintain civil order and keep his state in step with the government of Jefferson Davis for more than two long years after Lincoln issued the powerful edict.

4

"TO THEIR HANDS I AM CONTENT TO LEAVE IT"

The success that Abraham Lincoln had achieved by appointing Andrew Johnson as military governor in Federal-held eastern Tennessee in early 1862 led the president to hope that he might accomplish similar results by naming such a governor in Union-occupied eastern North Carolina. As he had attempted in Tennessee, Lincoln wished to establish in eastern North Carolina a loyal government that would treat for peace and lead the state back into the Union. Like Tennessee, North Carolina had a large Unionist element prior to the outbreak of the war, and Governor Vance, an old-line Whig, had been a reluctant secessionist.

When the war began, Lincoln believed that a majority of the inhabitants of the new Confederacy remained loyal to the Federal government after their states seceded. They had, he felt, only acquiesced to de facto secession enacted by a small class of slaveholders, who did not speak for the population at large. Lincoln hoped that as United States troops penetrated into the South—as they did in coastal North Carolina—those Southerners who remained loyal to the Union would cooperate with the invading army, accept wartime reconstruction, organize loyal governments, and bring their states back into the Federal fold.[1]

To carry out his plan for wartime reconstruction and reunion in North Carolina, Lincoln, on the recommendation of members of his cabinet, chose Edward Stanly as military governor. Stanly was a native North Carolinian, born in New Bern in 1810. He practiced law in Washington, North Carolina, and was elected to Congress from Beaufort County in 1837 as a Whig. He served in the state House of Commons from 1844 to 1846. The North Carolina legislature elected him state attorney general in 1847, but he resigned after only one year and returned to the General Assembly. In

5. Vance rebuffed overtures by Edward Stanly, United States military governor in eastern North Carolina, to discuss peace negotiations and wartime reconstruction in the Tar Heel State. North Carolina Office of Archives and History, Raleigh.

1849, he was elected to Congress, where he supported the Compromise of 1850 and other efforts to avoid dissolution of the Union. Stanly was re-elected to Congress in 1851, but with the decline of the Whig Party in North Carolina, he left the state and settled in California in 1853 to practice law. Four years later, he ran unsuccessfully for governor of California as the candidate of the new Republican Party, speaking out in favor of maintaining the Union amid the growing sectional discord. But he disagreed with the Republican Party's opposition to the extension of slavery into the territories acquired as a result of the Mexican War, and he opposed any attack on slavery where it already existed in the South.[2] In Stanly's mind, the "sole purpose of the [Civil] war was to preserve the Union, not to disturb the institution of laws of the Southern states."[3]

In response to Lincoln's call, Stanly arrived in Washington, D.C., in May 1862, where he met with Secretary of State William Seward and Secretary of War Edwin Stanton. With little instruction from either, he was dispatched to New Bern to assume the office of military governor. Stanton directed General Burnside to cooperate with Stanly in restoring Federal control in eastern North Carolina.[4]

From the beginning, Stanly received little popular support or encouragement for restoration of a loyal government in eastern North Carolina. Nevertheless, he reinforced Lincoln's own ideas about the strength of Unionism in the Tar Heel State. "A large majority of the people want the Union restored," he reported to the president.[5]

Much of Stanly and Lincoln's conception of the depth of Union sentiment in North Carolina resulted from the election of Vance as governor as the Conservative Party candidate in 1862. The Conservatives' overwhelming victory over the Confederate Party in the gubernatorial race seemed to be an indication of North Carolina's reluctant support for the Confederacy. It might signal the possibility of appealing to Vance and the Conservatives to consider abandoning the war and bringing North Carolina back into the Union.[6]

Upon hearing of Vance's election in August 1862, Lincoln summoned Stanly to Washington to discuss the situation in North Carolina. Before Stanly departed for the capital, however, Lincoln wanted him to contact Vance. "I would very much like for you to see Col. Vance, the newly elected Governor of North Carolina, before you come, if such a thing is practicable," the president instructed the military governor.[7] Apparently Lincoln wanted Stanly to sound out Vance on the depth of the latter's commitment to the Confederacy and the likelihood of his cooperation in peace negotiations and restoration of North Carolina to the United States. Stanly, however, did not contact Vance until he returned from his interview with Lincoln.

On October 21, 1862, Stanly wrote Vance a solicitous—almost toadyish—letter requesting a meeting with the Tar Heel governor. "The strong affection which I have inherited & cherished for the people of my native State, has induced me to come here, by request of the President of the United States," began Stanly. He went on to "earnestly solicit the favor of an interview with you, at such time or place, hereafter to be designated as may be agreeable to you." Stanly maintained that his first objective was to launch talks that might lead to "an honorable peace." As a show of good faith, he informed Vance that "authority has been given me to negotiate for an exchange of political prisoners." He asked that if Vance could not personally attend the suggested conference, he send delegates to confer about possible peace discussions.[8]

In a vitriolic reply, Vance informed Stanly that he had no intention of meeting or sending delegates to discuss peace negotiations. Such actions, he declared, would be "incompatible with my views of duty." He informed Stanly that "If the measures which you propose to discuss relate to a general peace between the Confederate States and the United States, then it is needless for me to inform you that I have not the power to confer with you authoritatively. By the Constitution of the Confederate States to which the State of North Carolina has unanimously acceded, the power to make war & conclude peace has been delegated to the President & Senate—To their hands I am content to leave it." To suggest that North Carolina might enter into separate peace talks with the Lincoln government, Vance emphatically told Stanly, was "still more inadmissible." The state had "dissolved her connection with the old government and entered into a solemn compact with the new government of the Confederate States. Her obligations in this new relation are obvious & her honor is pledged to redeem all these obligations faithfully with the last dollar & the last drop of blood, for the general good."

Vance chastised Stanly for even implying that he might negotiate with the Lincoln government behind the backs of Confederate authorities. "Your proposition," he declared, "is based upon the supposition that there is a baseness in North Carolina sufficient to induce her people to abandon their confederates & leave them to suffer alone all the horrors of this unnatural war, for the sake of securing terms for themselves—a mistake which I could scarcely have supposed any one so well acquainted with the character of our people as yourself could have committed." Thus insulted by Stanly's overture, Vance informed Lincoln's military governor that further proposals for peace talks "will be promptly forwarded to the proper [Confederate] authorities if entrusted to me."[9]

Possessing a temper and sensitivity equal to those of Vance, Stanly took offense at the Tar Heel governor's rebuff and on November 7 wrote him a letter complaining about the rude tone of Vance's response to his proposal. "There is nothing Sir, in your position or in mine, that justifies you in using the language complained of to me," he protested. Stanly reiterated his belief that most North Carolinians repudiated the concept of secession and could be persuaded to rejoin the Union.[10]

But not to be bested in a clash of tempers, Vance on November 24 fired off another angry response. "I have only to say Sir," he retorted, "by way of conclusion to this correspondence, which I thought had ended with my reply to your first, that you should by this time have been convinced that your mission to North Carolina was a failure, miserable and complete." He informed Stanly that he, Stanly, was despised in the Tar Heel State. "Do you know sir," he lambasted Lincoln's military governor, "that your name is execrated and only pronounced with curses in North Carolina?" Those heated words apparently ended all correspondence between the two men.[11]

Stanly thus came to the realization that, despite Vance's prewar opposition to secession and his support among the state's Conservative leaders, the Lincoln government could expect no cooperation from the Tar Heel governor in ending North Carolina's participation in the war and restoring the state to the Union. He informed Secretary of War Stanton that his attempt to solicit Vance's participation in discussions of peace had failed, and he sent copies of their letters to the secretary. Yet Stanly did not give up all hope of establishing a loyal government in North Carolina. "I still believe," he wrote Stanton, "if the people of North Carolina could be allowed free expression of their wishes and opinions they would decide to separate themselves from any associations with the rebel states." He would welcome any suggestions from the president about how to continue their efforts to restore North Carolina to the United States.[12]

At Lincoln's urging, Stanly held congressional elections on January 1, 1863, in the state's occupied district. The candidates were former North Carolina Whig legislator and Unionist Jennings Pigott and Charles H. Foster, an odd political opportunist who for some time had been trying to have himself elected governor of occupied North Carolina. All white men who had been state residents for one year could vote in the congressional contest. Only three of the eleven counties in the district held the election. A mere 864 votes were cast, and Pigott won overwhelmingly. But dubious and unenthusiastic about such an election, the United States House of Representatives refused to seat him.[13]

Furthermore, by the time the election took place, Stanly had become disenchanted with Lincoln's plans for North Carolina. He and the president had drifted apart in their opinions about the objective of the Federal war effort. The issue that divided them was the fate of the enslaved African Americans in the state. When Lincoln first appointed Stanly as military governor, the two agreed that the chief war objective was the restoration of the Union, without any program for the abolition of slavery. But eventually the plight and future of the thousands of slaves who fled to Union lines in North Carolina and elsewhere had to be addressed.

Stanly's first trouble involving escaped slaves occurred when an argument arose between him and Vincent Colyer, superintendent of the poor in Federal-controlled North Carolina, over schools for blacks in New Bern. Colyer and some New England troops also became outraged when Stanly returned fugitive slaves to masters in the area. Colyer traveled to Washington, D.C., and complained to abolitionist senator Charles Sumner of Massachusetts about Stanly's actions. Sumner took Colyer to see Lincoln, and Radical Republicans in Congress began clamoring for Stanly's dismissal.[14]

In a report submitted to Stanton on June 12, 1862, Stanly gave the following explanation for his instructions to Colyer to stop teaching African Americans to read and write:

> A gentleman of good Samaritan inclinations and acts [Colyer] had established a school for negro children. He called and informed me what he was doing, and asked my opinion. I approved all he had done in feeding and clothing destitute white and black, but told him I had been sent to restore the old order of things. I thought his negro school, if approved by me, would do harm to the Union cause. In a few months we shall know the result of the war. If by Southern folly emancipation comes, their [blacks'] spiritual welfare would not suffer by the delay, for I desired he would give such oral instructions in religious matters as he thought best.
>
> Another reason I urged [Colyer to close the schools] was, that by one of the cruel necessities of slavery the laws of North Carolina forbade slaves to be taught to read and write, and I would be most unsuccessful in my efforts if I encouraged the violation of her laws. . . . . If the old residents ever return, those negroes who have been taught to read and write would be suspected and not benefited.

Stanly informed the secretary of war that until Colyer fled to Washington to complain about his actions to Sumner and the other radicals in Congress, he had assumed that he and Colyer had agreed on the necessity of closing the schools. "In the interview with the manager of the schools," he told Stanton, "I made no use of threats, used no discourteous language, and treated the gentleman referred to with all kindness. He called the next morning and informed me he had suspended teaching the negro children. I approved what he had done. . . . Not a word was said, nor any intention given, of any intention to 'enforce the laws of this State.'"

Regarding the return of fugitive slaves, Stanly claimed that one master approached him "who had four slaves taken from him, and told they were free by a rude soldier, who cursed his wife." Before the slaveholder could search for his property in New Bern, Stanly stressed, "I suggested, first, he must take the oath of allegiance; this he agreed to do." Stanly then told the slaveholder, who had just pledged his loyalty to the Union, that he could search for his slaves, "advising him to use mildness and persuasion." According to the military governor, one of the slaves "voluntarily returned to the home of a kind master."[15]

Although concerned that Stanly might deny education to blacks or return fugitive slaves, Lincoln nevertheless did not give in to the demands of Sumner and other radicals that he remove Stanly. But neither Lincoln nor Stanton made an effort to bolster Stanly's efforts with specific instructions regarding the treatment of escaped slaves. Yet, having received at least the tacit support of Lincoln, Stanly remained at his post until the president took the one step that he could not accept—the final issuance of the Emancipation Proclamation on January 1, 1863. He informed Lincoln that he could not endorse emancipation as an objective of the Federal war effort. Emancipation, he insisted, would destroy any chance for reconciliation and restoration of North Carolina to the Union. To bring about such a reunification had been the purpose of his mission as military governor. To accomplish that mission, he had avoided exciting the state's slaveholders over the possibility of abolition. He had also made conscientious efforts to protect the other property and rights of the people who lived within his jurisdiction by imposing strict regulations on United States occupation troops.[16]

In the final analysis, however, such efforts had no impact in swaying Governor Vance and his fellow Conservatives even to consider negotiations for peace. Perhaps if Stanly had remained as military governor until late 1863 and at that time had approached the Conservatives about negotiations for peace and reconciliation, he might have received some encouragement from members of the party—especially if he remained adamant about restoring the antebellum status quo, including the preservation of slavery. By the fall of 1863, resounding Confederate defeats at Gettysburg and Vicksburg had led to a growing feeling among North Carolinians that the war was turning against the Confederacy. The people were also becoming increasingly despondent and disgruntled over battlefield losses, conscription, desertion, impressment, tax-in-kind, and other issues. Many had begun to agitate for a peaceful conclusion to the fighting. They found a spokesman in William W. Holden, editor of the *North Carolina Standard*. Holden had begun calling for peace negotiations, and organized peace meetings convened in many communities.[17] Holden had denounced Stanly in June of 1862, calling his appointment "a wicked attempt to subjugate our people."[18] A year later, however, Holden was openly advocating any negotiations that might lead to peace. "[W]e have no idea that we can obtain 'peace upon our own terms,'" he proclaimed. "The most powerful nations seldom succeed in doing that. What the great mass of our people desire is a cessation of hostilities, and negotiations. If they could reach that point they would feel that the conflict of arms would not be renewed, and that *some* settlement would be effected which would leave them in the future in the enjoyment of 'life, liberty, and happiness.'"[19]

But even had Stanly remained in North Carolina in 1863 and held out the olive branch to Holden and his followers, it is doubtful that the editor of the *Standard* could have engendered enough popular support for peace to influence the state's leadership to enter into negotiations with the military governor. Such a plan certainly would not have elicited a favorable reaction from Governor Vance. As Vance's blistering response to Stanly's original overture indicated, he was in no way disposed to cooperate with the Federal government in negotiating a separate peace for North Carolina.

Holden and his followers, however, persisted in their efforts for peace negotiations. North Carolinians loyal to the Confederate cause saw this movement as a treasonous effort to reconstruct the old Union and demanded that Vance subdue Holden and his followers. Vance wrote confidentially to William A. Graham on August 13, 1863, asking his advice about how to respond to the peace movement. He informed Graham that he considered peace meetings "*ruinous* in the last degree." In his opinion, "They will cause the army to melt away by desertion, will create, perhaps dissensions & civil war at home, and will defeat any & all efforts for peace, unless it be on the basis of absolute submission to our enemies—which is all that has ever been offered us." Vance could see no purpose in peace meetings "except to encourage our enemies, ruin our army, & hasten our subjugation." He told Graham that he intended to oppose any "clamours for peace, originating in a desire for reconstruction." His administration would consider only a peace that could "be obtained upon the basis of separation & [Confederate] independence." Vance asked Graham to let him know to what extent "I will be sustained by *my friends* and former supporters" in adopting such a position.[20] Confederate officials in Richmond also became alarmed at the unrest stirred up by the editor of the *Standard*. Jefferson Davis wrote to the governor on July 24, 1863, to inquire if rumors were true that "Holden is engaged in the treasonable purpose of exciting the people of North Carolina to resistance against their government, and cooperation with the enemy."[21]

In early August Vance traveled to Richmond to confer with Davis about Holden and the peace advocates and to express the state's dissatisfaction over the lack of appointments of North Carolinians to government and military positions in the Confederacy.[22] Returning to Raleigh, the governor composed a letter to be made public that denounced the peace movement but did not attack Holden personally. In the letter, written to John H. Haughton, lawyer, planter, and former state senator with Unionist sympathies, Vance expressed in detail his opinion "as to the best means of obtaining a speedy, lasting just & honorable peace." He insisted that the Confederacy should not humble itself to propose peace negotiations with the United States. He asserted that "as the matter now stands and has stood from the beginning, I can only look upon propositions of peace coming from us, no matter how pure and patriotic the motive which induces them, as involving national dishonor, ruin and disgrace." He maintained that "our only hope for national honor, for happiness, for peace itself lies in a cordial [sic] undaunted & vigorous prosecution of the war until our enemies offer us peace." To ask for peace talks, Vance argued, would only weaken the war effort by encouraging a defeatist attitude among the people and desertion from the army. If the war was resulting in some difficulties on the Confederate home front, "the North gives unmistakable signs that she finds it quite as difficult to keep up the strife as we. The blood which flows through the streets of her cities, the bold and defiant tone of her press and politicians towards Lincolns administration, the thousands of Federal bayonets gleaming throughout the land to enforce conscription and 'preserve order,' as they significantly term it—all show that they are having their own troubles also." Thus the people of North Carolina should forget about peace meetings and stand fast with the Confederacy until the Federals, exhausted from war, cried enough and sued for peace with terms favorable to the South.[23] Dissuaded from publishing the letter by William A. Graham, who apparently found its message against peace proposals to be too strong, Vance instead called a meeting of Graham and other Conservatives to develop a policy to combat the peace initiatives.[24] Principally on the advice of Graham, Vance on September 7 issued a public proclamation discouraging peace meetings but not criticizing Holden.

In his message, Vance exhorted North Carolinians to remain loyal to the Confederate war effort and forgo any peace meetings that might divide and turn them against each other. "A great and glorious nation is struggling to be born," he declared,

and wondering kingdoms & distant empires are stilled with listening hope & admiration watching this greatest of human events. Let them not, I pray you, be shocked with the spectacle of domestic Strife and petty, malignent [sic] feuds. Let not our enemy be rejoiced to behold our strong arms and stronger devotion which have often made him tremble, turned against ourselves. Let us rather show that the God of Liberty is in His Holy Temple—the hearts of freemen—and bid all the petty bickerings of earth keep silence before him.[25]

Shortly after Vance's proclamation appeared, Georgia troops passing through Raleigh broke into the *Standard* office and scattered Holden's papers and the ink and type from his press. The ransacking soldiers, from the command of Gen. Henry Benning, were responding to resolutions adopted in Virginia by Confederate army officers, most of whom were from North Carolina. The resolutions called for the suppression of Holden and the peace proponents. On the day following the attack on the *Standard* office, allies of Holden sacked the office and destroyed the presses of the *State Journal*, a Raleigh newspaper that had joined the campaign to gag the *Standard*. The trouble intensified when angered soldiers from a passing Alabama brigade announced plans to seize Holden, whose friends vowed to protect him. During all three altercations, Vance personally managed to calm mobs and restore quiet in the capital.

Holden himself expressed gratitude for the governor's actions in preventing bloodshed and preserving public order. He promised to support Vance as long as the state's chief executive adhered to the true principles of the Conservative Party. For the time being, no more peace meetings convened.[26]

Although Vance early dismissed peace talks as a viable option for ending the war, Holden's success made him well aware that a serious and potentially dangerous peace movement was arising in the state. As a politician committed to the success of the Confederacy, as well as concerned about his political future, he could not afford to ignore the rumblings among those who were dissatisfied with the war and wanted to see it brought to a peaceful conclusion. After all, much of eastern North Carolina was in Federal hands. Stanly's effort to create a loyal government in the region had failed. But if the war dragged on and turned decisively against the Confederacy, sentiment for reconciliation might establish itself in that area and spread to the rest of the state. He also had to deal with the reality that considerable war opposition existed among folk in the Mountains and in the Quaker Belt of the Piedmont.

Furthermore, in the November 1863 congressional elections, the peace proponents had seen their candidates win a large number of seats in the Confederate Congress. On November 17, Holden claimed six recently elected congressmen from North Carolina as sympathetic to his point of view on peace: James T. Leach, Thomas C. Fuller, Josiah Turner Jr., John A.

Gilmer, Samuel H. Christian (who died before taking office), and George Y. Logan. Of the ten congressmen elected from North Carolina in 1863, seven were new to the office. They included the aforementioned six plus James G. Ramsey. The three representatives who were reelected to the second Confederate Congress were William N. H. Smith, Robert R. Bridgers, and Burgess S. Gaither. Of all the congressmen elected in 1863, only Bridgers had been an original supporter of secession. All of the congressmen, with the exception of Bridgers and Gaither, favored some type of peace negotiations.[27]

Encouraged by this election of members of the peace faction of the Conservative Party to the Confederate Congress, Holden renewed his attack on the Confederate government, protesting such violations of personal liberty as conscription and impressment. In December he began calling for a state convention to initiate peace negotiations directly with the Federal government in the hope of bringing an unpopular and devastating war to an end. He vowed to oppose Vance in the gubernatorial election of 1864 unless the incumbent governor supported the state convention. Vance, however, refused to endorse the convention.[28]

But indications of popular support for possible peace talks led Vance to conclude that he and the Davis government needed at least to pay lip service to the idea of bringing an end to the war and its suffering through negotiations. Vance therefore—partly on the advice of Graham and other Conservatives "who advocate this course"—urged Davis to make a propaganda show of trying to hold such talks, as a means of maintaining the support of the Tar Heel populace that was growing increasingly discontented with the war. "After a careful consideration of all the sources of discontent in North Carolina," the governor wrote the Confederate president on December 30, 1863, "I have concluded that it will be perhaps impossible to remove it except by making some effort at negotiations with the enemy. . . . I am promised by all men who advocate this course that if fair terms are rejected it will tend to greatly strengthen and intensify the war feeling and will rally all classes to a more cordial support of the government. . . . I have not suggested the method of these negotiations or their terms, the *effort* to obtain peace is the principal matter."[29]

When Vance made his proposal to Davis, he well knew that the Lincoln government would never agree to a peace that included Confederate independence and left slavery intact—conditions upon which the Davis government uncompromisingly insisted. Consequently, peace meetings between representatives of the governments in Richmond and Washington had no real chance of success, even if Lincoln, who refused to recognize the legitimacy of the Confederate government, would agree to negotiations. But if the Confederate government would make peace overtures that were rejected—as Vance knew they surely would be—then Confederate and state leaders could report to their disgruntled citizens that they had made an effort to open peace discussions but had been summarily rebuffed by the Federals. Such a propaganda tactic, Vance asserted, might help quiet the dissent and disenchantment among the home-front population.[30]

On January 8, 1864, Davis responded to Vance in a long letter rejecting the governor's idea and explaining why it would not work. The president pointed out to Vance that previous attempts to open negotiations with Lincoln had failed. The Federals had refused even to grant interviews to Confederate commissioners, including Vice President Alexander H. Stephens. To try again "to send commissioners or agents to propose peace is to invite insult and contumely, and to subject ourselves to indignity without the slightest chance of being listened to." Lincoln's recent Emancipation Proclamation had made the possibility of peace talks even more remote. Davis maintained that even if "it were practicable to obtain a conference through commissioners with the government of President Lincoln, . . . Have we not just been apprised by that despot that we can only expect his gracious pardon by emancipating all our slaves, swearing allegiance and obedience to him and his proclamation and becoming in point of fact the slaves of our own negroes?"[31]

To Vance's observation that there were rumors that some members in the United States House of Representatives were displeased with Lincoln's prosecution of the war, Davis replied:

I have seen no action of the Federal House of Representatives that does not indicate by a very decided majority the purpose of the enemy to refuse all terms to the South except absolutely unconditional subjection or extermination—But if it were otherwise, how are we to treat with the House of Representatives? It is with Lincoln alone that we ever could confer and his own partisans at the North avow unequivocally that his purpose in his message and proclamation was to shut out all hope that he would *ever* treat with us on *any* terms. If we will break up our government, dissolve the Confederacy, disband our armies, emancipate our slaves, take an oath of allegiance binding ourselves to obedience to him and to disloyalty to our own states, he proposes to pardon us and not to plunder us of any thing more than the property already stolen from us and such slaves as still remain. In order to render his proposals so insulting as to secure their rejection, he joins to them a promise to support with his army one tenth of the people of any state who will attempt to set up a government over the other nine-tenths, thus seeking to sow discord and suspicion among the people of the several states, and to excite them to civil war in furtherance of his ends.

Davis went on to admonish Vance that he must move forcibly to quiet the peace proponents in his state. "I fear much from the tenor of the news I receive from North Carolina," he lectured the governor, "that an attempt will be made by some bad men to inaugurate movements which must be considered as equivalent to aid and comfort to the enemy, and which all patriots should combine to put down at any cost." He confessed to Vance "that my only source of disquietude on the subject arises from the fear that you will delay too long the action which now appears inevitable; and that by an over earnest desire to reclaim by conciliation men whom you believe to be sound at heart, but whose loyalty is more than suspected elsewhere, you will permit them to gather such strength as to require more violent measures than are now needed."[32]

On January 25, 1864, North Carolina's congressional delegation wrote to Vance informing him that Davis had shared his letter to Vance with them. The congressmen told the governor that the letter "contains information which would be interesting to our people and we are of the opinion that its publication would have a happy effect not only in our state, but upon public opinion throughout the Confederacy." They urged Vance to publish Davis's letter along with the governor's own correspondence of December 30, which Davis had not shown to them.[33] On January 27, Vance wrote to Davis asking his permission to "have my letter and yours published." Three days later, Davis telegraphed back that "I have no objection to the publication referred to if you think it advisable."[34]

Vance, however, developed serious reservations about the wisdom of publishing the president's letter. "After careful consideration," he wrote to North Carolina's congressmen on February 4, "I am doubtful of the propriety of so doing, for the reason that it contains an intimation of force to be applied in certain contingencies which I think better calculated to increase than allay irritation." In his opinion, he should not publish Davis's letter, and he asked the congressmen to look it over again. "However, so great is my respect for the opinion you express that if after a reexamination of the letter, you should still advise it I will publish it."[35] On the same day, Vance wrote to Jefferson Davis proposing that he not publish the president's entire letter but "have the substance of it published in the

Fayetteville Observer." Davis waited almost two weeks before "declining to have my correspondence thus changed for presentation to the public," and Vance could use the letter only "as it was sent to you."[36] With that, the congressional delegation evidently dropped the issue.

Apparently Jefferson Davis misinterpreted or, more likely, chose to ignore the real purpose of Vance's letter of December 30: to suggest that the Confederate government help quiet the peace advocates in the Tar Heel State by placing the responsibility for continuation of the war squarely on the Lincoln government. Instead, Davis seized on Vance's letter as an opportunity to reprimand the young governor for not doing enough to silence disloyalty in his state. The president also, in effect, went over Vance's head to North Carolina's congressional delegation in order to drive home his concerns about the peace movement in the state.

Vance learned a valuable political lesson in making his failed suggestion to Davis. He realized that he had been naïve and mistaken in raising the idea of peace negotiations, even though he was suggesting only a peace meeting *effort* for propaganda purposes. By showing Vance's letter to the North Carolina congressional delegation, Davis subtly called Vance's loyalty into question and placed the blame for dissension in the state on the governor's timidity in dealing with the dissenters.

Vance had made it clear to Edward Stanly in 1862 that he would not consider any peace negotiations without the involvement of the Confederate government. Now, having been burned by Davis's response to his suggestion about peace overtures, he was just as adamantly resolved to leave any future plans for such negotiations entirely to the government in Richmond. With that position firmly in mind, he turned his attention to the upcoming gubernatorial campaign for his reelection in 1864.

5

"MY LIFE POPULARITY AND EVERYTHING SHALL GO INTO THIS CONTEST"

As 1863 ended, Vance might have had second thoughts about whether he really wanted to run for reelection in the August 1864 gubernatorial race. His first term as governor had saddled him with tremendous problems and responsibilities. The effort to balance the complaints and needs of North Carolinians with the demands for support from the Confederate government had been exhausting. His health and outlook declined. "I have been sick and gloomy," he told Edward J. Hale, his political confidant and editor of the *Fayetteville Observer*. In December Vance became bedridden as the result of a "severe cold" and an operation in which he had a "large tumor" removed from his neck. "Six months ago you would have learned of my illness through the *newspapers*," he lamented, as if he felt he was going unnoticed and unappreciated.[1] To add to his despondency, apparently he also was having doubts about his ability to win reelection if he opposed a peace convention. Perhaps, he told his mentor David L. Swain, he would "quietly retire to the army and find death which will enable my children to say that their father was not consenting to their degradation."[2] But Vance quickly rallied and began planning his tactics for the upcoming election.

By late 1863, Holden had let the governor know in no uncertain terms that he and his allies would oppose Vance's reelection in 1864 if he refused to support a state peace convention. Vance was equally determined that he would never endorse such a meeting. "I can not of course favor such a thing for any existing cause," he wrote to his advisor William A. Graham on January 1, 1864. "I will see the Conservative party blown into a thousand atoms and Holden and his understrappers in hell . . . before I will

6. Edward J. Hale, editor of the *Fayetteville Observer*, served as a
political confidant for Vance during his campaign for reelection in 1864.
North Carolina Office of Archives and History, Raleigh.

consent to a course which I think would bring dishonor and ruin upon both
state & Confederacy!" He continued: "Is Holden the leader of the Conservative party? If so I don't belong to it. Why will old Whigs and Union men
surrender the leadership of their party to a man who has denounced them
all his life, who has done more to produce our present troubles than any
man in it, and who is moreover a known demagogue & a man of bad character?"[3] Vance asked Swain's advice about his course of action in the coming election. He worried that "The final plunge which I have been dreading
and avoiding that is to separate me from a large number of my political
friends is about to be made. It is now a fixed policy of W. Holden and others
to call a convention in May to take N.C. back to the United States, and the
agitation has already begun."[4]

Vance implied to Graham and Swain that Holden's announcement in
December to seek a state convention had precipitated the governor's break

7. William A. Graham—Confederate senator, former North Carolina governor,
and former United States senator and secretary of the navy—gave Vance considerable
political advice throughout the war. North Carolina Office of Archives and History,
Raleigh.

with the editor of the *Standard*. But in actuality, Vance had already fore-
cast his estrangement from Holden as early as August 1863. On the eleventh day of that month, Vance wrote confidentially to Hale: "I believe . . .
the split with Holden is decreed of the Gods—I have made up my mind to
it and am prepared for it any day—tho' I don't intend to 'precipitate it.' . . .
He is for submission, reconstruction or any thing else that will put him
back under Lincoln & stop the war—and I might add—punish his old
friends & co laborers the Secessionists." Vance urged Hale to begin attacking Holden and the peace men in the columns of the *Observer*: "Pitch into
them—Cry aloud and spare not—My life popularity and everything shall
go into this contest."[5]
But in January 1864, the governor did not immediately proclaim his

8. William W. Holden, editor of the *North Carolina Standard* and proponent of peace negotiations, ran against Vance in the heated gubernatorial election of 1864. North Carolina Office of Archives and History, Raleigh.

opposition to Holden and the peace convention. In a private letter to Hale on February 11, however, he revealed his grasp of the situation in the upcoming election and his tactics for waging a successful campaign. Although Holden had not publicly announced an intention to run against Vance in the election, the governor knew that eventually the editor of the *Standard* would do just that. But Vance discounted Hale's worry that the state's secessionists might run a third candidate in the election. The supporters of the Davis government, Vance maintained, would have no choice but to vote for him in preference to Holden. He intended to be reelected by winning the votes of both the secessionists, called "destructives," and the members of his own party, the Conservatives, including those Conservatives who might be considering Holden and peace negotiations.[6]

As Vance saw the matter, his greatest difficulty in triumphing in the election lay in garnering the votes of those old Union men in his own party who might be receptive to the idea of reconciliation with the United States. As he stated to Hale earlier, "The convention question is to be my test." He feared that the Conservative Party might split into two factions: moderates, who would support continuing the Confederate war effort and would agree only to a peace based upon Confederate independence, and "ultras," who were opposed to Davis's conduct of the war and might favor a state peace convention. Vance believed that in order to win the gubernatorial race he had to hold those two factions together. "I do not wish," he declared to Hale, "this rupture to be upon any *minor* issue. In other words and to make myself plain, I do not wish to fritter away my strengths or lose a friend by fighting the ultra *conservatives* upon any but the *main points*. Let them abuse Jeff Davis and the Secessionists to their hearts content so they but oppose this Convention movement & keep to their duty on the war question. And whilst I would disapprove of this as vexatious, I hold it would be bad policy to waste my strength by quarreling with them." Cautious lest he alienate any voters, Vance stressed that "so far I have not courted the Secessionists or quarreled with many friends for things that have even threatened to compromise me, but have suffered in silence."

As Vance and his wife worried at the bedside of one of their children who was "dangerously ill," he vacillated in publicly announcing his platform.[7] He also felt uncertain about how and when to proceed in his race for reelection and wanted to wait for advice from his Conservative supporters. Such advice was not long in coming. John D. Hyman, a friend and former co-editor of the *Asheville Spectator* who soon became editor of the pro-Vance Raleigh *Conservative*, wrote to Vance on February 17, 1864. "By your silence you are daily losing friends," Hyman warned the governor. "The Democratic and secession party allege that Holden is your spokesman and that you are in favor of a convention; while a large number of conservatives are committing themselves to a convention, whether by signing petitions or participating in public meetings held at Holden's suggestion—whereas they would commit themselves in opposition if they knew you were opposed to it."[8] Five days later, on February 22, Vance publicly denounced Holden's peace convention, when he made his first campaign speech in Wilkesboro, the seat of Wilkes County.

In the meantime (as noted in chapter 2) Vance's campaign had been potentially threatened when the issue of Confederate suspension of habeas corpus arose again. The Confederate Congress's first laws suspending the writ had been allowed to expire in 1862 because of public opposition. But on February 5, 1864, at President Davis's request, the Confederate lawmakers enacted a third law suspending habeas corpus in thirteen specific cases. The eleventh clause of the act was directed at suppressing peace activities in the Confederacy. Holden immediately denounced the new habeas corpus act as another example of the hardships and violations of constitutional rights that the Confederate government was imposing on North Carolinians.[9]

Vance quickly realized that he would have to neutralize the issue of suspension in order to prevent Holden from gaining political support. Convinced that the act was directed at North Carolina's disaffected citizens, Vance—as discussed earlier—wrote to Davis on February 9 urging him to restrain from enforcing the new law. Suspending the writ of habeas corpus now, he cautioned the president, would only enhance, not retard, disloyalty and peace sentiment. The problems in North Carolina, he insisted, could not be solved by suppression of civil rights. The state would remain loyal to the Confederacy so long as Davis dealt fairly and cautiously with its residents. Vance pointed out to the president that he and other supporters of the Confederacy were already working in the state to prevent the calling of a peace convention.

Vance then launched into a long explanation of why some North Carolinians had become disenchanted with the Confederate war effort. He maintained that, from the beginning, the Davis government had been suspicious of the Old North State because it had been reluctant to leave the Union. As a result, the governor complained, those Tar Heels who were originally opposed to secession had been excluded from high civil and military positions in the Confederacy. He also contended that the Confederate policies of conscription, impressment, and tax-in-kind had been harshly and unfairly imposed upon North Carolinians.[10] Davis defended himself in detail against Vance's charges that he and his officials were biased against North Carolina.[11] A series of angry letters then passed between the equally stubborn and temperamental governor and president, in which each blamed the other for the disaffection in North Carolina.[12]

Davis's concern about the peace movement in the Tar Heel State led the Confederate War Department to order a brigade commanded by Gen. Robert F. Hoke to encamp near Raleigh. Many Conservatives believed that it was Davis's intention to have Hoke arrest and retain Holden according to the provision of the recent habeas corpus law. Apparently, however, the logic of Vance's February 9 letter to Davis—despite the subsequent heated and argumentative exchanges between the two men—convinced the president not to have Hoke arrest Holden, who temporarily suspended publication of the *Standard* and his clamor against the Confederate government.[13] "I suspended the Standard," Holden informed merchant and former Whig

Calvin J. Cowles of Wilkesboro on March 18, "on account of the suspension of habeas corpus abolishing civil law. I felt that if I could not continue to print as a free man I would not print at all." But Holden also implied that Vance approved of Hoke's deployment, and that the governor's refusal to protest the general's presence near Raleigh contributed to Holden's decision to shut down the *Standard*. If that is true, it is conceivable that Vance took advantage of Hoke's arrival to intimidate and temporarily silence Holden while he got his own campaign under way.[14]

Vance began his campaign for reelection in the midst of a stronghold of peace sentiment. Wilkes County stood in the west and at the edge of the Quaker Belt—prime Holden country. In his February 22 speech at Wilkesboro, the governor set the tone and agenda that would prevail throughout his campaign. By selecting a place in the heart of Holden's support region to launch his campaign, Vance was directly challenging his opposition. From that point on, he ceased to vacillate and began a direct public attack on Holden and the idea of a state peace convention. In his speech, he denounced the secessionists who had started the war but at the same time condemned the movement calling for a peace convention. He asserted that the Confederacy could win its independence if the people would only persist in their support for the Richmond government. He told the crowd of two thousand onlookers that he had "no more doubt about the establishment of the independence of the Southern Confederacy than I have of my own existence, provided we remain true to the cause we have solemnly undertaken to support." He pointed out to his listeners that if North Carolina made a separate peace with the Federals without the cooperation of the other Confederate states, the results would be conflict and anarchy within the state. Vance went on to chastise the Davis government for its recent law authorizing the suspension of habeas corpus. But he qualified his remarks with an appeal to the citizens of North Carolina to obey all laws of the Confederacy and the state, including those relating to habeas corpus and conscription. North Carolinians, he insisted, must not allow their dissatisfaction with the progress of the war and with laws emanating from Richmond to lead to disorder and civil strife among themselves. "I have come among you," he told the Wilkesboro crowd, "to beg you in the name of reason, of humanity, to obey the law; to recognize order and authority; to do nothing except in the manner prescribed in the Constitution; to bear the ills you have rather than fly to evils you know not of; in short . . . to implore you 'to do nothing rash.'"[15]

The next few days saw the governor give this speech again at Statesville, Taylorsville, and Salisbury. Upon Vance's return to Raleigh, Holden

—seeing plainly that the man he had supported for the office of chief executive two years earlier was now not going to advocate a state peace convention—announced in early March his intention to run against the incumbent in the gubernatorial race.[16] Although Holden had not resumed
regular publication of the *Standard*, he brought out a special edition on
March 3 announcing his candidacy. The editor felt that his platform should
be obvious to the voters. "My principals [*sic*] and views, as a Conservative
'after the straitest [*sic*] sect,' are well known to the people of the State," he
informed his readers. "These principles and views are what they have been.
They will not be changed." Holden declared that he would not actively
campaign against Vance but would remain at home and await the outcome
of the election. He would not campaign because "I am not disposed, at a
time like this, to invite the people from their employment, and add to the
excitement which prevails in the public mind, by haranguing them for
their votes. We need all our energies to meet the common enemy, and to
provide means of subsistence for our troops in the field and the people at
home. Let the people go calmly and firmly to the polls and vote for the
men of their choice. I will cheerfully abide their decision, whatever it
may be."[17]

After Holden's announcement, Vance wrote to Graham that "The man
who has been deepest in my confidence and whom my friends have persisted in apologizing for, has at length shown his purpose."[18] Of course,
Vance was not at all surprised at Holden's announcement that he would
run, and he had to be pleased that the editor of the *Standard* was not going
to campaign. To be sure, Holden was no match for Vance in public speaking
and would never draw the same large crowds, and any debate between the
two candidates would assuredly have gone to Vance. But by remaining at
home, Holden gave Vance free rein to use his colorful crowd-pleasing
speaking ability to gather votes, unfettered by the sober challenges of a
persistent opponent. Public appearance was particularly important in the
hinterland, where not everyone read the Raleigh *Standard*.

Some of Holden's supporters recognized that he was giving Vance a
decided advantage by not taking to the campaign circuit, and they implored him to begin stumping the state. Holden responded to their advice
in another special edition of the *Standard* on April 20: "I have received
several invitations to address the people as a candidate for Governor. Under the circumstances, I most respectfully decline to canvass the State. This
determination was made known in my [notice] announcing myself a candidate. . . . I am not afraid to meet Gov. Vance, or any other candidate who
may be supported by the Destructives or partizans of the Confederate ad-

ministration; but I am not vain enough to hope that I could change or control the opinions of the people by a canvass." The *Standard* editor went on to point out that neither candidate for governor had campaigned in 1862. Nor had the gubernatorial candidates in Virginia, Alabama, and Georgia done so in the recent elections in those states. Apparently Holden failed to realize that, with the changes that had occurred in North Carolina politics since 1862, he was making a tactical mistake in allowing Vance to use his best weapon—taking his cause directly to the voters—unchallenged.[19]

Holden did not begin republishing the *Standard* on a regular basis until May 18. That delay also proved to be a mistake, for as Holden biographer William C. Harris has written, it "permitted Vance to steal the march on him precisely at the time when North Carolinian outrage at Confederate transgressions was at its height and could have been used to good effect against Vance."[20] While the *Standard* remained silent, Vance's own newspaper, the *Conservative*, promoted his reelection and attacked Holden as a political chameleon and poor leader. Through the newspaper, Vance persisted in his efforts to obtain the support of the "ultra" Conservatives who might be persuaded to support a state peace convention. The *Conservative* effectively portrayed Holden as someone who was willing to cooperate fully with the Lincoln government and thereby negotiate away all rights of the state.[21] Early in his campaign, Vance had determined to undermine Holden's candidacy by depicting him as a "Lincolnite." As Vance informed Hale back in December, "I want the question narrowed down to *Lincoln or no Lincoln*."[22] The Raleigh *Confederate*, the organ of the "destructives," also lambasted Holden with an almost-fanatical zeal that helped ensure the secessionist vote for Vance. The *Wilmington Journal*, too, supported the governor's reelection. With this dual approach to the campaign, Vance and his supporters hoped to attract votes from both the secessionists and the Conservatives.[23]

While Holden remained at home, Vance stumped the state vigorously, responding to many invitations to speak and drawing large crowds throughout the spring and summer. In March, he also campaigned among the North Carolina troops in Virginia, where he vowed that North Carolina would never abandon the cause of Confederate independence.[24] On April 27, the *Conservative* clearly stated the platform on which Vance was campaigning—a platform that offered something to both Conservatives and secessionists. According to its planks, North Carolinians should obey all laws, "whether good or bad," as long as such laws were in effect. Civil law should take precedence over military law. But the Confederate government should implement "A speedy repeal of the act suspending the writ of habeas corpus." North Carolinians should not initiate any "separate state action through a convention" to seek peace. Nor should there be any "counter revolution" or "combined resistance to the government." The citizens of the Tar Heel State should maintain "An unbroken front to the common enemy." The "proper authorities" could seek "timely and repeated negotiations for peace." But there could be no "reconstruction or submission." All negotiations must be based on the "perpetual independence" of the Confederacy. Finally, North Carolinians should maintain "Opposition to despotism in every form, and the preservation of our Republican institutions in all their purity."[25]

To further appease the "ultra" Conservatives, Vance changed his mind about not publishing the contentious correspondence between him and the Confederate president. The *Conservative* then published letters between the governor and Jefferson Davis in which Vance set forth the problems and dissatisfaction with the war that were afflicting the people of his state. His complaints to Davis and his suggestion that the president make a token effort at peace negotiations with the Lincoln government bolstered Vance's support among discontented voters who might be inclined to drift into the Holden camp.[26]

The issue of habeas corpus, however, continued to worry Vance's Conservative supporters, who fretted that he had not spoken out strongly enough against the suspension of the writ. Early in the campaign, Vance had actually defended the constitutional right of the Confederate government to suspend habeas corpus. "With regard to the suspension of *habeas corpus*," declared the *Iredell Express* following Vance's campaign speech in Statesville, "we understood him to regret the necessity of it, which induced Congress to suspend the writ, but he read the opinion of an able lawyer that the act is constitutional, of which there is no doubt."[27] Ultimately responding to the advice of his associates, Vance defended the sanctity of the writ of habeas corpus in an April speech in Fayetteville, in the columns of the *Fayetteville Observer* that same month, and thereafter in the campaign. At the same time, he tempered his defense of the writ by insisting that North Carolinians should support the Davis government and accept nothing short of Confederate independence. Responding to the governor's address to the General Assembly in May, the state legislators passed a resolution against the suspension of the writ of habeas corpus and a bill making it a misdemeanor to ignore a writ issued by a state judge. At the same session, the legislature passed a resolution expressing its "most hearty approval and cordial sympathy" for Vance's position and stating that any peace negotiations should be made only on the basis of Confederate independence.[28] Thus, in effect, the legislature's resolutions endorsed Vance's platform and thereby bolstered his campaign against Holden.

Vance never relented in his attack on Holden and his state peace convention. At the same time, the governor publicly maintained that he was open to possible peace negotiations as long as they were based on Confederate independence and were undertaken in cooperation with the Davis government. He also portrayed himself as a protector of habeas corpus and the civil rights of the people. He stressed to the voters that Holden's peace convention was aimed at initiating peace negotiations directly with the Lincoln government without cooperation with the other Confederate states and the Davis government. If that occurred, Vance claimed, North Carolina would find itself clashing with the remaining Confederate states in a "new war, a bloodier conflict" than the present one. Civil disorder greater than that which had already occurred, and possibly anarchy, would result in the state. At best, the Tar Heel State would be ravaged by both Federal and Confederate troops. Furthermore, he insisted, a state convention would have no powers that the state legislature did not already have. It would accomplish nothing but the state's withdrawal from the Confederacy and its return to the Union under the same restrictions of states' rights and personal liberty that had led to secession in the first place. In addition, Vance attempted to discredit Holden by accusing him of being a member of the radical anti-Confederate group the Heroes of America, or Red Strings.[29]

Having much of his political thunder stolen on the issues of a peace convention and habeas corpus, Holden could only respond to Vance's platform by accusing the governor of having a wasteful and corrupt administration and of neglecting the state's business by staying so long on the campaign circuit. He also claimed that Vance was really the candidate of the "destructives" and not a true Conservative. More war, not peace, was Vance's objective, Holden asserted. He announced to North Carolina soldiers that their governor wanted them "to fight till hell froze over, and then fight upon the ice." The editor of the *Standard* spent much of his effort defending himself against the charge that he wanted a separate peace. He struggled in the columns of the *Standard* to convince the voters that his proposed peace convention would not lead North Carolina into separate negotiations. Instead, it would unite the Tar Heel State with the other Confederate states and the Davis government in seeking negotiations that would bring the war to a peaceful conclusion. Of course, as Vance knew, there was no significant popular support for a convention move-

ment in the other Confederate states, even in Georgia, where the states'
rights and anti-Davis governor Joseph Brown presided.[30]

Vance was shrewd enough to realize that, although he would wage his
campaign primarily on the basis of loyalty to the Confederacy and continuation of the war, he could not ignore the peace advocates in the state.
After all, in the November 1863 Confederate elections, the state's peace
proponents had seen their candidates win a large number of seats in the
Congress. Vance also wisely listened to the advice of his Conservative supporters, who warned the governor against allowing Holden to portray him
as opposed to any peace arrangement. "If your friends are not up and moving, we will be beat at the next August elections—Mr. Holden and his
friends are moving Heaven and Earth to identify you with ultra and Extreme men of the Confederacy," John A. Gilmer, a former Whig and U.S.
congressman who became a Confederate congressman, warned the governor in April 1864.[31] But Vance never had any real commitment to the peace
process. Any rhetorical sop that he threw to the 1864 electorate regarding
peace negotiations was simply intended to attract support from those voters who might be disillusioned and disaffected by the continuance of the
war.

In the end, Vance ran a nearly perfect campaign. He realized early that
Holden would be his opponent in his bid for reelection. He also grasped
that the secessionists would vote for him as an alternative to Holden, and
that he did not have to concentrate on wooing their vote with extreme
rhetoric in support of Davis and the war effort. He marshaled media support by establishing the *Conservative* in Raleigh and encouraging its editor, Hyman, and Hale, editor of the *Fayetteville Observer*, to promote him
and attack Holden. He listened to his Conservative advisors and took care
not to alienate the "ultra" members of the party by completely discount-
ing any possibility of a peace convention that might hold terms favorable
to the South. He also heeded Conservatives' advice to speak more emphatically in the defense of the writ of habeas corpus. By so doing, he denied Holden and his allies those issues with which to assail him. At the
same time, although Vance and Jefferson Davis engaged in heated exchanges over habeas corpus and North Carolinians' role in the war in general, his correspondence with the president did not precipitate any break
with the government in Richmond. In fact, Vance's appeal may have prevented Davis from having Holden arrested under the provisions of the
1864 law on suspension of the writ of habeas corpus. Vance canvassed the
state widely during the campaign. He did not slight the importance of the
army's vote and made a special effort to address North Carolina troops in

the field. Finally, he effectively utilized his greatest campaigning asset, his charismatic speaking ability, to sway large crowds of voters.

Vance's campaign was assisted in the summer of 1864 by the improvement of the Confederate situation on the battlefield and by a rumored decline of support in the North for continuing the war. Tar Heel citizens heard rumors that enthusiasm for the war was waning in the Union. If Lincoln suffered defeat in the presidential election in November, Confederate independence might be a real possibility. Encouraged by such news, North Carolinians were further swayed to accept Vance's call for perseverance in support of the Confederate war effort.[32]

Vance thus won the August gubernatorial election overwhelmingly, receiving 77.2 percent of the civilian vote. Of the soldiers' votes, Holden garnered only 1,824 of the nearly 15,000 cast. There is some evidence of possible fraud in some of the army voting, but this would not have changed the outcome of the election.[33] Upon hearing of the soldiers' vote, plantation mistress Catherine Ann Devereux Edmondston of Halifax County recorded in her diary that Holden "has been beaten so far by Vance that his votes are not even counted. . . . I could never believe that North Carolina was in any danger of electing a man like him for its head—the illegitimate son of a wicked woman, devoid alike of the instincts & breeding of a gentleman, a mere agitator for his own selfish ends. Never was more noise made over a more contemptible individual. I hope never to hear of him again!"[34] Vance carried all but three counties in the state: Wilkes (the site of the governor's opening campaign speech), Randolph, and Johnston. His votes totaled 57,873, while Holden received only 14,432.[35]

News of the victory brought congratulations from several sources. On August 6, Milledge L. Bonham, governor of South Carolina, telegraphed: "Hurrahs for the Glorious Old North State & Govr. Vance[.] I feel assurd & told your people you would" win the election.[36] Edward J. Hale wrote to the newly reelected governor: "We have indeed gained a great victory over disaffection at home & confident hopes & expectations in Yankee land. I confess that the thoroughness of the defeat, the using up, of Holden has surprised me. His incessant boasts of strengths [had convinced me] that he could not be beaten out of sight. God be praised! What a terrible blow it would have been to the cause if he had raised a respectable vote!"[37] General Robert E. Lee expressed his pleasure at the outcome of the election. "The result of the late election in N Carolina," declared the general, "is well calculated to cheer and sustain the people of the Confederacy. It dissipates the hopes that our enemies had cherished of a division of our efforts and councils, and convinces them that three years of war have in no degree shaken the resolution of our people to resist."[38] From Chapel Hill, Cornelia P. Spencer wrote to the governor, "expressing my own individual pleasure & exultation at your reelection. It was so triumphantly carried that we are a little ashamed now of having ever been uneasy" about the outcome.[39] The Raleigh *Confederate* rejoiced that "The majority for Governor Vance is unprecedented, and . . . must strike every true man with the highest gratification—not as a party triumph but as a thorough vindication of the patriotism and loyalty of the people of North Carolina. . . . The people of North Carolina are now united in a solid and boldly expressed determination to stand by our common government in all its just and proper efforts to maintain the cause, our rights and our independence."[40] With that vote of confidence from the electorate and various friends, advisors, and officials, Vance would in the coming months continue to lend his support steadfastly to the Confederacy's efforts to win its independence.

6

"THROUGH A MOST RIGOROUS
AND DANGEROUS BLOCKADE"

One of Vance's greatest administrative successes was adequately supplying North Carolina troops through the operation of the state's blockade-runners. Vance's predecessor, Gov. Henry T. Clark, had agreed with the Confederate government to supply North Carolina's troops with clothing and blankets in exchange for a payment to the state of fifty dollars annually for each soldier. The state used the money to purchase raw materials and contracted with local cotton and woolen mills to produce the soldiers' goods. But shortly after Vance took office, the Richmond government requested that he relinquish the state contracts to the Confederacy, which would then take over furnishing Tar Heel troops. Vance responded that he would have to bring the matter before the state legislature, but before the state lawmakers convened, the Confederate government ceased payment for the supply of North Carolina troops. Vance, however, refused to turn over the contracts, and eventually the Confederacy renewed the agreement whereby the Tar Heel State could supply its own soldiers and receive payment from the Confederate government.[1]

During the first month of his administration, Vance found the state faced with a shortage of leather and cotton and wool thread with which to make shoes, uniforms, and blankets. State adjutant general James G. Martin had approached Governor Clark about obtaining for the state a blockade-runner to transport materials and supplies from England. Clark declined to take that action. Vance, on the other hand, seized on the idea and began efforts to secure a vessel and appoint agents to purchase supplies in England.[2]

For the state's foreign commissioner, he and General Martin chose John White, a reliable merchant from Warrenton. Vance contracted with White to travel to England for the purpose of purchasing and shipping back to North Carolina whatever supplies the governor ordered.[3] To accompany White, Vance appointed Thomas Crossan, a former naval officer who had commanded the gunboat *Winslow* in coastal North Carolina and served as a lieutenant colonel of coastal artillery. Crossan's mission was to purchase and equip a blockade-runner for the state.

To finance blockade-running for North Carolina, the state legislature appropriated $2 million with which Vance bought and stored cotton. The state then issued warrants, or bonds, based on the cotton. Investors in England who purchased the warrants could collect 7 percent interest annually on their investment or, upon sixty days' notice to White, collect the cotton from Wilmington. Each bale of cotton weighed at least four hundred pounds, and a £100 bond secured twelve bales of cotton.[4] Vance instructed White that if he could not persuade investors to purchase the North Carolina bonds, then he should consult with the Confederacy's foreign commissioner to England, James M. Mason. The governor had been informed by a "gentleman from England" that North Carolina might "be able to negotiate a loan through Mr. Mason."[5]

When he reached England, White entered into a direct agreement with Alexander Collie and Company of London and Manchester, which established a line of credit with the North Carolina commissioner and accepted the cotton bonds as collateral. "After many unavoidable delays and disappointments," White wrote to Vance on May 20, 1863, "I have at last succeeded in obtaining a loan of money from Mess. Alexr. Collie & Co. of London and Manchester, which has enabled Col. Crossan to purchase a steamer and me a portion of goods required by the State. The loan or advancement made by them is predicated upon the Sale of Cotton at 5 pence Sterling per pound." White managed to secure a better exchange rate than that obtained by the Confederate government for its bonds. "I consider the Sale as proposed," he declared, "at least 12½ perct. better for the State, than the terms made by the Govt. at Richmond with Mess. Erlanger & Co."[6]

For the sum of £35,000, or $175,000, Crossan purchased the iron-hulled, side-wheeled steamer *Lord Clyde*. The ship had been built in the summer of 1862 and had operated for several months between Dublin and Glasgow prior to its sale to North Carolina. Crossan loaded the vessel with supplies and sailed it to Bermuda and then on to Wilmington.[7] White reported that "Col Crossan will take out with him from 100 to 120 tons assorted merchandise, which will leave of what has now been bought I suppose about 150 tons that I expect to ship by a sailing vessel to Bermuda to be there in time for Col. Crossans second cargo."[8] At the end of June 1863, the *Lord Clyde* arrived at Wilmington with a cargo of dry goods, blankets, and shoes. The cloth went to the state's factories to make blankets and uniforms.

At Wilmington Crossan changed the registry of the *Lord Clyde* and renamed the vessel the *Advance*. According to historian Stephen R. Wise, that "name . . . would often be confused with the ship's sponsor, Governor Zebulon Vance. People often tried to match the name of the steamer with that of the governor, but she was referred to in all correspondence and official port records as the *Advance,* and it was under this name that she became one of the war's most successful blockade runners."[9]

After the first *Advance* shipment arrived at Wilmington, Vance wrote to White that "I am much pleased with the result of your negotiations and approve most cordially of your whole conduct." He told his agent that the legislature had given him "full authority . . . to run the vessel when and how I may think best, and I shall therefore keep her going until we get in the balance of the purchases." He informed White that he was sending him "the balance of the bonds amounting to one million, but desire you deposit them only as you need money, and to buy only as I may order, as an accident might happen to Crossan at any time. I presume from your [May 20] letter that you are not bound to take the whole loan at once, but may take it up from time to time, depositing bonds as you go. On the whole I will say that much being left to your discretion, my desire is that you should not keep far ahead of your shipments, either in money or supplies; that you should deal cautiously & wait for advices."[10]

Just prior to this letter to White, the war had taken a decided turn against the Confederacy with the fall of Vicksburg and Lee's defeat at Gettysburg. Vance, however, attempted to downplay the importance of those defeats to White. His motive apparently was to encourage his agent to bolster the confidence of English investors, who might become cautious in investing in Southern bonds and extending credit because of the recent battlefield setbacks. It is possible that Vance as late as July 10, when he wrote White, might not have been aware of all the details of Lee's defeat and subsequent retreat. But more likely, he deliberately discounted it to White. "The fall of Vicksburg," he told his agent, "though creating some despondency has not discouraged us, and General Lee is compensating us by his invasion of Northern territory. On the whole our prospects are better than they were this time last year. Our people are adapting themselves to a state of war, our resources are developing wonderfully, our army is becoming veteran & invincible, and our crop prospects, with the harvest already in, almost excelled belief. You may assure, I think, the generous merchants who have befriended a people in their death struggle for liberty and independence, that their investment is a safe one." He assured White that "the war is evidently nearing its close," with victory for the South in sight.[11] Whether or not Vance actually believed the war would soon be over, he realized how important it was not to scare off merchants and investors, such as Alexander Collie and Company, with bad war news, lest North Carolina fail to receive its needed supplies. It is not easy to believe that by July 10 Vance did not know about the outcome of Gettysburg. Many North Carolina citizens certainly had heard of the results of Lee's disastrous attack on Cemetery Ridge. For example, Anna Long Thomas Fuller of Louisburg noted in her diary on July 4: "On the 1st, 2nd [and] 3rd, the great battle of Gettysburg was fought. Our loss was very heavy. It casts its shadow over many homes in our community."[12] But Halifax County plantation mistress Catherine Ann Devereux Edmondston did not receive news of Lee's defeat until July 10, the same day Vance wrote to White. Until then she had heard reports that Lee had prevailed, capturing 40,000 Union prisoners, and that Gen. George G. Meade was falling back toward Baltimore.[13]

In any event, Vance's hope that White might, by talking optimistically, dissuade investors from believing the war was turning against the South was, at best, naïve. White wrote the governor on August 7, 1863, that he was short of funds primarily because news of Confederate battlefield defeats had scared off investors in cotton bonds. "Our recent reverses," he told the governor, "has [sic] sent the Confederate cotton loan down to a very great discount, & it has also had the effect to deter Capitalists from buying N.C. cotton bonds. The whole amount issued is £150[,]ooo Sterling but not quite £100[,]ooo has yet been disposed of."[14]

Nevertheless, Vance persisted in encouraging foreign investors by giving the war news a twist in favor of the Confederacy. In August 1864, he wrote to Alexander Collie: "I cannot close without saying a word in regard to the 'Situation'—I am happy to say that it is promising. Grants great and bloody campaign against Richmond is an acknowledged failure. Instead of our capitol being in danger, Genl. Lee spares 25[,]ooo men [who] under a new & rising General (Early) are now in Pennsylvania avenging in the ashes of their towns the desolation of many a Southern village. There is hardly the semblance of a Yankee army west of the Mississippi and Genl Sherman has been halted in front of Atlanta by a severe and bloody check. Our army is in good spirits and *abundantly fed*. Crops of Indian corn are fine and our people more hopeful than ever." He told Collie to discount any rumors of disaffection in the South and cited his recent reelection as evidence of North Carolina's commitment to the Confederate cause.[15]

The *Advance* made eight successful runs between Wilmington and Bermuda between July 24, 1863, and August 6, 1864. In October 1863, Vance appointed John J. Guthrie, a former Confederate naval officer, as captain of the steamer to replace Crossan. Federal vessels finally captured the *Advance* when she left the North Carolina port on September 10, 1864. But during the time that the ship was operating, her cargoes provided significant quantities of supplies for North Carolina soldiers. On one trip, the vessel carried 1,700 blankets, 2,000 pairs of shoes, 30,000 yards of flannel, 5,000 pairs of socks, 96 dozen cotton and wool cards, and a large quantity of bagging and rope for cotton bales. The state-controlled factories used the imported cloth to turn out uniforms for Tar Heel troops. North Carolina sold any surplus cloth to the Confederacy at a low price.[16] In October 1863, Vance boasted to his political confidant Edward J. Hale, editor of the *Fayetteville Observer*: "No accident or misfortune befalling me, I am now in condition to ensure clothing for our troops to January 1865."

Although on the whole North Carolina's blockade-running activity was successful, problems in procuring certain items did arise. In particular, Vance was disappointed in the shoes and blankets that came through the blockade. He told Hale that even though sufficient clothing for the soldiers had arrived, the quantity of shoes and blankets was inadequate. "Our cargoes were not well assorted & sufficient of these articles were not brought in before. 18[,]000 prs. shoes & boots, a quantity of leather & 17,500 blankets are at Bermuda & expected by steamer next week."[17] He wrote to White on October 18, 1863, that "The number of shoes and blankets heretofore sent is far less than I desired, though I can't tell what you have behind. I will say in general that they should far exceed in amount any other articles. The shoes are mostly too narrow and the blankets too large and heavy." At the same time, he instructed White that "we have cloth enough and you need buy no more."[18]

White had considerable difficulty in securing cotton and wool cards. The cards were meant for distribution to households, where North Carolinians used them to convert cotton and wool into thread to be woven for family clothing. Any surplus of thread could be used by the state's factories to make clothes for the soldiers. Vance reminded White on July 10, 1863, that he had asked him to purchase cotton and wool cards and a machine and supply of wire for making them. "If you have not acted upon this already," he told his agent, "please buy at once fifty thousand pairs each of woolen & cotton cards and a machine & wire, & ship at once to Bermuda. I presume that by buying the teeth set in leather without the wood finishing, this number will not be a very large bulk." Still frustrated about the shortage of cards, Vance wrote to White again in September: "The only remaining article I am anxious about is the cotton & wool cards—I was sorry to learn that you had not purchased them. Please make every effort to get them & send them in—Perhaps you had better purchase them through agents in New York—they are better & cheaper than the English." Vance noted that with "plenty of cards for our housewives our people would be greatly relieved in the way of clothing and prices would be greatly diminished. I can not impress too strongly upon you the importance of these articles to our people. I hope before this you have done something toward securing a supply."[19]

White, who had not received the governor's original orders for the cards, responded on October 31 that he had ordered 25,000 to 30,000 cotton and wool cards. Because there was no ship leaving immediately for Bermuda, he sent the cards to Liverpool to ship by way of Halifax, Nova Scotia. But the Liverpool steamer was full. He promised to send the cards to Bermuda by the first vessel bound for that island port from either London or Liverpool, and other shipments would follow. "The machines for making cards," he reported, "I find can be bought for about £20 each[.] [I]n place of one, I have orderd. five with the wire &c. necessary to keep them going for a year. One man can attend to 10 or 12 of the machines in operation, as well as to one. They will be ready for shipment in about 2 weeks."[20]

The difficulty of procuring sufficient cotton and wool cards had plagued the state since early in the war. The legislature passed a resolution in January 1863 instructing Vance to obtain machines capable of manufacturing the cards. Hearing that Georgia had such machinery, Vance wrote to Gov. Joseph E. Brown asking for details and about the possibility of getting such devices for North Carolina. Brown answered that his state had bought a half interest in the Pioneer Card Manufacturing Company, which had one machine for making the cards. The machine operated at the State Armory in Milledgeville. When it was functioning properly, it produced about twenty-four pairs of cards each day, which, Brown said, "we sell at $6 per pair, for *leather* or *skins* suitable for making" other cards. Georgia gave "a preference in making sales to widows of deceased soldiers and wives of soldiers now in the service." That state had attempted to build additional machines, but so far they were not operational. Brown had no machinery or spare cards to sell to North Carolina, but Vance was welcome to send a mechanic or machinist to make drawings of the Georgia machine in the hopes of building similar ones for North Carolina.[21]

A Durham County machine manufacturer, John A. McMannen, visited Milledgeville and inspected its card-making machinery but apparently found it unsatisfactory. He concluded that "our only resource for obtaining cards is in foreign importation & running the blockade."[22] Vance ordered another machinist, named Brown, to travel to Milledgeville to have a look at the machines. Machinist Brown took apart one of the devices and made drawings. "Though the machine is complicated," the Georgia governor wrote to Vance, "I trust he may find no difficulty in making one."[23] But any attempts to build card machines proved unsuccessful, and North Carolina continued to rely primarily on imports for its cotton and wool cards, which the state never had in adequate supply.

In addition to White, Vance appointed another agent, Duncan K. McRae —a lawyer, politician, and former Confederate colonel—to travel to Halifax, Nova Scotia, to sell rosin and turpentine bonds and to obtain arms and equipment for North Carolina troops. A third commissioner, George N. Sanders—a self-promoter and adventurer of questionable motives—contracted with North Carolina to sell naval stores bonds and to cooperate with McRae. Sanders had already performed one foreign mission for the Confederate government. McRae met him in Richmond in 1862, where Sanders convinced the commissioner that naval stores bonds would find a ready market in England. McRae urged him to contact Vance, who approved Sanders's scheme of selling naval stores warrants and entered into a contract with him. The governor instructed Sanders, a Kentuckian, and McRae to go from Wilmington via Nassau to Halifax, a shipping port for blockade-runners en route from England to Nassau, Bermuda, or Havana. At Halifax, the two commissioners were to sell the state's bonds and purchase arms to be shipped to Wilmington.[24] In January 1863, McRae arrived in Nassau, from where he was to travel on to meet Sanders at Halifax. McRae reported that, if he could sell his bonds, there were supplies at Nassau that North Carolina might wish to purchase and ship at a good rate in blockade-runners "so successfully run by *certain owners*." He noted, however, that "I shall probably be obliged to go to Europe to sell the scrip."[25]

On March 12, 1863, Vance wrote to McRae that "circumstances occurring since your departure render it unnecessary for us to purchase the number of arms originally contemplated. I think one fourth (say 2500) will be sufficient investment at present—the Legislature having declined to raise any State Troops. Should you succeed in effecting a loan on your Scrip, you might invest it in shoes, blankets and gray cloth of the Army and cotton wool cards for the people." If McRae could not obtain a loan on the basis of state bonds, Vance instructed him to "suspend all further efforts and Consult with Mr. [James M.] Mason of Va. our [Confederate] Commissioner to England, as I have adopted another plan, to be tried in case you and Mr. White have both failed." The governor did not specify what his alternative plan was, but apparently it included cooperation with the Confederate government in obtaining supplies by running the blockade. Vance did make it clear that he had become suspicious of Sanders, who, without instructions, had sailed to England. "For various reasons upon reflection," Vance told McRae, "I have concluded that I would prefer you to have negotiations of the Scrip instead of Mr. Saunders [Sanders]. I had no intention of letting Mr. S. hawk our paper about through Europe. I know you will appreciate my reasons. Should you be in Europe (and I am writing as though you were) I desire you to act with Mr. White, put your fortunes together, Ship your purchases together &c."[26]

In July Vance instructed McRae to close his operations and return home on the earliest available steamer. He told the agent not to sell the turpentine and rosin warrants or bonds, but if McRae had already done so, he was to "recant if possible or get off as lightly as may be."[27] But the governor's instructions did not reach McRae in time to prevent his selling many of the bonds and using the loan to buy and ship an additional "twelve hundred rifles and ammunition to suit."[28] As he had done with White, Vance attempted to downplay to McRae any reports of recent Confederate battlefield defeats. "We have lost Vicksburg," he told McRae, "by starvation of the garrison and invaded Pa. Defeating the enemy, capturing large numbers of prisoners and scaring the Dutch almost into a cocked hat."[29]

"I regret that you sold the bonds at all," Vance lamented in September, when he learned that his July letter had arrived too late to halt McRae's purchases. He pointed out that "Mr. White had succeeded so well with his loan, it was altogether unnecessary and besides I find it exceedingly difficult to get and keep the turpentine, and it will be attended with considerable loss to the State—But let it go." He went on to say, with some exasperation, that North Carolina did not need to keep two agents "abroad for the same purpose." Vance also implied that he had received reports that McRae was having problems in supervising Sanders's activities, which so far had produced few results for North Carolina. He admonished McRae "to see that the State suffers no damage by him." Vance had advanced Sanders five thousand dollars in state bonds, but the agent had not "complied with his agreement in any one particular." McRae, therefore, should ensure that Sanders was "held *to it strictly*." In an increasingly irritated tone, Vance seemed to want to blame McRae for Sanders's performance.[30] Both McRae and Sanders had written to Vance about the difficulties they

were having in cooperating. Sanders accused McRae of fraudulently selling the naval stores bonds and cheating him out of a commission.[31]

Taken aback by Vance's annoyed words, McRae wrote to ask if he had
"properly construed" the governor's instructions to mean that he was to
relieve Sanders of his bonds. Vance snapped back that he indeed intended
for McRae to take over negotiations of Sanders's bonds but "did not design
to deprive him [Sanders] of any just and reasonable compensation which
might be due him."[32] Offended by Vance's chastisement, McRae defended
his actions in going to England as the only way to sell his turpentine and
rosin bonds and as necessary in order to catch up with Sanders, who had
preceded him there. He reminded the governor that his original assign-
ment had been to obtain a loan on the bonds and purchase arms and ammunition. He could hardly be blamed if Vance's subsequent order not to
sell did not reach him in time to prevent his doing so. McRae felt that
Vance disapproved of his performance as a trade commissioner for the
state.[33]

Retreating a bit from his irritable accusations, Vance wrote McRae a
partially conciliatory letter. "I was totally unconscious," he halfheartedly
attempted to soothe his commissioner,

> of saying anything . . . which would have lead you to suppose that I
> disapproved of your official action, except the proceeding to Europe
> instead of to Halifax, in which of course you did for the best—being
> compelled to follow the contractor Mr. Sanders. To say that this met
> my approbation entirely would remove a good portion of the right,
> which I claimed and exercised of removing the negotiations from the
> hands of Sanders. . . .
>
> I can but think therefore that you are hasty in inferring my disap-
> probation of your operations, which so far as I have been able to see,
> appear to have been advantageous to the state. Of course no blame
> can attach for your failing to comply with instructions never recd. . . .
>
> And I am sure I did not say, or *mean* to say that any harm had been
> done the state by the presence of two agents in Europe operating in
> the same market, but only expressed what I feared would have been
> the case, as a reason for giving you sole charge of the bonds, and
> which *might* have induced me to order differently had I known origi-
> nally of Mr. Sanders purpose to go directly to Europe.[34]

By early 1864, White, McRae, and Sanders had been relieved of their
duties abroad and returned home. To act as North Carolina's agent abroad,
Vance appointed Joseph H. Flanner, former president of the Wilmington

Steamship Company and purser of the *Advance*. To replace Flanner as purser, the governor named Thomas J. Boykin, who had been a surgeon in Vance's old regiment and then chief surgeon of the Department of the Cape Fear, with headquarters at Wilmington. On February 1, 1864, Vance wrote Alexander Collie that Flanner would be replacing White, and that "I desire no change made in the present management of the state's affairs."[35] To Flanner he gave instructions that he was to cooperate with Collie as White had done. Vance also wanted his new commissioner to "investigate" some accounts that McRae had "left" as "unfinished business" with I. A. Weston of London. "In a word," the governor told Flanner, "whilst I do not wish any change made of the parties who are now acting for us without the best reasons for doing so, I desire to know that all continue to deal fairly with the state and obey my instructions, and to this end you are invested with power to investigate their transactions from time to time, and to give fresh instruction should it be deemed necessary. You will advise me of your progress and observations by every steamer."[36]

Upon McRae's return to North Carolina, Vance asked Kemp P. Battle, president of Chatham Railroad, and Sion H. Rogers, the state attorney general, for their advice about "just compensation for his service."[37] Shortly after his foreign purchasing duties ended, McRae became editor of the Raleigh *Confederate*, a strong voice in support of President Davis and Confederate independence.[38] In late 1864, White returned to England as North Carolina's agent for supplies, replacing Flanner. He left the North Carolina coast on October 26, 1864, but contracted yellow fever at Bermuda. He spent some weeks recovering at Halifax and did not reach England until the day before Christmas, only a short time before Fort Fisher fell to Union attack and the port of Wilmington closed. Word from him would not reach North Carolina until late May 1865.[39]

Until the port was closed, supplies for North Carolina soldiers continued to flow through the blockade. Alexander Collie and Company had soon realized the profits that could be made in blockade-running and purchased a number of steamers to carry on the trade in Confederate ports.[40] Vance also saw the advantages of not confining the state's shipping activity to one vessel. He understood that North Carolina had a much better chance of getting supplies through the blockade if it used a number of ships. Consequently, with authorization from the state legislature, he purchased for the state one-fourth interest in four of the Collie Company's steamers—the *Don*, the *Hansa*, and "two others now building," the *Annie* and the *Edith*. Alexander Collie had proposed the arrangement, suggesting that North Carolina buy one-quarter interest in four of his steamers.

Vance sold one-half interest in the *Advance* to Power, Low and Company of Wilmington for $350,000 in state bonds.[41]

The partnership between Collie and Company and North Carolina benefited both parties. Collie turned a profit, and North Carolina received the supplies it needed for its soldiers. Under the arrangement, North Carolina owned one-fourth of the cotton being shipped out of Wilmington and took possession of all the cargo arriving in the Tar Heel port. The governor boasted to his confidant Edward J. Hale in early 1864: "Though [I am] not much of a business man you may rest assured I keep my eyes open. After making five round trips, I have sold half the Advance for $350,000 in State Bonds—she cost originally 90,000 all told!" Vance had recently sent sterling funds to North Carolina soldiers imprisoned in the North to buy clothing for the winter. He "loaned Gen Johns[t]on & Longstreet 10,000 suits of clothes, complete." And he had "on hand now 14,000 English blankets & 5,000 over coats & some 50,000 suits of ready made clothes."[42] Vance reported to Seddon that "I have now at Bermuda and on the way there, Eight or ten Cargoes of supplies of the very first importance to the army and the people. Consisting chiefly of some 40,000 blankets, 40,000 prs. shoes, large quantities of army cloth, leather and 112,000 pairs of cotton cards, machinery & [fittings] to refit twenty six of our principal cotton & woolen factories, dye stuffs, lubricating oils, &c. In addition to which I have made large purchases of bacon."[43]

But the prickly Vance was not always satisfied with the arrangement with Collie and Company. His temper flared when Theodore Andreae, Collie's agent in Wilmington, trod on his authority. In February 1864, Andreae dispatched the *Hansa* to Nassau instead of to Bermuda to pick up a "cargo of army supplies." The *Hansa* returned from Nassau without any supplies for North Carolina, which enraged Vance, who had intended for the vessel to sail to Bermuda. Andreae explained that the steamer on the way out of port had grounded near Smithville (present-day Southport) and burned a large quantity of its coal. The captain, F. Atkinson, sent an urgent message to Andreae explaining that he did not have enough coal to reach Bermuda and asking if he should proceed instead to Nassau, which was closer. Rather than have the vessel return to port for more coal and run additional risk of being captured at the mouth of the Cape Fear, Andreae ordered Atkinson to proceed to Nassau.[44] Displaying the characteristic insecurity that led him to become incensed when he perceived a lack of deference to his authority as governor, Vance proclaimed that Andreae's actions "looked to me rather like a very flagrant violation of the rights of N.C." He threatened that "if my orders are not obeyed I'll have to change my agent," apparently ignoring the fact that Andreae was Collie's agent and that North Carolina owned only one-fourth of the *Hansa*. The governor reminded Andreae that the state's contract with Collie and Company gave him control over the steamers in Confederate waters. "If that did not constitute power of control," he fumed, "please give to me your ideas of what would be an actual power. I preferred you should do the business at Wilmington both as a matter of convenience & because I thought you could do it better than I could. But if I find a continued disregard to my interests in this matter, if the vessels are to risk the blockade at the expense of the State without any return, I shall certainly assume the powers which belong to me and take control of the Steamers in Confederate waters." From now on, he should be consulted about the routes of the *Don* and the *Hansa*, he growled.[45]

Unable to accept Andreae's explanation and still seething from what he saw as a personal affront, Vance wrote to Collie complaining about his agent and asking for his dismissal. "I have just cause for complaint against your agent here Mr. Andreae," he wrote on February 8, 1864, as he laid out his case for Andreae's removal. "By the terms of the contract entered into between us in regard to the steamers Don & Hansa," he explained,

> I was to have all the inward capacity of the vessels for the bringing in of my freight from Bermuda. But in defiance of my express command Andreae has on one pretence or another sent the Hansa both trips since my part ownership to Nassau, where I had no freight. I am consequently running all the risks of the blockade for the benefit of the other part owners—and getting none of my supplies in. This course I shall not submit to, and should I conclude to exercise the power vested in me by the contract, and take charge of the vessels when arriving at Wilmington to the exclusion of your agent, you must not regard it as evincing any disregard of your interest, but only a necessary attempt to protect those of this state.
>
> Should your connection with the blockade-running business in N.C. be continued long I respectfully advise that you substitute for Mr. A. an agent who would inspire more confidence & respect than this gentleman has been able to do.[46]

In his attempt to have Andreae fired, Vance followed his customary practice of appealing to the superiors of officials with whom he had conflict—or from whom he had suffered personal insult—to reprimand and remove those persons from service in North Carolina.

But apparently Alexander Collie managed to stroke Vance's fragile ego, and the governor and Andreae reconciled their differences. In a more placid tone, Vance then wrote to Collie that "I have come to a definite and satisfactory arrangement with Mr. Andreae and I apprehend no further misunderstanding."[47]

The shortage of cotton and wool cards remained a serious problem for North Carolina. Vance wrote to Collie on February 8, 1864, that of the 100,000 pairs of cards he had ordered, "only eight thousand pairs have been received and the 'Don' just in reports none in Bermuda." The card-making machines ordered by John White in 1863 also had failed to reach North Carolina. Vance asked Collie to determine the cause of the delay and expedite their shipment. "If the cards & machinery are not already shipped," he implored Collie, "please forward them without regard to expense, for if I do not get them in by the 1st. of May I despair of getting them at all." As Vance's request implies, he was worried that the port of Wilmington might soon fall to Federal attack, and North Carolina needed to get as many necessities as possible through the blockade before that catastrophe occurred.[48] He had expressed the same concern to John White in September 1863: "The blockade running is becoming more and more perilous, & should Charleston fall soon the business will be about closed. In view of this danger, you are instructed to make no more purchases of goods for the present. The amount received and not at Bermuda—with home supplies—will keep our troops well agoing for twelve months and of course it is not desirable to have goods on hand which we can not ship."[49] He told Secretary of War Seddon in January 1864 that he anticipated the port of Wilmington would be closed by the spring.[50]

North Carolina needed iron. But Vance did not want any shipped at present because "the great difficulty of getting it in quantities sufficient to meet our wants, and the greater necessity for other articles, induces me to decline shipping it." He predicted that "Bacon will be our great want this spring & summer, though I fear to keep much at the Islands as it easily spoils."[51] Exhibiting his customary fiscal conservatism and a possessive caution regarding funds and supplies, Vance never wanted to risk losing cargoes and the state's investment. But as long as Wilmington stayed opened and running the blockade remained a reasonable risk, he continued to buy and ship goods cautiously.

Despite his concerns about the Federals' capturing Fort Fisher and closing the port of Wilmington, Vance persisted in portraying the progress of the war optimistically to his English investors. He discounted any rumors of disaffection among North Carolinians and reassured Collie that

Our prospects have improved materially since the beginning of the winter. Our troops are better clothed and equipped than at any time since the beginning of the war, and nearly two thirds of our entire army have already voluntarily reenlisted for the war, disdaining to be conscribed. We shall enter on the spring campaign with largely inferior numbers it is true, but with an army largely increased, excelling in discipline and baptized in the fires of three years of constant strife and with the spirit of resistance in the people strong and determined. I beg to assure you that the statements you see in Yankee newspapers about disaffection in N.C. are entitled to little weight. Our people are very fearful of a destruction of their civil rights & liberties, and are struggling to preserve them, our enemies will take this for disaffection.[52]

The routine of the state's blockade-running activity was disrupted when the Confederate government began to interfere in North Carolina's operations. The government in Richmond did not run its overseas trade with the same efficiency as did some of the individual states, including North Carolina. In late 1863, the Confederate government appropriated one-third of the cargo space of blockade-runners entering Southern ports. State-owned vessels were exempted. As far as Vance was concerned, that exemption should extend to steamers that were partially owned by the states—including the *Advance* and the Collie vessels in which North Carolina owned one-fourth interest. Seddon learned that the *Don* was about to leave Wilmington and that Vance was opposed to enforcing the Confederacy's claim to space on the vessel. He telegraphed the governor: "I regret to learn that because of an interest of your state in the Steamer Don objection is made to its conformation to the regulations about taking out government cotton[.] [T]he necessities of the Govt really require adhearance to this regulation & [I] really hope that you will not encourage or allow in your name the infringement of it[.]"[53]

Ignoring Seddon's wishes, Vance ordered Andreae to load the *Don* "at once" with cotton, "one fourth for the State . . . and send her to Bermuda as soon as possible, to return with Cargo of freight for the State &c."[54] He then fired off a letter to Seddon, protesting the Confederate government's efforts to claim part of the space on the *Don, Hansa,* and *Advance.* "It is a little remarkable to me," he wrote Seddon, "that the entire importing operations of this State, which have been so successful and so beneficial to the cause, seems [*sic*] to have met with little else than downright opposition." This recent imposition by the government was just another in a list of self-defeating maneuvers by the Richmond administration interfering in foreign trade by the states—trade that was benefiting the Confederate cause. First, Vance ranted, Confederate commissioner Mason "laid the strong hand on my agents and positively forbade them putting a bond on market for five months after they landed in England. Then came vexations and irritating quarantine delays at Wilmington (enforced by the military, not the civil authorities) though our foreign depot was at great cost and inconvenience made at Bermuda instead of Nassau to avoid this. Then seizing of my coal at Wilmington occurred, and the denial of facilities to get it from the mines &c." He warned Seddon that if the one-third regulation was imposed on the outgoing *Don*, then "I shall certainly countermand the Sailing of the two other steamers now expected, and would suggest for the benefit of the Dept. that it would be much better to purchase than to seize an interest in the property of Strangers [Collie and Company], who are engaged in bringing us indispensable Supplies through a most rigorous and dangerous blockade."[55]

When Collie received word of the controversy between Vance and the Confederate government, he offered to sell one-fourth of the space in his company's steamers to the Confederacy. That arrangement would mean that North Carolina would have one-fourth and the Confederate government would have one-fourth of the cargo space to ship cotton in the four steamers. Collie and Company would retain one-half of the space. "I hope you will accept this proposition," Vance told Seddon.[56]

The War Department, however, declined the offer and insisted that all private steamers—including those partially owned by the states, such as the *Advance* and the Collie vessels—had to relinquish one-third of their cargo space to the Confederacy.[57] In early March 1864, the Confederate government, "instead of the one-third capacity hithertofore occupied in private steamers," began claiming one-half of the space. The navy's paymaster immediately demanded one-half of the space on the *Hansa*, which was on the verge of loading cotton for an outward trip.[58] "Is it possible that such an unblushing outrage is intended by the government?" the furious Vance inquired of Seddon. "I have no comment to make on such a proceeding further t[h]an that I will fire the ship before I will agree to it."[59] Seddon answered that the Confederate Congress had approved the president's action in appropriating space in private blockade-runners, and that the government would not relent from its position. He told Vance to direct all future complaints to the secretary of the treasury, who now had "authority over the subject."[60]

Vance was not the only governor to become upset over the new Confederate shipping regulations. Gov. Joseph E. Brown of Georgia urged all the governors "to unite in asking Congress when it assembles to remove this restriction."[61] Vance appealed to Confederate senator William A. Graham to propose legislation "to relieve the State from the [requisitions] and absurd 'regulations' upon the blockade trade." In the meantime, he had "directed all our ships not to return unless the restrictions are removed, and large quantities of merchandize & machinery are lying at the islands and will I fear cause great loss to the state."[62] Governors Clark of Mississippi and Watts of Alabama joined Vance and Brown in seeking action from their congressmen. As a result, Congress passed a bill repealing the cargo regulations, but the president vetoed it.[63] When Vance and five other governors met in Augusta, Georgia, in October 1864 to attempt to resolve difficulties affecting the war effort, they again asked Congress to repeal the restrictions on vessels plying their ports. In March 1865 Congress passed another bill repealing the restrictions.[64] But by that time, the port of Wilmington was closed, the war was nearly over, and North Carolina was out of the blockade-running business.

During the controversy with the War Department, Vance also went directly to President Davis with his complaint about the Confederate policy on cargo space. He reminded the president that North Carolina undertook blockade-running "when the Confed. Govt. with the offer of liberal contracts to individuals had failed to obtain the requisite ships and supplies, and when the necessities of our armies were pressingly great. Now that the Confed. Govt. has no ships, little money abroad, and inflexible terms which will drive the fleet now so usefully employed in evading the blockade away and prevent others from entering the trade it is more than ever necessary for this State to continue to relieve her troops and people by persisting in her own enterprises." The new Confederate regulations would cripple effective blockade-running, he claimed, and "The vessels in which N.C. is interested cannot and will not operate under those terms."[65]

But Davis stood his ground. He reminded the governor that Congress had approved the regulations regarding blockade-runners. He maintained that the law pertaining to shipping had to be enforced with uniformity. If "certain persons have been exempted because they were part-owners with a State in a vessel, or because they were shippers in a vessel owned in part by a State, while others were left to strict government of the regulations, such regulations would have been direct contravention of the law." He insisted that he had no authority to change or abolish the regulations. "Even if this could be done," he stressed to Vance, "you will readily see how injurious would be the effect. Such consideration could not be extended to

North Carolina alone. All other States would have to be put upon the same footing. And thus a premium would be offered to ship owners to dispose of part interests to States on such terms, that all the ships engaged in running the blockade would ere long be owned in part by States; and there would be nothing left for the Confederate Government to regulate."[66]

Of course, Vance did not carry out his bombastic threats to "fire" or remove from service the North Carolina blockade-runners. He grudgingly accepted the Confederate mandate. Nevertheless, he did ask for special dispensation for the *Advance*. Vance contended that the *Advance* was already fulfilling the requirements of the Confederate government for the use of cargo space for shipping cotton. He pointed out that the A. L. Davis and H. Fitzhugh Company—in partnership with Power, Low and Company—had filled half of the vessel. This was done according to "a contract for importing supplies for the Confederate Govt. and the sale to them was encouraged by . . . the Secty. of War . . . as favorable to the wants and interests of the Confederacy." Therefore, he asked that the *Advance* be exempted from turning over half of its space to the Confederate government for the shipment of cotton.[67] Secretary of the Treasury Christopher M. Memminger, as directed by the president, denied the governor's request.[68] But in July 1864, the Confederate authorities relented and allowed the *Advance*—which was then returning to Bermuda after repairs in England—to operate under the "Davis and Fitzhugh contract." Vance was sure that such an arrangement "will no doubt work to the mutual advantage of the Genl. and State governments, as well as for the private interest in the ships."[69]

Vance and some of his associates were a part of the "private interest" involved in the *Advance*'s shipments. For example, on one occasion, the governor wrote to John White that he and his friend Dr. Edward Warren, surgeon general of North Carolina, had shipped onboard the *Advance* "six bales of cotton" belonging to Warren and "five bales" belonging to him. "Please have the funds separated," he instructed White. "Dispose of all & any more I may ship to best advantage & deposit to my order." In a postscript, Vance informed White that two more of his bales should have reached their destination, presumably Bermuda—"making in all thirty bales—for my ac't."[70]

By September 1864, the governor knew that he would not be shipping any more cotton on the *Advance*, for the vessel was captured while leaving the port of Wilmington on September 10. At that time, Capt. Joannes Wylie commanded the vessel, which fell prey to the swift blockade ship the *Santiago de Cuba*. For months, Vance blamed the loss of the *Advance* on the Confederate navy. According to him, the navy had seized the state's hard coal at Wilmington for the use of its two gunboats the *Chickamauga* and the *Tallahassee*. Thus forced to use a soft coal that produced an easily detected black smoke, the *Advance* was sighted and overtaken by the *Santiago de Cuba*. But as historian Stephen R. Wise has shown, Vance's "accusation was false. . . . As it was, the *Advance* was lost two months before the Navy began impounding coal."[71] Vance had wanted the two gunboats disarmed and converted into transports or blockade-runners. He appealed to President Davis, who turned the matter over to Secretary of the Navy Stephen R. Mallory. The secretary retained the vessels with the intention of having them harass Northern coastal shipping.[72]

As Vance must have realized, the capture of the *Advance* was merely sounding a death knell for blockade-running off the North Carolina coast. In the early fall of 1864, the Federals had drawn their blockade alarmingly tight. Virtually all ships leaving the mouth of the Cape Fear River were spotted, and most were fired upon. "Things continue so uncertain with regard to blockade running that I am at a loss what to do since the loss of the Advance," the governor wrote to Alexander Collie on November 2, 1864.[73]

But until the final months of the war, Vance operated the state's shipping through the blockade with success. Tar Heel troops generally were well supplied. Problems of logistics and transportation within the Confederacy were primarily responsible for the failure of clothing, blankets, and other equipment to reach North Carolina's soldiers. Not everyone, however, considered Vance's efforts to be best for North Carolina or the Confederate government. State treasurer Jonathan Worth maintained that blockade-running had seriously injured North Carolina's finances.[74] President Davis also chafed under Vance's obstinate attempts to prevent him from commandeering space for Confederate cotton in the state's blockade-runners.

In a later generation, historian Frank L. Owsley lambasted Vance and the other governors for a lack of cooperation with the Davis administration in keeping the Confederate army adequately supplied. Owsley contended that the government at Richmond should have been the central directing agency for the procurement and distribution of supplies, and that the states should have played a cooperative and subordinate role. He maintained that the states "did not show sufficient confidence in the Confederate government to allow it to do the common purchasing," and that lack of support "lowered the confidence of the foreign powers in the stability of the government, which in turn hurt its credit." But Owsley did not address the question of whether or not the states had good reason for their lack of confidence. "It is true," he admitted, that the Davis government initially acquiesced to the states' clothing and equipping their own troops. "But this was not expected to be a permanent arrangement. The Confederate government planned to take over the whole business as soon as it 'got on its feet.'"[75] That conclusion, however, ignores the blunt reality that, because of inefficiency in its supply operations, the Davis government never did get on its feet. Had the Confederate government managed to clothe, feed, and equip its army, that capability would have relieved a considerable burden from the state. North Carolina simply did for itself what the Confederate government could not do—that is, it sufficiently equipped and supplied its soldiers. As a Confederate supply agent, as well as political envoy, in England, James M. Mason proved largely ineffective. Vance's agent John White, on the other hand, moved quickly and efficiently to sell the state's cotton bonds, procure needed supplies, and purchase a ship for transporting them. He obtained a much better rate of interest on North Carolina warrants than Mason secured on Confederate bonds. Nevertheless, Vance encouraged his agents to cooperate with Mason as much as possible.[76] Even if North Carolina was forced by circumstance to pay its own way in the war, it does not necessarily follow that the state and its governor were at odds with the Confederate administration. In fact, Vance's willingness to accept the responsibility of keeping the state's soldiers well equipped and in the fight is an indication of his commitment to the Confederate cause.

No records have been discovered to date giving an accurate approximation of how many supplies the state of North Carolina managed to procure through the blockade. Twenty years after the war, Vance gave this accounting:

> Large quantities of machinery supplies; 60,000 pairs of hand cards; 10,000 grain scythes; 200 barrels of bluestone for wheat-growers; leather and shoes to 250,000 pairs; 50,000 blankets; grey-wooled cloth for at least 250,000 suits of uniforms; 12,000 overcoats, ready-made; 2,000 best Enfield rifles, with 100 rounds of fixed ammunition; 100,000 pounds of bacon; 500 sacks of coffee for hospital use; $50,000 worth of medicines at gold prices; large quantities of lubricating oils, besides minor supplies of various kinds for the charitable institutions of the State.

He recalled that "Not only was the supply of shoes, blankets and clothing more than sufficient for the supply of the North Carolina troops, but large quantities were turned over to the Confederate government for the troops of other states." At the end of the war, according to Vance, the state "had on hand ready-made and in cloth 92,000 suits of uniforms, with great stores of blankets, leather, etc."[77]

In operating state blockade-runners effectively and ensuring that North Carolina soldiers received supplies, Vance was following the dictates of the state legislature, which as North Carolina's chief executive he was required to do. But he also complied in virtually every case in which the War Department, through official correspondence, asked him for provisions or supplies. In December 1864, the War Department begged Vance for "any commissary you may have at hand." Seddon stressed that "there is at present lamentable Deficiency of provisions, especially of meat . . . and there is imminent danger, that unless unusual sources of supply can at once be commanded, the armies . . . cannot be maintained in service."[78] Vance immediately gave orders to turn over half of the provisions that the state had at home and all the bacon that the state had shipped as far as the blockade-running islands to the relief of the Confederate army.[79] Throughout the war, Vance consistently responded to Confederate pleas for supplies. For example, in the winter prior to the Battle of Chickamauga, he shipped 14,000 complete uniforms to Gen. James Longstreet's corps. Later he gave an additional 10,000 uniforms to the Army of Tennessee.[80] In the fall of 1864, the amount owed to North Carolina by the Confederate government for supplying the state's own troops had reached $2,400,000.[81]

Owsley and other detractors of Vance have pointed to the large quantities of uniforms and other materials that the governor supposedly withheld from the War Department as evidence of a lack of cooperation that hindered the Confederate cause. Owsley insisted that "while Confederate soldiers from other states were freezing and dying from exposure," North Carolina had on hand "large stores of clothing and blankets," constituting "a surplus sufficient to meet the needs of the troops for the entire year 1864."[82] In Owsley's defense, Vance's own boasting after the war about his success in running the blockade and equipping North Carolina's soldiers led, in part, to his reputation among Owsley and others that he undermined the Confederate war effort by hoarding materials.[83] However, despite Owsley's rhetoric or Vance's postwar boasting, it is doubtful that North Carolina possessed more undistributed supplies and equipment than the Confederate government had in its coffers in the final days of the war. And there is no evidence that Vance was any more possessive and obstinate in releasing such supplies to soldiers in the field than were some Confederate authorities. For example, Gen. Joseph E. Johnston found the Richmond bureaucracy most unsupportive in the last days of the Carolina campaign. He requested that the Department of the Navy turn over to him a large store of supplies that was stockpiled at a landlocked naval depot at Charlotte, but Secretary of the Navy Stephen R. Mallory refused. General Lee and Secretary of War John C. Breckinridge (who replaced Seddon) also denied Johnston stores collected at North Carolina depots. They reserved those supplies for the Army of Northern Virginia. Johnston's army was forced to subsist off the countryside, and Vance assisted the general by furnishing him wagons and draft animals.[84] Thus the persistent Owsley portrait of Vance as the Scrooge of the Confederacy, whose miserly with-holding of supplies helped bring about Southern defeat, is inaccurate. On the contrary, Vance's skillful management of the state's blockade-runners helped to keep North Carolina soldiers equipped and in the field, thereby prolonging the Confederacy's struggle for independence.

7

"WOMEN HAS NERVED THE ARM
OF THE STALWART SOLDIER"

No one had more reason to be discontent with the purpose and progress of the war than the white women of North Carolina. With husbands, fathers, and sons away in the army, many Tar Heel women found themselves having to assume sole responsibility for operating farms and businesses, as well as feeding and clothing themselves, children, and the elderly with little or no help or resources. As the conflict wore on and food and other necessities became increasingly scarce, women throughout North Carolina complained to Vance of their plight.

Eventually they began to stage demonstrations and "riots" to secure food and supplies. These disturbances took place in a number of towns and cities. Perhaps the most notorious of the so-called food riots occurred in Salisbury in March 1863. A group of women calling themselves "Soldiers' Wives" marched downtown and demanded to purchase supplies from local merchants at government prices.[1] When the merchants refused to sell at those prices, the women "then forced our way in and compelled them to give us something." From the merchants and the local depot they "succeeded in obtaining twenty three blls of flour two sacks of salt and half a bll of molasses and twenty dollars in money, which was equally divided among us."[2]

A similar raid soon took place at Greensboro. Nancy Mangum of nearby McLeansville reported to Vance on April 9 that "a crowd of we Poor women went to Greenesborough [sic] yesterday for something to eat as we had not a mouthful meet nor bread in my house. . . . I have 6 little children and my husband in the armey and what am I to do." The Greensboro women had less success than their sisters in Salisbury. Local authorities arrested them and jailed them for a short time. "[T]hree and four men gatherd hold of one woman and took their armes away from them and led them all up to gail," reported Mangum. And some authorities "threatened to shoot us and drawed their pistols over us."[3] Following the Greensboro incident, Vance publicly cautioned women that "Broken laws will give you no bread, but much sorrow; when forcible seizures have to be made to avert starvation, let it be done by your county or state agents."[4] In Yancey County in early 1865, fifty women raided government warehouses and seized sixty bushels of wheat. In western Yadkin County, a female band carried off the tax-in-kind corn in wagons.[5] In April 1864 the Bladen County Court sentenced five women to five months in jail for seizing seven sacks of grain from a Bladenboro warehouse.[6]

Initially, county courts attempted to provide relief for families made destitute by the war. But the demand for aid quickly grew beyond the capacity of the counties alone. In December 1862, the state passed a law appropriating $400,000 to be used in purchasing provisions to feed the poor. Four additional acts "for the relief of the Wives and Families of Soldiers in the Army" followed. Under these laws, the county justices of the peace supervised the distribution of relief, and they could claim state support in either cash or provisions. The state appropriated $1 million in February 1863, $1 million in December 1863, $1 million in May 1864, and $3 million in the last months of the war in 1865. But these funds proved inadequate; more relief was sorely needed. The Confederate government's tax-in-kind exacerbated the problem.[7]

Martha Futch of New Hanover County wrote to her husband, John Futch of the Third North Carolina Regiment in the Army of Northern Virginia, that she had twice tried unsuccessfully to obtain food relief from county agents. Her father resolved to persuade authorities in Wilmington that she and her family were in serious need of assistance. "[A]nd dear husband," she wrote on February 19, 1863, "I shal come to see you if you aint back by April." But Martha Futch never saw her husband again. Worried about his wife and family at home and having suffered through the Battle of Gettysburg, during which he watched his brother die, John Futch deserted from the army. Attempting to make his way home, he was captured, and on September 5, 1863, he was shot by a Confederate firing squad.[8]

Many women complained to Vance that the county justices were hoarding or not distributing money, food, and supplies fairly. Some claimed that the officials were speculating with state supplies for their own profit. Women therefore frequently found little or no relief from the government. Until the last days of the war, they continued to raid businesses, warehouses, and cotton and grain mills throughout the state.[9]

To feed and care for their families, some women sought war work. In Cumberland County, a group of them formed the Cumberland Hospital Association to employ poor women to fill a state contract to sew shirts for North Carolina soldiers. The state quartermaster, Henry A. Dowd, agreed to pay the seamstresses five cents a shirt for "cutting and baling" and one dollar "for making." But the association found that the pay was not enough to cope with inflation and speculation prices. "The exorbitant prices of provisions," association president Mary F. Lutterloh wrote to Vance in November 1864, "induces us to apply for corresponding advance in the price of labor to save our poor from suffering." She went on to say that the "Association has been paying 7 cts to our cutter for cutting and baling—3 cts of which were paid by the state and 4 cts were added by the Association to save her from suffering, and we now ask for an advance, and also that the state shall pay all the expense," because the increase from three to five cents made by the state would not be sufficient. Apparently considering herself superior in social class, however, Lutterloh took care to dissociate herself from the poor working women on whose behalf she wrote. "I trust I need not assure you Sir," she informed Vance, "I have no personal interest to subserve in this matter, but have written in behalf of our seamstresses, who are seriously affected by the low price of labor." Probably not overly concerned about the plight of the seamstresses, Vance merely referred the request to Dowd.[10]

Many working-class women resented the Confederate law that exempted large slaveholders from the draft. Martha Coltrane of Randolph County, for example, protested the special consideration that slaveholders were receiving by being exempt from conscription. Without the help and support of conscripted male family members, she explained to Vance, the wives, children, and elderly parents of nonslaveholders were forced to endure a great deal more than the families of wealthy planters, whose menfolk remained at home. She was especially alarmed that the new act conscripting men between the ages of thirty-five and forty-five would draft her husband into the army. She wrote the governor that

> This is a great undertaking for me as i never wrote to a man of authority before necessity requires it of me as we are nonslave holders in this section of the State i hope you and our legislature will look to it

and have justice done our people as well as the slaveholders i can tel you the condition of my family and you can judge for your self what its condition woul be if my husban is called from home we have eight children and the oldest is not forteen years old and an old aged mother to support, which makes eleven in our family and without my husband we are a desolate and ruined family for extortion runs so hie here we cannot support and clothe our family without the help of my husband i hope you will look to the justice of the peepils of this section of the state and i trust you will hold the rane in your own hands and not let the confederate congress have the full sway over your State i appeal to you look to the white cultivaters as strictly as cngress has to the slaveholders and i think they men from 35 to 45 be hel as reserves at hom to support ther families if the are called from home its bound to leave a thoasn families in a starving condition in our county we trust in god and look to you for some help for our poor children.[11]

Despite hardships, however, some North Carolina women applied their labor to support the Confederacy. Throughout the state, women formed relief organizations to provide assistance to Confederate soldiers. One such organization was the Soldiers' Relief Society of New Bern. A number of local women met in that town on September 3, 1861, to form a volunteer agency "for the purpose of providing suitable food and nourishment for the sick soldiers now encamped in [and] about this town." The society divided New Bern into districts and assigned members to each district to attend to the needs of soldiers there. The women supplied money and provisions to the men and collected needed funds through concerts and other events.[12] For much of the war, members of the Ladies' Soldiers Aid Society of Wilmington boarded the southbound train at its regular stops in the port city. They dressed the wounds of the injured and provided food in the station yard.[13]

A number of female North Carolinians served tirelessly in Confederate hospitals both inside and outside the state. After the First Battle of Manassas, several women from Charlotte's Hospital Association left the Queen City and traveled to Yorktown, Virginia, to work as nurses in the Confederate hospital there. Back in Charlotte, other members of the society, under the leadership of Mrs. J. H. Wilson, collected food and supplies for the Yorktown hospital. The association secured "special rates" from the railroads and an express company to transport the donations. Another North Carolina nurse, N. H. Whitford, volunteered and labored long hours at the

Yorktown facility. She acknowledged to Gov. John W. Ellis that it was not customary for women to take such an active role in military and public affairs. But she nevertheless sought his permission to volunteer. "Do you think such a move on my part unmaidenly, or indelicate?" she cleverly placated the governor. "I act from the purest motive, a desire to do good. . . . Nothing but heartfelt interest in our poor suffering soldiers . . . would ever have induced me to address you on such a subject."[14] Women also volunteered at the "wayside hospitals" that sprang up along the Wilmington and Weldon Railroad and the North Carolina Railroad. At the Rowan Wayside Hospital, for example, 140 Salisbury women provided nursing and other assistance for wounded troops.[15]

One of the women in North Carolina most active in support of the Confederate war effort was Mary Anne Buie of Richmond County. A shrewd businesswoman of considerable energy, a newspaper columnist, and a former teacher and principal of female academies in South Carolina and Georgia, Buie referred to herself as the "Soldiers Friend," and she created a soldiers' relief fund, calling upon Southerners to contribute liberally.[16] Foreshadowing her like-minded sisters of the postwar Lost Cause movement and the United Daughters of the Confederacy, she proposed to Vance that he aid her in writing a patriotic history of North Carolina's role in the war, lest the Tar Heels' glorious deeds go unrecognized. She also maintained that "the patriotic people would not hesitate to erect a Monument at Raleigh to the gallant Dead of N.C. no matter where they sleep or when they fell whether at picket post, on hospital *cot* at the flaming battery, or on the gory fields or ploughed by canon ball in victories or defeats." Buie was convinced that "the honor of the South was at stake." North Carolinians were fighting a valiant struggle, she maintained, and women were unselfishly contributing to that struggle through hard work, sacrifice, and moral support of the state's troops in the field. "May I say [I am] proud of my sex in this war," she wrote Vance in September 1862. "The fair creatures have resolved to wield their potent influence which has spread like a gentle dew reviving the spirit of [a] thousand drooping heads. Women has nerved the arm of the stalwart Soldier going forth to conquer or die."[17]

Buie publicly lambasted anyone of prominence or means who would not contribute to her soldiers' relief fund, especially men like a certain Colonel Crenshaw of Richmond, who, although he was making a nice profit with his blockade-runners *Hebe* and *Venus*, refused to contribute. In response to Crenshaw's refusal to "subscribe to her fund," Buie prayed that his vessels would be destroyed at sea. According to one observer, "the old *witch was gratified"* when the *Hebe* and *Venus* wrecked upon the same shoal.[18]

But the bombastic and patriotic Miss Buie also saw the war as an opportunity to engage in some profitable speculation of her own. In August 1864 she wrote to Vance asking for a letter of recommendation to overseas investors. She intended to depart Wilmington on the blockade-runner *Dominion*, and she claimed that she already had letters of introduction from Governors Bonham of South Carolina and Brown of Georgia, as well as from Gen. P. G. T. Beauregard "& others of the army and officials." She also asked Vance to permit her to ship some of her personal cotton aboard the *Advance* "for my benefit." She employed flattery to sway the governor. "I am truly proud of your success," she coyly stroked his ego, "& now permit me to say I see your destiny if your life is spared you will be either President or Vice in the next nomination[.] [Y]ou have struck the right chord & your music pleases the whole South[.] I have written many notices of you in the Geo and S.C. papers in a few words praised you for clothing the soldiers, & taking care of the families[.] [Y]our name is familiar all over the land & in Europe," she continued. Buie reminded Vance that she was "a favorite" of President Davis and that the ladies of South Carolina and Georgia had presented her with a "set of silver" for her soldiers' relief work.[19]

Perhaps a little less aggressive than Buie, but nevertheless ambitious and persistent, a number of other North Carolina women saw the war as an opportunity to advance their own interests. Delia Jones of Clayton, for example, attempted to use the circumstances produced by the conflict to step outside the traditional sphere for women. She wrote the following to Vance on January 6, 1863: "Thinking that the number of young men called into the military service must necessarily diminish the number of Secretaries, copyists, &c required in public & private offices, I write to inquire if any such office as a woman could fill is now vacant. I would like to engage in something of the kind, being a swift penman & accustomed to writing a good deal." Vance responded by instructing an aide to "answer this letter, that the Gov has nothing at present which she could do."[20]

As the war neared an end and Confederate troops desperately sought supplies from North Carolina, Vance made a public appeal for private donations of food for the army. Although the contributions were few from a hard-pressed population, he found the women of Raleigh to be the most sympathetic and responsive to his request. "The first answer," he wrote to Gen. Robert E. Lee, "was from a poor widow of the city, who hard pressed to live in these distressing times, as I know she is, came yet to offer me two pieces of bacon and a barrel of meal. Such offerings on the sacred alter [sic] of country, hallow our cause, and I hope will secure God's blessing upon it."[21]

Led by a clique of "elite" women—Ella Harper, Till Abernathy, Laura Norwood, and Mary Fries Patterson—the women of Caldwell County in western North Carolina engaged in "activities . . . to make public endorsements of both secession and the Confederacy while remaining within established gender roles." They demonstrated "allegiance to the Confederacy" by supplying the needs of soldiers—clothing, blankets, haversacks, and food—through their local soldiers' aid society, which included women "from all social groups in the county." The members of the aid society also raised money to help pay for the construction of an ironclad vessel to protect coastal North Carolina. Although the Caldwell elite did not accept the lower class of women as social equals, allowing them into their "network of family and friends," the poorer class nevertheless accepted their upper-class sisters' leadership in lending support for the Southern war effort. As the war drew to an end and the Confederacy faced defeat, and as the county endured Union raids, the women of Caldwell increasingly became disheartened, accepted the inevitable, and longed for the return of their husbands and sons. But for much of the conflict, they had supported a cause in which they, like their menfolk, had believed.[22]

Women's responses to the war were as varied and complex as those of men. Some women suffered great hardships, begged their men to come home, and might have damned Jefferson Davis, Vance, and all Confederate armies and officials for bringing on their plight. One poor woman wrote to Vance in January 1865 that "you and some of they [sic] rest of those big bugs will have to answer for they blood of our dear ones who have been slain. Pease [sic] must come on some terms, and you have they power to make an effort towards pease."[23]

But many women, such as the patriotic Cornelia Phillips Spencer and Catherine Ann Devereux Edmondston, supported the Confederacy and its leaders from the outset of the conflict until its bitter end. Others accepted the dire circumstances inflicted on their families and neighbors by the war as God's will or the price that had to be paid for Southern independence. Still others, such as the ambitious Mary Buie and Delia Jones, viewed the upheaval of war as a catalyst for change and opportunity. It would be an oversimplification to conclude that a definitive antiwar unity existed among North Carolina women, or that gender played a decisive role in undermining the Confederate war effort and bringing the war to an end.

To be sure, North Carolina women experienced much hardship that led them to demand and seize food supplies, as well as to complain to the governor in an attempt to relieve the suffering of their families. But expressions of such dissatisfaction—by either word or deed—did not automatically translate into a lack of nationalistic support for the Confederate cause. As historian Jean V. Berlin has written of Confederate women, "To suggest that they hastened or postponed defeat is to ignore the complex interplay of Confederate ideology, religion, domestic politics, and military events in late 1864 and 1865." According to Berlin, women "focused their rage and disappointment solely on the North, not on the institutions that failed them at home."[24]

Indeed, many of the letters that North Carolina women wrote to Vance reflect a Confederate nationalism that blamed Northern aggressors for the suffering on the state's home front. Mary Bell of Macon County, whose husband, Alf, was in the army, blamed President Lincoln for the hardships that she and other wives were suffering. "I believe that we have a just God," she declared, "and that sooner or later, Abraham Lincoln will meet with his just rewards. I may be called heartless and wicked, and doubtless am, but it does one good to think that a retribution awaits such tyrants as old Abe."[25] The greatest concern of North Carolina women was for their households. But as important as a family and its welfare were to them, it does not necessarily follow that because women valued the protection of their children and husbands, they would automatically have to defy and undermine the Confederate war effort. In fact, as Berlin has pointed out, "the integrity and safety of their own Households [constituted] one of the central tenets of Confederate nationalism." The household, Berlin observes, was "the basic unit of Southern society," and "Thus Confederate nationalism had to call on the devotion of Southerners to their home and its protection."[26]

Tar Heel women generally did not blame Vance or the Richmond government for the hardships inflicted on their families by the war. Indeed, Vance's papers indicate that women were far less likely to take him to task over home-front problems than were male correspondents. William A. Smith, a Johnston County planter, member of the secession convention, future legislator, and postwar Republican, is an example of the latter. Smith wrote to Vance in January 1863 complaining about the injustice of impressment and taxes, as well as the hardships imposed by speculation and inadequate poor relief. The people of Johnston County appealed to Vance to correct those evils. Otherwise, the county might be forced to secede from North Carolina. "Of course," exclaimed Smith, "no one at this day, will deny our right, Garenteed to us by the noble *blood of South Carolina*[.] Please let me know wether we shall plant any crops this year, or shall we all plunge head long into anarchy & confusion and the strongest take all and let the helpless perish as they deserve for being helpless and Weak."[27]

Catherine Edmondston praised both Vance and Jefferson Davis for their efforts in service of Confederate independence. As the war neared its end, she applauded Vance's proclamation "announcing to us how the Peace negotiations have failed & calling on us to be of good cheer & stand by one another & vigorously to prosecute the war & assuring us of ultimate success. All right and true. We *will* succeed." In contrast to Lincoln, whom she considered lacking in ability and polish, she exalted Davis as a man of accomplishment and good pedigree. "What a blessing that our exponent, our head, is a *gentleman*, a man not only of good sense but of good breeding," she wrote.[28] At the fall of the Confederacy, she upheld that the mistakes that Davis might have made in prosecuting the war were "honest mistakes," and she could still "reverence him" as "our exemplar & our head."[29] Any shortcomings that the president might have, she maintained, were limited to his selection of a wife, whose behavior—not the president's—was undermining the Confederate cause. Edmondston particularly rankled at Varina Howell Davis's departure from Richmond for the safety of Raleigh in May 1863 as the Confederate capital was threatened by Federal attack. "I fear she is not a woman of the true stamp," cried Edmondston on May 13. "I fear she does not strengthen her husband, or she would never have abandoned her post & set such an example for the rest of the women of the Confederacy."[30] Edmondston attributed the first lady's lack of fortitude and loyalty to her Northern ancestry and schooling. Varina Davis's father was a native of New Jersey and the son of a governor of that state. He had moved to Natchez, Mississippi, after the War of 1812, and Varina had attended a boarding school in Philadelphia for one year.[31] "Mrs. Davis is I hear a Philadelphia woman!" the Halifax County plantation mistress complained. "That accounts for her white nurse & her flight from Richmond. I fear she is not worthy of her husband, for I learn that she is neither neat or ladylike in her dress, travels in old finery with bare arms covered with bracelets. Would that our President, God bless him, had a truehearted Southern woman for a wife. She would never have deserted him!"[32] Edmondston had nothing derogatory to say about Vance's wife, whose "true" Southern background and retiring manner apparently made her acceptable as the spouse of a Confederate governor.

When North Carolina women expressed their outrage over a lack of food or other dire circumstances, they usually complained about corrupt and insensitive county and town officials or unscrupulous merchants and speculators. Their dissatisfaction did not usually include a condemnation of Vance or the Confederate government. "You are the choice of our Husbands and Sons," Salisbury's "Soldiers' Wives" wrote to the governor, "and we too look up to you Sir with perfect confidence as being able and willing to do something for us."[33] Tar Heel women tended to view the hardships and problems that afflicted them as moral failing by extortionists and inattentive county officials rather than as shortcomings of the South's political leaders. They looked to Vance and Jefferson Davis as the sources of their salvation rather than the causes of their desperation.

North Carolina women frequently decried men who failed to show the proper patriotism for the Confederacy. They denounced deserters, especially if their own husbands or sons were serving in the army. Mary Jane Hogan took Vance to task for his proclamation that granted amnesty to deserters who would return to duty. Her husband, she lectured the governor, had died in Confederate service. It was therefore only equitable and just that deserters should suffer death by execution.[34] Jane Sugg of Randolph County proclaimed that she "could nock them [deserters] in the head with a ax just as fast as they could bring them tow me and never flinch at it. . . . I wish the deserters had to dig up Randolph with there teeath and carry it off with there mouths."[35]

Some North Carolina women saw Confederate defeat as the will of God. "I believe God has permitted this calamity to befall us for some wise purpose," Anna Long Thomas Fuller of Louisburg wrote in her journal upon hearing of Lee's surrender in April 1865. "I trust we shall see it, [and] be a better people."[36] A poor woman from Charlotte maintained that God was allowing the South to lose the war as punishment for the sin of slavery. She wrote Vance "that I believe slavery is doomed to dy out that God is agoing to liberate niggars, and fighting any longer is fighting against God."[37]

For most Tar Heel women, the solution to the suffering of their families lay not in political opposition to the Confederacy but in social morality. A few women did demonstrate for William W. Holden when that peace candidate ran against Vance for the governor's office in 1864.[38] But by and large, women shunned the political arena (in which they had no vote anyway) and leveled their anger at profit-seeking merchants and speculators. Even so, their raids on stores and warehouses were relatively peaceful, despite hyperbolic accounts rendered by the press and some outraged men who were unnerved by the new assertiveness demonstrated by the state's female population.[39] The Salisbury "Wives" claimed that any reports to Vance that they were "plunderers of the town disturbing the peace and quiet of the community" were not true. Their raids, they reported to the governor, were not the violent episodes reported by male merchants and the press. Instead, they resulted from "Having been forced into measures not at all pleasant to obtain something to eat by the cruel and unfeeling Speculators who have been gathering up at enormous prices not only bread stuffs but everything even down to eggs chickens & vegetables to carry out of our state for the purpose of Speculating upon them." The women sought Vance's help in redressing the evil of speculation and assured him that "we ask not charity we only as[k] for fair and reasonable prices for provisions and leather for Sir many of us have been shoeless this whole winter except the cloth shoes we can make ourselves which are not protection even against the cold."[40] Tar Heel soldiers too complained to Vance about speculation and the suffering it was causing their wives and families at home. One North Carolina soldier, J. R. Robertson, wrote to the governor protesting that poor men were being forced to fight for "nothin" except to preserve the "Rich mans property & negars," while the wealthy "Big men" remain at home to "cheat & speculate out of the pour soulgers [sic] wives." If he was not given a furlough soon to go home and relieve his wife's "suffering," he intended to desert.[41]

In Bladen County in February 1863, a group of women and men joined together to form a band of "Regulators." They threatened to raid the corn supplies of the wealthy slaveholders in the area, who they claimed were hoarding corn and speculating. Only Vance's intervention, the "Regulators" maintained, would prevent them from taking the law into their own hands. They had offered to pay two dollars a bushel for corn but were refused because "the slave ones has the plantations, & the hands to raise the bread stufs & the common people is drove of[f] in the ware to fight for the big mans negro & he at home making nearly all the corn that is made & then because he has the play in his own fingers he puts the price on his corn so as to take all the soldiers wages." The "Regulators" warned that "we hoos sons brothers & husbands is now fighting for the big mans negros are determined to have bread out of there barns & that at a pric[e] that we can pay or we will slaughter as we go." They asked Vance to enforce a two-dollar maximum charge for a bushel of corn.[42]

In response to many complaints by women and their husbands in the army, Vance attempted to thwart speculation by imposing by proclamation an embargo on certain items that could be sold out of state—particularly in Virginia—for larger profits than could be made locally. The embargoes, which were authorized by the state legislature, lasted for a period of thirty days and were renewed by new proclamations from the governor. The articles prohibited for export varied from time to time. They included such items as salt, bacon, pork, beef, meal, flour, wheat, potatoes, shoes, leather, hides, cotton cloth, yarn, wool cloth, and lard.[43] But the embargoes proved ineffective in halting speculation. In instances in which he felt a request was justified, Vance had the authority to issue permits to certain exporters exempting them from the embargo on some items. Militia officers found it difficult to enforce the prohibition, and speculators such as George W. Swepson and John M. Morehead frequently disregarded or found ways to circumvent the embargoes.[44] Swepson was a prominent textile manufacturer, banker, broker, and railroad promoter who embezzled state money in a major railroad fraud after the war. Morehead was a wealthy textile manufacturer and railroad investor, a former governor, a state senator, and a member of the Confederate Provisional Congress.[45] Vance was well acquainted with both men. He issued an exemption permit to Swepson and on one evasive occasion had difficulty recalling to a militia officer whether or not he had given Morehead a permit.[46]

One item that was frequently in demand and specified in Vance's embargo proclamations was salt. Salt was needed especially in the pork-packing winter season, when hogs were slaughtered and the meat preserved. North Carolina established a number of saltworks on the coast near Wilmington. On January 12, 1863, the state salt commissioner, John M. Worth, reported to Vance that the state works at Wilmington were making about 300 bushels of salt per day. He was selling the salt at around five dollars per bushel and within four months should be able to pay back the state treasury for its funds invested in the works. Private salt makers, however, claimed that it cost about eight dollars per bushel to make salt. "I have no advantage over them," Worth told the governor, "except labor of conscripts—which cannot amount to 50 [cents] on the bushel."[47] In September David G. Worth, who had replaced his uncle John as commissioner, reported that the works at Wilmington had produced about 5,000 bushels of salt, which had been distributed to the counties. But the want of good transportation by road and rail and a shortage of firewood seriously hindered production and distribution. On one occasion, a shortage of salt occurred when the workers at Wilmington fell victim to "a most malignant fever," which "killed many" and resulted in the suspension of production.[48] Further shortages resulted when Gen. William H. C. Whiting, commanding at Wilmington, interrupted work at the salt manufactories in his district. In January 1863, Vance protested to Gen. Gustavus

W. Smith, commanding the Department of North Carolina and Southern Virginia, that "Genl Whiting had Seized all the teams, hands and boats belonging to the State Salt Agent and completely stopped the works. This is a great calamity to our people, to stop the making of 350 bushels of Salt per day right in the midst of pork packing season."[49] Although the hands returned to work, Whiting persisted in attempts to terminate the saltworks and draft the workers for the defense of Wilmington. Whiting also questioned the loyalty of the salt workers and suggested that they might be Union collaborators.[50] His attacks on the works and the workers, combined with clashes over the impressment of slave labor, conscription, and the issue of habeas corpus, led to much friction between Whiting and Vance, who at one point called upon the War Department to remove the general from North Carolina.[51] The Confederacy, however, kept Whiting at his post.

North Carolina also operated a saltworks at Saltville, Virginia, and imported some salt from Turks Island in the Bahamas. "We shall need every bushel we can get next fall," Vance wrote Nicholas W. Woodfin, the state salt agent at Saltville in March 1863. "Notwithstanding that Salt is now down to $5. Per bushel in Wilmington for domestic and $8 for Turks Island, the packing season having passed."[52] With Union attack threatening Wilmington in late 1864, Whiting again ordered the saltworks in his district to be shut down and the workers to join in defense.[53] This time the works remained closed. Vance, facing the coming hog-killing season, struggled to compensate for the shortage by transporting sufficient salt from the works in Virginia. But the failure of efforts at transportation and finally the conscription of the workers to help defend against the Union attack in Virginia stymied his efforts.[54] "Having broken up my salt works at Wilmington," he telegraphed Secretary of War Seddon, "you have now conscribed my hands at Saltville, and stopped those there. Please inform me where N.C. is to get salt or how people can live without it?"[55] Of course, a shortage of salt was only one of the dire circumstances facing North Carolina, as Wilmington soon fell in the new year, and the war came to an inglorious end for the Confederacy in April 1865.

With foodstuffs in short supply throughout much of the war, North Carolinians—women and men—protested the distillation of corn and other agricultural products into liquor.[56] Vance attempted to enforce the state's law of 1862 prohibiting distilling. "We learn," declared the Raleigh *Progress* in November, "that Gov Vance said recently that he had determined that not another still should run in the State during his term. He thinks as all other honest people do that bread is better than whiskey."[57]

Vance generally denied requests by citizens for dispensation to distill liquor. But because of the state's incapacity to enforce the prohibition law in outlying areas, North Carolinians continued to make and sell whiskey in significant quantities, much to the consternation of wives and mothers who were desperately trying to feed their families.

Vance clashed with the Confederate War Department when it attempted to use tax-in-kind grain to distill liquor in North Carolina for the use of the Medical Department. "I learn," he protested to Secretary Seddon, "that large distilleries are in operation at Charlotte and Salisbury in this state, making spirits of tithe grain by order of the war Dept." He pointed out to the secretary that the state's laws "positively forbid the distillation of any kind of grain within its borders under heavy penalties." If the Confederate authorities did not order the distilleries to shut down, then he would order state officials to close the facilities and punish the operators. "It seems to me," he told Seddon, "if spirits are so absolutely requisite for the Medical Department, that grain sufficient might be found in remote and plentiful districts, and leave for the use of the people every grain which is accessible. Be this as it may, I am sure you will agree with me in saying that no person can under authority of the Confederate Government violate State laws with impunity."[58]

Seddon, however, replied that the Medical Department "has no contract for alcoholic stimulants in the State of North Carolina." The distillery at Salisbury—none existed at Charlotte—was "owned by the Medical Department, and is engaged in the manufacture of whiskey and alcohol for the sole use of the Sick and wounded of the army." The Confederate government had purchased the distillery "for the purpose of dispensing with the system of contracting for alcoholic stimulants," because "a large quantity of whiskey manufactured by contractors is of an inferior quality, and their contracts were not in other respects faithfully carried out." In addition, "a large quantity of whiskey made by contractors has been sold to private parties, when it should have been delivered to the Government, thereby consuming grain that was required to fill their contracts." Taking up Vance's gauntlet of states' rights versus Confederate authority, Seddon further pointed out that the attorney general of the Confederacy had ruled that "a State has no power to interfere with the Confederate government in the manufacture or even contracting for such supplies" and "that the Government distillery at Salisbury, should not be interfered with or the supply of grain cut off." However, a states' rights battle between the governor and the War Department was averted when Seddon announced that the government's distillery would be moved further south, "where corn is more abundant." He told Vance that "I trust your objections will under the circumstance be withdrawn," and the governor dropped the matter.[59]

North Carolina women did not hesitate to protest to Vance about such problems as shortages, speculation, and distilling. On occasions they also raided stores and warehouses in order to feed their children. But contrary to any dubious press reports or protests by merchants and speculators about hysterical hatchet-wielding females violently attacking storage facilities, women were much more likely to find themselves the recipients of violence than the instigators. Men often resorted to violence against women who asserted themselves or were perceived to have violated their traditional gender roles. Confederate soldiers tortured a number of Mountain women and girls during the Shelton Laurel massacre in Madison County in the winter of 1863. They inflicted the torture in retaliation for a raid by Union sympathizers on salt stores in the county seat of Marshall. The Confederate soldiers also killed a number of the women's male relatives who had participated in the raid. They executed Nancy Franklin's three sons before her very eyes.[60]

In the Quaker Belt counties of the Piedmont, where deserters and peace supporters were prevalent, the militia or Home Guard frequently tortured women to obtain information about male relatives who had deserted. Col. Alfred Pike gave the following report about his interrogation of the wife of deserter Bill Owens:

> I went with my squad to Owens spring where his wife was washing & inquired of her as to Owens whereabouts, she said he was dead and buried. I told her that she must show us the grave. She thereupon began to curse us and abuse us for every thing that was bad. Some of my men told me that if I would hand her over to them they would or could make her talk. I told her to go some twenty steps apart with them, she seized up in her arms her infant not twelve months old & swore she would not go—I slaped her jaws till she put down her baby & went with them, they tied her thumbs together behind her back & suspended her with a cord tied to her two thumbs thus fastened behind her to a limb so that her toes could just touch the ground, after remaining in this position a while she said her husband was not dead & that if they would let her down she would tell all she knew. I went up just then & I think she told some truth, but after a while I thought she commenced lying again & I and another man (one of my squad) took her off some fifty yards to a fence

& put her thumbs under a corner of the fence, she soon became quiet and behaved very respectfully.[61]

Judge Thomas Settle reported other outrages by the Home Guard against women in the region who had supported deserters or draft dodgers. He wrote to Vance that "I found in Chatham, Randolph, and Davidson that some fifty women in each county & some of them in delicate health and five of them advanced in pregnancy were rudely (in some instances) dragged from their homes & put under close guard & there left for several weeks. The consequence[s] in some instances have been shocking. Women have been frightened into abortion almost under the eyes of their terrifiers."[62]

Vance attempted to address the concerns of women faced with home-front deprivations and to correct the problems of food shortages. When crops in western North Carolina failed because of drought in 1863, the legislature appropriated funds to purchase corn in eastern North Carolina and transport it the western counties "to feed the wives and children of soldiers." Vance responded to that legislation and ordered the supplies moved by rail.[63] But the Confederate Quartermaster Department complained that the eastern corn was needed by the army and that "too large a quantity" had been "sent to the western part of the state." With the approval of Secretary of War Seddon and Quartermaster General Abraham C. Myers, Maj. Charles S. Carrington of the Quartermaster Department called on Vance and asked him to stop shipping the corn to the west and allow it to be used to feed troops in North Carolina and Virginia.[64] Prior to leaving Richmond for Raleigh, Carrington assured Myers that "when a proper representation" of the army's need "is made to the patriotic Governor of North Carolina I believe that he will arrest the further removal of corn necessary to the armies of the Confederate States, and give all the assistance in his power to direct the transportation now employed in this service & necessary to place this corn within reach of the armies."[65] Carrington's intuition about Vance's Confederate patriotism and commitment to the army's welfare proved correct. After the major's visit, Vance informed Seddon that "To surrender the whole" of 5,000 bushels of eastern corn already purchased but not yet transported westward "would so effectually close up the chances of the people for bread that I feel great reluctance in doing so even for so vital an object as the feeding of the army." Nevertheless, Vance "agreed to continue purchasing and to turn over to [Carrington] as the necessities of the service might require." He hoped to supply the army's needs by "organizing a corps of provision agents throughout the interior to see what can be bought and how much is hoarded that may be seized and trust that the result may be such as to enable me to surrender to the Army the whole of the crop of the east."[66] As in this instance, Vance usually attempted to work out a compromise between the needs of the Confederate government and those of the home-front populace of his state.

At times the governor's temper flared when Confederate troops summarily impressed food and supplies from North Carolina's civilians. In January 1863, he heatedly expressed to the Confederate War Department his objections to cavalry officers' impressing forage from western North Carolina families with husbands and fathers in the army. He wrote to Seddon: "There are a large lot of broken down Cavalry horses belonging I think to Genl [Albert G.] Jenkin's command quartered in the Counties of Wilkes, Yadkin, Ash[e] and Surry in this State. The officers controlling them are pressing corn and forage at prices less by one half than the current rates in that country. As that country was almost ruined by drouth last season, there will be the greatest difficulty in feeding the wives and children of the absent Soldiers." Vance suggested that the horses be removed to the eastern part of the state "where there is a great abundance" to forage.[67] When Seddon did not respond to his complaint by the end of three weeks, the annoyed governor wrote to the secretary that he had "not had the pleasure of a reply." He informed Seddon that the "deprivations are still continued," and that although he had "every possible disposition to aid in the support of the army, I have the strongest reasons conceivable—the existence of my own people—for declining to permit these horses to remain in that section of the State. When the question of starvation is narrowed down to women & children on the one side and some worthless Cavalry horses on the other, I can have no difficulty in making a choice. Unless they are removed soon, I shall be under the painful necessity of calling out the militia of the adjoining Counties and driving them from the state. I hope however to be spared such a proceeding."[68]

When Seddon asked for an explanation from his subordinates, the officers commanding the cavalry troops denied they were unfairly impressing forage and even questioned the loyalty of western Carolinians. They also implied that Vance was opposing the feeding of their horses because they were the mounts of Virginia cavalry.[69] Miffed by the accusation, Vance responded to Seddon: "I beg leave to disabuse your mind of the impression which it seems to entertain, that I object to these impressments because they were for *Virginia* cavalry. By no means. I did not term them such, at least not so intend to term them. I have no prejudice against troops from any state engaged in defending the common cause. But I *am* unwilling to see the corn taken from the mouths of women and children for the use of *any* troops, when these troops might be easily removed to regions where there is corn to sell."[70] Ultimately, the commanding general in western Virginia agreed to return the horses to that state "to enter on active service" within "a few weeks."[71]

Vance also protested to the War Department that the deprivations inflicted by detached troops—especially cavalry—were devastating families and turning many North Carolinians against the Confederate cause. "The Department," he complained to Seddon on December 21, 1863,

> I am sure can have no idea of the extent and character of this evil. It is enough in many cases to breed a rebellion in a loyal country against the Confederacy, and has actually been the cause of much alienation of feeling in many parts of North Carolina. It is not my purpose now to give instances and call for punishment of the offenders—that I do to their commanding officers, but to ask if some order or regulation cannot be made for the government of troops on detached service, the severe and unflinching execution of which might not check this stealing, pilfering, burning and sometimes murderous conduct. I give you my word that in North Carolina it has become a grievance, intolerable, damnable and not to be borne! If God almighty had yet in store another plague—worse than all others, which he intended to have loose on the Egyptians in case Pharoah still hardened his heart, I am sure it must have been a regiment or so of half-armed, half disciplined Confederate Cavalry! Had they been turned loose among Pharoah's subjects, with or without an impressment law, he would have become so sensible of the anger of God that he never would have followed the Children of Israel to the Red Sea, No Sir not an inch!! Cannot officers be reduced to the ranks for permitting this? Can not a few men be shot for perpetrating these outrages as an example? Unless something can be done, I shall be compelled in some sections to call out my Militia and levy actual war against them.[72]

Despite such indignant threats, Vance never detailed the militia or Home Guard to combat marauding Confederate troops. As in most cases where he clashed with Confederate authorities, he—after a temperamental outburst—retreated to a policy of conciliation and cooperation with the

War Department. He usually made every effort to provide the army with needed supplies. For example, on April 27, 1863, he wrote to the secretary of war:

> It affords me great pleasure to assure you that the crisis in regard to provisions in this State has passed over, and the conviction is now firm in all minds that there is not only enough but to *spare*. The passage of the impressment act and the near approach of a harvest which promises to be abundant, have brought to light many hoards that the fear of famine kept out of the market.
>
> The call for aid to the army has met with a liberal response from our generous people and I trust all fears may be dismissed.
>
> The quantity of provisions on hand were not large belonging to N.C. They were purchased under authority of an Act of our Legislature to prevent suffering in the families of soldiers and consequent disquiet and desertion in the Army. The demand has been much less than I expected, and in a few weeks I shall be able to see what can be dispensed with. I hope to be able to turn over some 250,000 lbs bacon and some Corn to the Confederacy. Precisely how much I can not now say. The purchase of Govt. agents can also be increased when the State and most private individuals cease to be in the market.[73]

Vance acknowledged the problems women expressed to him about shortages and the feeding and care of their families, and he, in cooperation with the state legislature, made an effort to address their suffering. But despite the many appeals and protests made by Tar Heel women, any responsibility that Vance felt for relieving the hunger and other deprivations of his people never took precedence over his commitment to supporting the Confederate army in the field. At one point he publicly implored women to cease writing despairing letters to their husbands and other male relatives in the army.[74]

Despite their hardships and those of their families, women in North Carolina largely stayed the course of supporting the war until near the end of the conflict. Their will to continue the struggle for Southern independence broke down only when the will of the general population—male and female—began to dissolve as the reality that the war was indeed lost became obvious to everyone. Certainly, Vance never thought that women had undermined the Confederate war effort. In the early days of Reconstruction, he urged North Carolina writer and journalist Mary Bayard Clarke to use her pen to encourage Tar Heel women to resist military reconstruction with the same fervor with which they had supported the

Confederate cause. Clarke obliged him with an article published in the *Old Guard*. Reflecting on women's role in the sectional conflict, she wrote that "although southern women did not in person wield the sword, or enter the legislative halls, their steady unchanging influence did more to fill the ranks of the Confederate army than all the edicts of its Congress, or acts of its Conscript Bureau." She instructed postwar women that they should again do their duty and show that same fortitude against their Federal conquerors. In particularly, she implored North Carolina women to reject the attentions of northern men who now occupied the state. Instead, they should remain devoted to the saintly image of "our great and glorious General, Robert E. Lee. . . . Let him be your guide in defeat as he was your star in the hour of triumph; and like him, so act and speak as to wring from your conquerors, whether they will or not, that respect which generous spirits spontaneously yield to dignified misfortune."[75] More than two decades after the war, Vance glorified before a northern audience the sacrifice and patriotism that the women of North Carolina endured and displayed for the Confederate cause. "They submitted," he proclaimed, "to the privations and hardships of the situation with a cheerful patience which shamed the boasted courage of man."[76]

8

"I AM NOT OUT OF HEART"

Any public optimism about Confederate success that might have surrounded Vance's reelection soon dissipated. In the autumn of 1864, the war increasingly turned against the Confederate states as Atlanta fell, Gen. William T. Sherman began his march from Atlanta to Savannah, and the Army of the Potomac tightened its grip on the Army of Northern Virginia in the trenches around Petersburg and Richmond. Amid those setbacks, Vance struggled to support the Confederacy in its attempt to thwart the Federal advance on all fronts.

Desertion, which had plagued North Carolina since virtually the beginning of the war, now became epidemic among the state's soldiers. Vance and his supporters realized that, more than ever, the problem was undermining the war effort. Deserters in large numbers were leaving the battlefields and camps and returning to North Carolina, where they were stealing, terrorizing local populations, and otherwise engaging in acts of violence, especially in the Quaker Belt and the Mountains. "Look at the conduct of the deserters," Edward J. Hale wrote to Vance on August 11, 1864. "I hope . . . that you will be able to send a force into Moore or Montgomery [County] to give them a thorough drubbing—Kill two or three dozen of them & the rest will cast off very quickly." He lectured the governor that "There has been no signal defeat & punishment of the rascals," which was "the reason they are so bold."[1]

To bolster his efforts in using the militia and Home Guard to track down and arrest deserters, Vance on August 24 issued a public proclamation addressing the ills of desertion and offering an incentive to deserters to return to their units. He proclaimed that "many soldiers from the troops of this state have deserted their colors and comrades, and are now lurking in the woods and mountains, some of them subsisting by forcing their friends to violate the laws by aiding them, and others by violent depredations upon peaceful citizens." Such men were "entailing shame and obloquy upon themselves and their posterity, outraging the laws and peace of society, and damaging the cause of their hard pressed country." Nevertheless, Vance continued, Gen. Robert E. Lee had issued General Order No. 54, promising a "full and free pardon" or the "infliction of only the mildest penalties of military law" to all deserters—except those guilty of capital crimes—who voluntarily returned to their regiments within thirty days. "And I hereby warn," Vance stressed, "all such who refuse to comply with these terms that the utmost power of this State will be exerted to capture them or drive them from the borders of a country whose high honor and spotless renown they disgrace by refusing to defend, and the extremist [sic] penalties of the law will be enforced without exception when caught, as well as against their aiders and abetters in the civil courts."

In his proclamation, the governor ordered all the units of the militia to hunt down deserters, and he instructed civil magistrates "to be diligent in proceeding against all such as violate the statute against harboring, aiding or abetting deserters." He cautioned magistrates that if they were not diligent in their duties regarding deserters, he would withdraw his "executive protection" that theretofore had kept them from service in the Confederate army.[2]

Vance also asked the Confederate War Department to establish a military court in western North Carolina to arrest, try, and punish deserters. He wrote to Secretary of War Seddon that it "is deemed important that deserters taken with arms in their hands, in that District, should be tried and punished. First, for the moral effect and secondly to prevent the escape of desperate men from poorly guarded prisons or while being transferred to some distant point of trial." He informed the secretary that many apprehended deserters were escaping from county jails in the west. Recently, a "number of deserters, while being transferred from Asheville to Camp Vance [near Morganton], overpowered the Guard, composed of Junior Reserves, killed two of the boys, and made their escape."[3]

The increase in desertion was but one indication that the war was turning decidedly against the Confederacy. The success of the constantly pressing Union armies was slowly wearing down Confederate forces and swelling the war-weariness and despondency of the Southern population. "I never before have been so gloomy about the condition of affairs," Vance wrote to David L. Swain on September 22, 1864. "Early's defeat in the Valley I regard as the turning point of this campaign & confidentially, I fear seals the fate of Richmond though not immediately." Unlike many Southerners, Vance considered it a foregone conclusion that Lincoln would prevail in the upcoming U.S. presidential election in November. He was sure that with Lincoln's victory over Democratic candidate George B. McClellan, running on a peace platform, war was certain to continue, and "abolitionism is rampant for four more years." Vance also insisted that by replacing Gen. Joseph E. Johnston with John B. Hood to lead the Army of Tennessee against Sherman's onslaught, Jefferson Davis had given control to "still a worse commander," who had lost Atlanta. The people of Georgia, Vance claimed, had completely given up the fight, and their soldiers were now "deserting by hundreds." Georgia's governor, Joseph E. Brown, furthermore was "a *humbug* & can do nothing but get in the way." If the Federals continued to advance "till the close of the year we shall not be offered any terms at all."

More than any other factor, "the bitter demoralization of the people" worried Vance. He observed that Sherman's line of communication was five hundred miles long, but the inhabitants of the invaded region had not seized that opportunity to rise up and raid and harass Sherman's columns. It perplexed the governor that "throughout our own country, not a bridge has been burnt, a car thrown from its track nor a man shot by the people whose country he has violated!" The people seem to "submit when our armies are drawn off." This refusal of the home-front population to engage in a type of partisan or guerrilla warfare, said Vance, "shows what I have always believed[—]that the great *popular heart* is not now & never has been in this war! It was a revolution of the *politicians* not *the people*; was fought at first by the natural enthusiasm of our young men; and has been kept going by state & sectional pride assisted by that bitterness of feeling produced by the cruelties & brutalities of the enemy."

Despite the progress of the Union campaigns and the lack of will among the Southern people to resist, Vance maintained that the Confederacy must strengthen its resolve and its efforts to halt the invasion of its heartland. Only by continuing to fight and making the United States pay dearly in lives, money, and morale could the Confederate states hope "to be offered any terms at all." The governor refused to give up his hope of continuing the fight until the Federal government, exhausted with waging war, could be brought to the bargaining table to consider seriously peace terms that might be favorable to the Southern states. "I am not out of heart," he told Swain. "As you know, I am of hopeful & buoyant temperament—Things may come around yet. Gen. Lee is a *great* man and has the remnant of the best army on earth bleeding, torn & overpowered though it may be."[4]

Nevertheless, if the Confederate states were to turn events around and have any chance at all of securing favorable peace terms, they had to rally around each other and the Davis government and strengthen their resolve and efforts to continue to wage war until the conflict ended. With that in mind, Vance proposed that the governors of the Confederate states east of the Mississippi River meet to discuss how they might revive the waning struggle for Southern independence. Vance dispatched letters to the governors of Georgia, Alabama, South Carolina, Florida, Mississippi, Tennessee, and Virginia suggesting that a conference be held "at some point such as Augusta during the coming month of October, when and where some general plan of action might be agreed upon for the relief of the country, and recommended to our several legislatures." On the proposed agenda would be the problems of desertion and poor relief. Of particular concern to Vance was the scarcity of soldiers to fill the diminishing Confederate ranks. He therefore wanted to discuss with the other governors the possibility of conscripting state officials who previously had been exempt from the Confederate draft. Those officials had been "withheld from service, not only on account of the necessity for them in administering the governments, but also because the principle of state sovereignty rendered it improper to allow the Confederate Government to conscript them." Vance wondered, "[C]ould there be a way prescribed to put, at least, a portion of them into service without injuring the efficiency of the State governments, and without infringing upon rights of the States and their dignity as sovereigns?" If the states adopted that course, however, "it is desirable that action on this and all kindred matters should be uniform, or as nearly as possible. It would avoid much discontent, for every man to know that he was required to do only that which every one else has to do, and the burthens of war are fairly distributed."[5]

On September 27, Gov. William Smith of Virginia responded to Vance's call for a conference of governors. Smith suggested Columbia, South Carolina, as the meeting site. He requested that they meet as soon as possible, because he intended to convene his state's legislature on the first Monday in November. He cautioned Vance that the conference "may give rise to much misrepresentation"—presumably meaning that Confederate officials might interpret the conference as an effort by the states to circumvent Confederate authority and possibly bid for peace. Nevertheless, he had "no solid objection" to the conference and could "well see that great good may result from it."[6]

Gov. Milledge L. Bonham of South Carolina responded the following day. He applauded Vance's idea of a governors' conference and suggested Augusta, Georgia, as the most convenient site for the meeting. In response to Vance's proposal about making conscription of state officials a part of the agenda, Bonham told the Tar Heel governor that South Carolina's state officers were already subject to the draft. He wrote "that in South Carolina no persons are reserved to the State but all have gone into Confederate service from the classes of Militia officers, Magistrates, Deputy Clerks, and Deputy Sheriffs, (except in one or two cases where the Confederate Government has detailed or Exempted them) and several other classes, all of which classes, I have understood in several States, have been reserved by the States or by the Executives thereof." With a subtle swipe at North Carolina, Bonham asserted that "Whilst I think each State should have a permanent force of its own, as matters now stand, it is better that every one who can be spared should go into Confederate service." All the Confederate states should relinquish to military service "the army of efficient officials and detailed men . . . whose duties can, as well, or better, be performed by infirm men, disabled officers and soldiers, citizens exempted by Confederate law from service in [the] field and persons over fifty years of age."[7]

On October 1, Gov. Joseph E. Brown of Georgia answered Vance that he was in agreement with holding a conference of governors. He requested that the meeting take place at Augusta on October 17, because the Georgia legislature would meet on the first Thursday in November, and he needed time to prepare for the session. Brown informed Vance that the North Carolina governor's concerns "in reference to State offices are not applicable to this State, where every officer civil and military who can possibly be spared and keep the State Govmt in existence, is, and for months past has been in military service as part of the militia of the State." Vance's remarks about state officials, however, "may be and probably are applicable to other States."[8] Gov. John Milton of Florida "cordially approved" of the conference. He wrote to Vance on October 11 that he would attend "if in my power to do so, but we are so constantly threatened with raids in different parts of the state, that my presence here seems to be almost indispensable."[9]

In the meantime, Gen. Robert E. Lee had written to Vance that the situation around Petersburg and Richmond had worsened and reinforcements from North Carolina were desperately needed.[10] Vance then attempted to convene the North Carolina legislature in a special session to consider permitting the conscription of certain exempted state officials into the Confederate army and sending the Home Guard beyond the state in emergency situations. The governor first sought the approval of his Council of State to call for the special session of the legislature. But the council ruled "that the absolute necessity required by law does not at the present time sufficiently appear to warrant an extra call of the General Assembly." Fenner B. Satterthwaite, president of the council, went on to say that the members endorsed the Augusta conference and expressed their willingness to convene again quickly if asked by Vance. "The Council beg to tender their sympathy to your Excellency," Satterthwaite told the governor, "in your situation and to state that in their opinion every possible object of public benefit or advantage is being accomplished under your Administration of the State Government."[11]

Such conciliatory words did not assuage Vance's annoyance at the council for failing to endorse a special session of the General Assembly. "After some little chaffing [sic] they refused out loud," he confided in Hale. "I think I shall have to cut loose from some of the old fogies & rely for counsil [sic] & advice from men nearer my own age & notions of things." Vance had no real indication that the state's lawmakers would authorize the conscription of state officials. Nevertheless, he wanted to place any blame for failing to do so squarely on their shoulders. "I do not know that the State will surrender any of its officers," he confessed to Hale, "but I want the Legislature to take the responsibility of refusing."

When the governors' conference convened in October, Vance had his course of action clearly in mind: "My intention is to compare notes, see how many men each State had retained in its service, how many it can spare & agree upon some common plan to be submitted to our several Legislatures." He was certain that he could ask North Carolina to submit to only those conscription policies that the other states had agreed to accept. Senator William A. Graham advised him to "pledge N Carolina to submit to whatever the others will submit to." But Vance still had reservations. "Will I damage myself by taking this course," he asked Hale, "and, what is more important, can I benefit the state and the country?"[12] Hale encouraged him to "go further than what Gov. Graham advises." The *Fayetteville Observer*'s editor felt that Vance should publicly proclaim that he was in favor of conscripting of state officials, even without similar action on the part of the governors in the other states. "We are too much & deeply interested in this matter of the defence of Va. to stand upon what others have done or failed to do," he told Vance. Still, Hale pointed out that bringing the matter of conscription of state officials before a special session of the legislature had certain pitfalls. "If it should refuse to do anything," he theorized, "the effect would be very bad—better it should not meet at all. And is there not reason to fear that they will lack the nerve to conscribe any class, especially such influential classes as the Justice & Militia officers?" But Vance might succeed in convincing the lawmakers "by your own strong convictions of the necessity." Hale also noted that the Raleigh *Conservative* opposed a special legislative session, but should the Augusta conference "result in an agreement to pursue a concerted line of policy," Vance could count on his support. "The *Observer* will second any movement calculated to promote the success of the great cause," he promised.[13]

Governors Vance, Bonham, Brown, Smith, Thomas H. Watts of Alabama, and Charles Clark of Mississippi assembled at the Augusta conference on October 17. Robert L. Caruthers of Tennessee and John Milton of Florida did not attend. In 1863 Caruthers had been elected governor of Tennessee, largely by a secessionist vote, but because of the Union occupation of Nashville, he was never inaugurated. Early in 1862, Federal troops had occupied much of Tennessee, and Lincoln appointed Andrew Johnson as military governor of the region. As a result, Isham Harris remained the last inaugurated governor of the state. Through Governor Brown, Vance invited Caruthers to the Augusta meeting. Brown forwarded Vance's invitation to Caruthers's brother-in-law General Marcus J. Wright, who was commanding at Macon, Georgia, but Caruthers did not attend the conference. Milton of Florida did not travel to Augusta apparently because he felt that the threat of Union raids in his state required his presence at home.[14]

At the conference, the governors passed resolutions promising to increase measures—including providing more troops—to support the Confederacy in continuing the war. The governors dispatched copies of their resolutions to the Davis government in Richmond. In addition to their declarations of support, they included a request asking the Confederate Congress to repeal the February 6 act that allowed the Confederate government to claim one-half of the cargo space of all privately owned blockade-runners. That space, the governors maintained, should be allotted to the states.[15]

When the North Carolina General Assembly met at its regular session in November 1864, Vance sent a message to the legislators asking them to bolster the war effort by sending more troops to the Confederate army. William A. Graham wrote to him that he found the governor's "recommendation wise and appropriate." But Graham also felt that "in any regulations on the subject of troops furnished to the Confed. Gov't, there shall be a respectable body guard reserved, of the sovereignty of the State."[16] In the Confederate Senate on December 1, Graham opposed passage of a congressional resolution asking the states to search among their exempted officials for additional troops for the army. He argued that the raising of troops by the states was the sole responsibility of the states. His motion to table the resolution was adopted.[17] The North Carolina legislature rejected Vance's proposal that members of the Home Guard be sent to reinforce Lee's dwindling ranks. The state lawmakers also declined his request to increase the age of conscription of North Carolinians to fifty-five. A movement even arose in both houses of the assembly "to initiate negotiations for an honorable peace." John Pool in the state Senate and Daniel Fowle in the House introduced resolutions calling for the election of peace commissioners to cooperate with similar officials from other states to negotiate peace with the United States. A close vote in the Senate tabled Pool's resolution. No vote on Fowle's proposal occurred in the House.[18]

In November Lincoln's reelection signaled to the Confederate states that any quick cessation of the war initiated by a U.S. presidential peace advocate had vanished. The future promised only further fighting. Despondency in the South grew as Lee's situation at Richmond daily became worse and Sherman pressed toward Savannah, leaving havoc in his wake.[19] In the minds of Vance and other North Carolinians, the port of Wilmington loomed as an imminent Federal target. The Wilmington and Weldon Railroad, which ran from the North Carolina port to Petersburg, was Lee's last vital supply line. By the end of 1864, the Union had closed all the Confederate ports except Charleston and Wilmington. Its seizure of an island in the Charleston harbor in 1863 and the subsequent increase in the naval blockade had seriously impeded blockade-running at the South Carolina port. Thus, in late 1864 Wilmington remained the final major lifeline of the Confederacy.[20]

Vance anticipated that a Union attack on Wilmington might take place in the near future. In November, he paid a visit to the port city to inspect the fortifications at Fort Fisher and other defensive works guarding the entrance to the port. On November 15, he reported to Jefferson Davis that he found the defenses "all in excellent condition so far as I am able to judge, there seems to be nothing wanting but troops." He observed that "a land attack in the rear of Fort Fisher . . . seems to be the point of real danger." He cautioned the president that, except for the garrison in the fort, only an inadequate force of state militia protected the major fortification. He therefore requested that General Lee dispatch "at least two brigades of veteran troops" to supplement those defending Fort Fisher. Vance acknowledged the pressure upon Lee's lines at Richmond. But he added, "Except for the moral effect involved in losing our capital I can not see that

9. The Federal capture of Fort Fisher in January 1865 closed the vital port of Wilmington and signaled the approaching end of the Civil War. North Carolina Office of Archives and History, Raleigh.

Richmond itself is of any greater importance to us now than Wilmington."[21] Davis responded to Vance's message on November 21, informing the governor that the "proper attention" was being given to his suggestions, "which the Secretary of War has been directed to communicate to Genl. R. E. Lee."[22]

On December 20, Gen. Braxton Bragg, then in overall command at Wilmington, sent Vance an urgent telegram stating that a U.S. expedition had assembled "a heavy fleet of armed steamers & transports" off Fort Fisher. Bragg proclaimed that "all the assistance you can give us is now needed."[23] Alarmed by Bragg's telegram, Vance immediately issued a public proclamation pleading for all men, "whether by law subject to military duty or not, who may be able to stand behind breastworks and fire a musket of all ages and conditions, to rally at once to the defence of their country and hurry to Wilmington." He reminded the public that "the organized forces of the State already ordered to the front may still be insufficient" to turn back a Federal attack on Fort Fisher and Wilmington. "Your Governor will meet you at the front and will share with you the worse [sic]," Vance boasted.[24] Despite his plea, however, no force of volunteers rushed to Fort Fisher.

On December 22, 1864, Vance delivered his second inaugural address to the people of North Carolina. In an speech much briefer and more despondent that his first one, he announced that "I make no new promises, lay down no new principles." He called for his citizens to remain united in resisting the Federal attempt to conquer and return them to the Union. He cautioned them to avoid "Depression, distraction, division; of sentiment & aim; leading to civil feuds, domestic violence and political death." He assured them that "If crushed by overwhelming numbers in the field of battle we are guiltless of the unavoidable result." But if the people became disunited through despair and disaffection, then only "internal & self destruction" awaited them. "Let all our movements whether peace or war," he declared, "be in solid column; our people at home as our brothers at the front standing *in line of battle, facing one way & together!*"[25]

True to his word when he called for volunteers to reinforce Fort Fisher, Vance rushed to Wilmington, accompanied by North Carolina's surgeon general, Edward Warren. Two companies across the Cape Fear River from Fort Fisher, along with the Seventh Battalion of Junior Reserves and a detachment of sailors from the CSS *Chickamauga*, berthed at Wilmington, reinforced the fort. From Virginia, the War Department detailed a division commanded by Robert F. Hoke to help defend the fort. But by the time Hoke and his troops arrived, the first attempt to capture Fort Fisher had already failed.[26]

In command of the naval arm of the U.S. expedition off Cape Fear was Rear Admiral David D. Porter. Gen. Benjamin F. Butler commanded the army contingent. Carrying out a bizarre plan conceived by Butler, the Federals began their attack of Fort Fisher on December 23, when the navy towed a ship filled with gunpowder and other explosives to within a few hundred yards of the fort. Butler's plan called for the explosion of the vessel to do great damage to the fort. But, ignited on December 24, the explosives had no impact on the fortifications. On Christmas Day, Porter's crews began bombarding the fort; however, that did little damage as the defenders took refuge in their bombproof shelters. Simultaneously with the bombardment, three thousand troops under the command of Gen. Godfrey Weitzel landed north of the fort and began marching south to assault the breastworks. When the troops drew within fifty yards of the fort, a nervous Butler ordered a halt. He instructed his men to retreat and reembark on the transports. Such was the general's haste that he left one detachment on the beach, and Porter had to send a vessel to evacuate the troops. The Union expedition then sailed away. Following its departure, Vance traveled down the Cape Fear River to inspect Fort Fisher. There he congratulated Col. William Lamb, the engineering officer commanding the fort, and Gen. William H. C. Whiting, who had direct command of all Wilmington's defenses.[27] Vance wrote to President Davis recommending that Lamb be promoted to brigadier general. "I was nearby during the recent attack upon the defences of Wilmington," he told Davis, "and people and soldiers alike were enthusiastic in praise of his [Lamb's] skill and gallantry."[28]

Further military events, however, would soon bring Lamb's army career to an end. On January 12, 1865, the U.S. armada appeared again off Fort Fisher. The navy was still under the command of Admiral Porter, but Gen. Alfred H. Terry led the army contingent this time. On the next day, Porter's gunners began bombarding the fort, concentrating on its land face. Terry landed his troops north of the fort, and they entrenched themselves behind a breastwork. On January 15, they began attacking the fort. Bragg ordered Hoke's division—much needed in defense of the fort—to remain at Sugar Loaf, a defensive position between Fort Fisher and Wilmington, in order to protect the city. After considerable bombardment and savage hand-to-hand fighting at the Confederate bastion, General Whiting formally surrendered Fort Fisher to General Terry in the late evening. With the fall of Fisher, the Confederates abandoned four lesser fortifications protecting the entrance of the Cape Fear River. The capture of Fort Fisher closed the port at Wilmington, and it would not be long before the Federals took the city itself.[29]

Around the time that Fort Fisher fell to Northern attack, Vance began to express concern about the condition of the Union soldiers held at the Confederate prison camp at Salisbury, in the Piedmont county of Rowan. The prison was an abandoned cotton factory that the Confederate government purchased in 1861 to confine Southern soldiers awaiting court-martial, deserters, disloyal citizens, suspected spies, and Federal prisoners of war. The first Union prisoners arrived in December 1861, and 1,500 were incarcerated there in March 1862. Conditions at the facility remained relatively good through 1863. But by the fall of 1864, the number of prisoners, many of whom were being moved south as the Army of the Potomac threatened Richmond, swelled to more than 10,000. That number far exceeded the capacity of the prison. Many inmates lacked shelter, adequate food, and proper medical care. Sanitation conditions were deplorable, and prison gangs robbed and even murdered fellow inmates. Guards were mostly old men and boys who were ill prepared to keep order. Between October 1864 and February 1865, 3,419 prisoners died.[30]

On February 1, 1865, Vance acknowledged that he had just learned of the plight of the prisoners at Salisbury. He wrote to Gen. Bradley T. Johnson, commandant of the prison, that "most distressing accounts reach me of the suffering and destitution of the Yankee prisoners under your charge. If half be true it is disgraceful to our humanity and will provoke severe retaliation. I hope however it is not so bad as represented, but lest it be so, I hereby tender you any aid in my power to afford to make their condition more tolerable. I know the great scarcity of food which prevails, but shelter and warmth can certainly be provided and I can spare you some clothing if the Yankees will deliver as much to N.C. troops in Northern prisons."[31]

On the same day, Vance wrote to Secretary Seddon expressing his concern about the conditions at Salisbury and especially his fear of "severe retaliation" when the Federals discovered the atrocious circumstances endured by their soldiers at the prison. He called on Seddon to move quickly to improve conditions.[32] The following week, John C. Breckinridge, who had recently replaced Seddon as war secretary, answered that he had instructed the adjutant general to order an investigation of the prison and to "correct the evils complained of."[33]

General Johnson was in Richmond pressing on the War Department the need to improve conditions at the Salisbury camp when Vance's letter to him arrived at the prison. In the commandant's absence, his subordinate, Assist. Adj. Gen. G. W. Booth, responded to the governor, reporting that the prisoners had sufficient wood for fuel. "Only two days have they been without and then unavoidable circumstances prevented its issue." He noted that some of the prisoners sold their wood to the camp sutler for tobacco. The prisoners' daily ration was one pound of bread, one pint of soup, and "small issues of meat or sorghum—sometimes small quantities of both." Booth further reported that the prisoners' lack of clothing was "truly deplorable—most of them having been prisoners some 6 or 9 mos." The Confederate government "cannot issue clothing to them," and in the past month General Johnson had requested through Confederate War Department channels that the Federals supply clothing. Drinking water, drawn from ten wells and a creek outside the prison grounds, was in short supply. "No stream of water runs thro' the prison." As to the shortage of shelter, Gen. John H. Winder, commissary general for all Confederate prisons east of the Mississippi, had prohibited "all improvements—buildings &c." in Confederate prisons under his command.[34]

Upon returning to Salisbury, General Johnson wrote to Vance, echoing Booth's report. "No one can feel more acutely than I do the condition of the prisoners of war here," he lamented. "General Winder . . . forbade any buildings to be erected here. A large percent [of prisoners] have therefore lived *in holes in the ground*. Were I to attempt to erect Barracks here Spring wd. come on before they cd. be finished. I must therefore try to get tents. Can you lend me or procure for me in Raleigh 150 or 200 wall tents. If so pray send them at once. I recently visited Richmond for the main purpose of pressing on our authorities our duties to ourselves & these people, laying before them the terrible suffering & mortality among them. I have procured from the Federal officer for distributing goods [for U.S. soldiers imprisoned] in Richmond 3500 blankets which will be here tomorrow, with the tents their condition will be tolerable, but nothing will alleviate it but speedy exchange."

Johnson had learned that Gen. U. S. Grant—general in chief of the Union army simultaneously directing the Army of the Potomac in Virginia—was willing to exchange prisoners "from us 3000 per week." He therefore telegraphed Gen. William M. Gardner, Confederate commandant of military prisons east of the Mississippi, "urging him to press for the immediate delivery of all the prisoners in North & South Carolina at Wilmington." Johnson acknowledged that Grant would agree to an exchange of prisoners only if captives from both sides were paroled and not allowed to return to their respective armies. "On this our authorities may stick," Johnson told the governor, "but we ought to agree to it at once. The prisoners here eat our rations & keep men out of the field to guard them. They are a terrible burden—it would be better to send them home at once on parole. But the men we get back will go home, reinvigorate the population for the war, work, help to raise provisions, and in an emergency, *defend themselves*, by guerrilla war, of which no parole can deprive them." He stressed to Vance that "if these people are not turned over to their authorities, they will be pressed back into No Ca who will have to subsist three armies—the Confederate, the Federal, & the Neutral, more terrible than either."[35]

No evidence has been found in Vance's papers to indicate whether or not he supplied the tents requested by Johnson. But, in any event, Johnson's hope for a "speedy exchange" was soon realized, when the Salisbury prisoners were exchanged at Wilmington in March 1865.[36]

The capture of Fort Fisher, coupled with Sherman's success on the march in Georgia, led some members of the North Carolina legislature to reconsider the idea of a peace convention. Vance immediately voiced his disapproval of such conventions. He was particularly concerned that if Georgia held a convention, North Carolina might follow suit. On January 15, he wrote Governor Brown: "The march of Sherman through Georgia,

his threatened advance through So Carolina and the recent disaster involved in the defeat of Genl. Hood and the fall of the principal defensive
work of Wilmington, have necessitated the desire of a State Convention
for vague and indefinable purposes. I do not think that a Convention can be
called in North Carolina unless your State should lead in the movement,
and I see many indications of such an intention among your people."
Vance went on to admonish Brown to do all he could to prevent a peace
convention in Georgia. "I suppose you are aware of my opinion in regard
to the danger of such a movement," he wrote Brown. "I regard it as simply
another revolution and by which we would incur not only the danger attendant upon a disunited Confederation, but also of domestic strife and
bloodshed."[37] Vance also cautioned South Carolina governor Andrew G.
Magrath (who had succeeded Bonham) that state peace conventions should
not be convened. He told Magrath that, instead of peace conventions, "The
Spirit of our people must be revived, their patriotism aroused anew and a
determination to suffer be enforced if we are to hope for ultimate redemp-
tion."[38]

Near the end of January, Vance learned of the upcoming Hampton
Roads Peace Conference to be held on February 3 in Virginia. At that
conference, three Confederate commissioners and critics of Jefferson Davis
—Alexander H. Stephens, John A. Campbell, and Robert M. T. Hunter—
would attempt to negotiate a peace with Lincoln and the Federal government. To a friend, Vance expressed his opinion of the pending conference. "Never was there a greater error," he protested. "It is most unwise to
suspend our preparations for the public defense. We should really double
our energies, & present to our enemies the energetic determination of a
great people, driven to the wall in the last stage of desperation and ready to
dare every thing! But alas! Alas! We hail the first step of our enemies
toward negotiation, on any terms, as an act of gracious kindness and will
tacitly accept our degradation beforehand!" As far as Vance was concerned,
the peace meeting was "a great swindle, and we are so anxious to be duped
that we can never plead *rape*. I believe however it will result in peace but
such peace as I for one will blush to accept."[39] But the governor's fears of
the success of the peace negotiations were not realized. The Hampton
Roads conference quickly failed when the Southern commissioners learned
that Lincoln would not compromise on his stipulations that the Confederacy—which he refused to recognize as a legitimate nation—lay down its
arms, renounce its independence, and accept emancipation of its slaves.[40]

In the vicinity of Wilmington in late January, General Terry and Admiral Porter awaited the arrival of reinforcements before attacking the port

city. General Grant traveled to Cape Fear to discuss future operations with the two commanders. Grant explained that he wanted to use Wilmington as a base to supply Sherman's advance into the Carolinas from Savannah. With control of Wilmington and the railroad leading from that port to Goldsboro in the interior of North Carolina, the Union army could make Goldsboro a supply depot for Sherman when he entered the Tar Heel State. At Grant's request, the U.S. War Department dispatched to the Cape Fear region Gen. John M. Schofield and his Twenty-third Corps, Army of the Ohio, which had been with the army in Tennessee. The department appointed Schofield commander of the Department of North Carolina. His objectives were to capture Wilmington and then press on to Goldsboro to reinforce and supply Sherman. A force from New Bern would drive eastward from the city to join Sherman at Goldsboro. Supported by Porter's gunboats on the river, Schofield began his attack on Wilmington on February 11.[41]

As the Federals pressed their attack, General Lee telegraphed Vance that more troops from Schofield's corps were on their way to Wilmington and that General Bragg was traveling to Raleigh to confer with the governor about defenses of the port city. "I can send no more forces from this army," lamented Lee. "Please bring every man from the state" to defend the city.[42] Then, with the fall of Wilmington appearing imminent, Lee again telegraphed Vance, asking, "What assistance can you give Genl Bragg?" Lee advised the governor that Sherman was on the march toward North Carolina, and "Supplies of all kinds should be at once moved from [Sherman's path] thoroughly and completely. Horses mules stock of all kinds should be driven off." Gen. P. G. T. Beauregard, then commanding troops in South Carolina and Georgia against Sherman's advance, had reported to Lee that Sherman would probably move on Charlotte and from there unite with Federal troops from the coast at Raleigh or Weldon, a junction of the Wilmington and Weldon Railroad. "This can not be done," declared Lee, "if all supplies are removed or destroyed."[43] Vance wired the general that he would give Bragg "all the assistance in my power." The governor had "called out every man liable to duty in the state." But "I cant destroy provisions without a force of cavalry."[44]

Meanwhile, at Wilmington, after the Federals captured Fort Anderson and forced the retreat of Hoke's men at Sugar Loaf, they reached the outskirts of the city on the evening of February 21. Bragg gave orders for Hoke and others to abandon the city, which was formally surrendered by Mayor John Dawson on the following morning. Bragg withdrew his troops westward toward Goldsboro to defend against the penetration of the Federals from the coast. With the capture of Wilmington, the Union virtually controlled all of coastal North Carolina, from which a sizable force could drive westward to cooperate with Sherman as he moved northward into the state. Vance wrote to John White, the state's procurement agent in England, that because the Federals had captured Wilmington and halted blockade-running, "Nothing remains but to *close up* our affairs as completely as possible and wait for a change. Our Accounts in England I suppose can easily be reduced . . . and what funds we have should be placed in safety to aid in the final adjustment of our indebtedness. Our goods on hand, whether in Europe or the islands, I leave to you to dispose of in any way deemed best."[45]

Amid such circumstances, Vance attempted to sustain and rally support among North Carolinians for maintaining the war effort. On February 14, he issued another public proclamation urging the state's citizens not to lose heart but to strengthen their resolve against a horrible fate that awaited them if they allowed the Union army to prevail. Once again, he reminded North Carolinians that their state had reluctantly seceded only when it was forced from the Union. Later, in hopes of reconciliation and bringing their wartime suffering to an end, he had encouraged the Confederate president to investigate peace agreements based upon Southern independence. Vance further noted that the Davis administration had attempted a number of peace talks with the Lincoln government—including most recently at a conference at Hampton Roads, Virginia—only to be rebuffed repeatedly by the Federals. The blame for continuing the war, he reminded his people, therefore rested entirely with the U.S. government, and the people of the Confederacy could expect no quarter from their enemy if they allowed him to prevail.

He pointed out that the Thirteenth Amendment, recently passed by the U.S. Congress and sent to the states for ratification, would change the U.S. Constitution "to decree immediately forever, the abolition of slavery." Not only would Southerners lose their slaves if the North won the war, but if victorious, the Federals intended to hang "every man, soldier, sailor or marine, civilians or others, who had been engaged in what they term rebellion." The Lincoln government would also confiscate land and other property throughout the South. Vance summed up the "consequences of our submission":

Four million slaves, two hundred thousand of whom have been in arms against us, turned loose at once in our midst, our lands confiscated, and sold out to pay the cost of the slaughter of their masters;

our women, children and old men reduced to beggary, and driven from their once happy homes, our mutilated and diseased soldiers, starving in rags from door to door, spurned by even pensioned negro soldiers, whilst the gallows grows weary under the burden of [our] wisest statesmen and bravest defenders, to say nothing of universal financial ruin and the intolerable oppression of a rapacious and vindictive foe in the hour of conquest! Great God! Is there a man in all this honorable, high spirited and noble commonwealth, so steeped in every conceivable meanness, so blackened with all the guilt of treason, so damned with all the leprosy of cowardice, as to say yes, we will submit to all this! And whilst there yet remains a half million men amongst us able to resist!

The governor denied rumors that "we are already subdued." Enough troops and supplies still existed to continue fighting and achieve victory, "So long as we remain one and determined." The loss of the major cities and ports of the Confederacy did not necessarily signal impending defeat. "For thank God, the Confederacy does not consist in brick and mortar, or particular spots of ground however valuable they may be in a military point of view. Our nationality consists in our people."[46] Vance called for public rallies in the counties to inspire people on the local level and strengthen their resolve in support of the Confederacy. A small number of people attended, and Vance spoke at some of the gatherings.[47]

President Davis telegraphed his thanks to Vance for his proclamation and urged the governor to continue to do all he could "to bring [a] large auxiliary force in to the field," as time "is all importance [sic] to a success—Which will revive confidence."[48] Increasingly concerned about his dwindling ranks, General Lee beseeched Vance to do more to restore morale in his state in order to curtail the epidemic of desertion among Tar Heel troops.[49] Secretary of War John C. Breckinridge and Commissary General Isaac M. St. John (who had supplanted Lucius B. Northrop) urged Vance to sell or "loan . . . reserve supplies" to the Confederate government.[50]

Vance struggled to comply with the requests of the Confederate officials. He asked Generals Beauregard and Bragg to keep him informed of Sherman's and Schofield's movements so that he could move supplies away from the Federal advance.[51] When Gen. Joseph E. Johnston soon took Beauregard's place as commander of the Confederate force (including the remnants of Johnston's old Army of Tennessee) defending against Sherman, Vance immediately inquired of him about the best route for evacuating state quartermaster stores. "Should Sherman come this way," Johnston telegraphed the governor from Charlotte, "I recommend the neighbor-hood of Danville [Virginia]. Should he turn towards Fayetteville[,] Salis-bury would be safe."[52] Johnston quickly concluded that Sherman's des-tination was Goldsboro, not Charlotte as Beauregard had predicted. At around the time Sherman entered North Carolina in early March, Gen-eral Lee placed Bragg's troops under the command of Johnston. Bragg remained with his army between New Bern and Goldsboro, while Johns-ton concentrated the rest of his force in the vicinity of Fayetteville, cor-rectly surmising that would be Sherman's next objective.[53]

As Confederate officers had asked him to, Vance made still another pub-lic appeal to the citizens of North Carolina to stay the course in support of the Confederate army and its efforts to halt the Federal advance. In an address to the people in late February, he cited Lee's requests that Tar Heels aid the Southern soldiers in the field and the defense of their state by con-tributing "such Commissary and Quartermaster stores as they can possi-bly spare" and by preventing such supplies from falling into Union hands. Vance outlined a voluntary plan for getting provisions to Confederate troops and keeping them away from the Federals. Every citizen who had the means should "pledge himself to furnish the rations of one soldier for six months." That individual should deliver to the nearest commissary agent "80 pounds of bacon and 180 pounds of flour, or their equivelent [sic] in beef or meal." He should deliver one-half of the pledged supplies immedi-ately and the rest within three months, unless he could provide the entire amount at once. Those North Carolinians contributing such provisions should strive to increase the size of their offerings, which "will be received either as sales, loans or donations." Even the poor could provide provisions by combining their efforts and feeding one soldier for six months.

To implement his plan, Vance called for counties and neighborhoods to hold public meetings to enlist subscribers. He cautioned that

> Should you not, Fellow Citizens, respond to this call, you may cal-culate, not only upon seeing your own sons in the Army suffer and be defeated in the field, for want of those supplies, but you will have the mortification to behold them seized and appropriated to the support of the enemy who comes to destroy us. Advancing as he does, through the interior of the land, without either water or rail-road communications in his rear, he is now subsisting by the plunder and the ruin of the people of South Carolina, and must necessarily do so when he enters our State. Be assured, therefore, that every pound of bacon and beef, and every bushel of meal, which you withhold

from your own Army, is a certain contribution to the maintainance [*sic*] of that of the enemy. You have, therefore, to choose whether you will feed your sons, who are bleeding in our defence, or our ruthless enemy who arms our slaves and lays waste our country.

To reassure North Carolinians that he did not expect them to make sacrifices he was not willing to share, Vance "tendered to the Commissary Department one half of my entire years' [*sic*] supply, and expect to put my own family upon the limited rations allowed to our soldiers, regretting that I have so little to offer."[54] He hoped that his public appeal for supplies would bring a favorable response from the people. But civilians' voluntary contribution of provisions on a significant scale never materialized.

In response to General Lee's pressing demands that he do more to apprehend and return deserters to Confederate ranks, Vance promised the general to call out the Home Guard in every county.[55] Lee reciprocated by dispatching troops to the Tar Heel State to assist in the hunt for deserters.[56]

With Sherman on the verge of entering North Carolina from the south, Confederate authorities increased their demands on Vance for support in repelling the Federal advance. One of the problems that had hindered the Confederacy in moving supplies since the beginning of the war was the variation in railroad gauges. The differences meant that supplies often had to be unloaded and reloaded before they reached their final destinations. A narrow gauge ran from Charlotte, through Greensboro, to Danville, Virginia. From Danville to Richmond a wide gauge was in operation.[57] That problem became even more serious in the final months of the war. In order to expedite the transport of provisions and equipment away from Sherman and to Confederate troops in North Carolina and Virginia, General Beauregard (before Johnston assumed command) had asked Vance to widen the gauge of the North Carolina Railroad running from Charlotte to Greensboro. With the concurrence of the North Carolina and Virginia legislatures, the Confederate government had financed the building of the line from Danville to Greensboro in 1862 and was responsible for its maintenance through the Piedmont Railroad Company.[58] Vance had only reluctantly agreed to the Greensboro-to-Danville segment, believing that the Confederacy should put its main efforts into maintaining the railroads in eastern North Carolina. "How far do you wish to bring the wide gauge?" Vance inquired of Johnston on March 1, adding, "I do not want it further east than Salisbury unless great necessity requires it."[59] Johnston responded that he considered the widening of the gauge to be "a military necessity."[60] General Lee wired Vance that he and the quartermaster general believed that "the widening of the gauge should continue to Danville if possible."[61] Secretary of War Breckinridge telegraphed the governor: "It is of great importance to have the gauge through to Danville, and I respectfully urge you to consent that it may be widened from Salisbury to Greensboro."[62]

In a March 3 letter to Confederate military engineer Gen. Jeremy F. Gilmer, Vance explained his reasons for not wanting to widen the gauge beyond Salisbury. Widening the road from Salisbury to Greensboro, he argued, would break "my connection with the West." He intended to "remove my stores and public records" to the western part of the state if Raleigh was threatened by Federal attack. But if Vance had to move his government west and the gauge was widened between Salisbury and Greensboro, he would have "to break bulk twice," once at Greensboro and then again at Salisbury. The Western North Carolina Railroad—with a narrow gauge— ran from Salisbury to Morganton in the far west. Furthermore, Vance surmised, "Should Sherman, as is most likely, unite with Schofield and advance upon Greensboro from this direction, all of the rolling stock in N.C. crowded upon Greensboro for safety would be destroyed, whilst the S.C. stock would be safe, having the road open behind it. I do not understand that it is in the interest of N.C. to make the sacrifice of her own property to save that of S. Carolina." He told Gilmer frankly that he did not consider extending the wide gauge to Greensboro to be a "military necessity." The state's rolling stock "is simply sufficient to transport everything desired between Salisbury and Greensboro," and if the gauge were widened, then many of the state's railroad cars—built for the narrow gauge—would remain idle. Vance vowed to stand by his refusal unless Confederate authorities could give him "further reasons" for widening the road.[63]

Even without Vance's approval, the Confederate authorities began widening the railroad east of Salisbury. The Tar Heel governor telegraphed Breckinridge in protest, requesting that work be halted "until the matter can be consulted upon."[64] Breckinridge answered that he had given instructions for a Confederate officer to explain the military necessity to Vance. The secretary of war also felt "compelled to take possession of some of the roads and increase the rolling stock to secure supplies." He promised to restore the old gauge "as soon as the emergency is over." At that point Vance backed down, stating that all he had wanted was an official explanation of why widening the gauge was necessary. "I do not wish to make unreasonable opposition to [a] change of gauge east of Salisbury," he replied to the secretary, "but have asked various officers for reasons for so doing & received none."[65]

Vance agreed more readily to General Johnston's request for supply wagons than he did to widening the railroad. On March 3, Johnston telegraphed the governor requesting "fifty additional good wagons and teams" to transport supplies "to make a prompt movement to meet" Sherman's advance "threatening your capital." Johnston asked that the wagons be "collected in the vicinity of Raleigh and Smithfield at [the] earliest possible movement [sic]."[66] Lee and Breckinridge had informed Johnston that the supplies at North Carolina depots were intended for the Army of Northern Virginia. Johnston, they said, must take his army's provisions from the countryside. But in order to get those provisions to his army, he needed additional wagons.[67] So he turned to Vance for help. Vance immediately responded that he could provide fifty, mostly two-horse, wagons, "if you will give authority to impress a few country waggons [sic] for post duty. [The] State has no authority to impress."[68] Using the wagons supplied by Vance, Johnston managed to feed his army.[69] But to one Confederate officer who helped himself to some of the state's wagons without asking first, Vance was not so accommodating or polite. "You have taken the liberty of impressing my wagons without my permission," he heatedly chastised the commandant at Fayetteville. "I send them back for State goods and notify you to keep your hands off them."[70]

As Union troops from New Bern advanced toward Goldsboro, they clashed with Bragg's force east of Kinston. Bragg, whose army included the commands of North Carolina generals Robert F. Hoke and Daniel H. Hill, intended to halt or at least slow the Federal advance to Goldsboro. In the subsequent Battle of Wise's Forks, the Confederates drove back the Federals but failed to turn their flanks. Schofield's reinforcements from Wilmington and New Bern turned the tide of the battle on March 10, and Bragg withdrew to Kinston and then to Goldsboro, where he awaited orders from Johnston.

In the meantime, Sherman was moving toward Fayetteville, which he reached on March 11. Johnston, waiting to determine whether Sherman would move toward Goldsboro or Raleigh, began concentrating his forces near Smithfield. At Averasboro on March 16, a portion of Johnston's force commanded by Gen. William J. Hardee engaged one wing of Sherman's army. Although the battle proved indecisive, it divided Sherman's army, giving Johnston an opportunity to strike while the Federals were most vulnerable. Johnston attacked at Bentonville, a small community west of Goldsboro. Initially, the Confederates gained the upper hand at the Battle of Bentonville, the largest land engagement to take place in North Carolina during the war. But Sherman managed to bring his entire army together on March 21 and drive off the Confederates. Johnston's army withdrew to Smithfield, and Sherman's men marched to Goldsboro, where they met Schofield's troops from Wilmington and New Bern. A repair of the rail line from New Bern soon brought needed supplies to the Union forces at Goldsboro.[71]

In anticipation of an advance on Raleigh by Sherman, Vance summoned his Council of State to advise him on the future course of action by the state government. When the council met on March 13, the members advised the governor to transfer department records and other "effects of the state" out of Raleigh. They stipulated "That the governor with such officers as attend him shall with said valuable effects retire to some point west of Raleigh their location to be selected by the governor and changed by him when necessary." The council stressed that it was essential for the governor and the state treasurer, Jonathan Worth, to "accompany said effects." If deemed essential by Vance, other officials could also evacuate to the west. Otherwise, "those officers who do not leave shall remain in their rooms . . . as they usually do in their daily business."[72] As the council recommended, Vance began transferring records and supplies to western depots on the North Carolina Railroad. To towns such as Graham, Greensboro, and Salisbury he moved "thousands of blankets, overcoats, uniforms, shoes, and boots, as well as medical supplies, tons of provisions, and a stockpile of arms and ammunition." He also transferred "state monies, stocks, securities," and state government records. Within a few weeks, there remained in the capital only "some commissary stores and essential daily records under the joint control" of North Carolina adjutant general Richard C. Gatlin and treasurer Jonathan Worth."[73]

On March 25, Sherman traveled from Goldsboro to City Point, Virginia, to discuss future operations with General Grant. After returning to North Carolina, he received word that Richmond had fallen on April 3 and that Lee was fleeing westward. Davis and his cabinet also were in flight from the Confederate capital. With Lee's and Johnston's armies remaining the final strategic objectives, Sherman began marching his troops to Raleigh in pursuit of Johnston.[74]

Prior to the fall of Richmond, Senator William A. Graham returned to North Carolina "thoroughly satisfied, that . . . Independence for the Southern Confederacy was perfectly hopeless." On March 20, he called on Governor Vance and emphasized that the "Military situation is by no means favorable; and I perceive no solution of our difficulties, except through the actions of the States." He suggested that Vance summon the legislature to consider separate peace negotiations. Vance listened to Graham but promised only to bring the matter before his Council of State. Because he had not heard from Vance about the opinion of the Council of State, Graham on April 6 "found the governor" on the train at Hillsborough, returning from Statesville, where Vance had moved his family to get it out of harm's way. The two men traveled on by train to Raleigh, where they dined together. Vance told Graham that the council was evenly divided on the question of calling the legislature into session to discuss a separate peace. But he added that one of North Carolina's Confederate congressmen, John A. Gilmer, had suggested a meeting with Sherman to discuss peace. Graham replied that Jefferson Davis "would probably complain of" such a conference and "should be apprized of it, if held." But Graham also suggested to Vance that "he should be in a position to act independently of the President." Vance expressed his reluctance to act without cooperating with Davis, but he agreed to consult the council a second time. Apparently Vance did not regret that the Council of State could not agree to call the legislature into session for peace discussions. Graham noted that "the result of the deliberations of the council was not disagreeable [to Vance]; but since the fall of Richmond he has a truer conception of the situation."[75] By this time, Grant's army had captured Richmond, and Jefferson Davis and his cabinet were fleeing southward into the Piedmont of North Carolina. Lee's troops would soon surrender at Appomattox. Even at that late hour, however, Graham misjudged Vance when he assumed that the governor might seriously entertain the idea of separate peace negotiations for North Carolina. Vance remained adamant that he wanted nothing to do with a state peace convention or any talks of reconciliation that did not involve the Confederate government.

On April 7, Vance—along with a number of young women, and Duncan K. McRae, editor of the pro-Davis Raleigh *Confederate*—boarded a train to Smithfield to review the troops of Johnston's army. With Johnston, the governor's party observed the corps of Gen. William J. Hardee. General Hoke's division gave three cheers for Vance. After a reception by Hardee, Vance addressed the North Carolina Junior Reserves Brigade, urging the boys "to fight till Hell freezes over." That evening the governor's party attended a cotillion and returned to Raleigh.[76] Vance had asked Graham to accompany him to the review before returning home to Hillsborough, but Graham declined, because, as he told David L. Swain, he could not see "any good to be accomplished there. Gen'l Johnston, I know, and appreciate him highly, but his Generals, I learn, at least many of them, [are] drunken men of desperate fortunes, who have no idea but to continue the war indefinitely."[77]

With the Confederacy's situation worsening by the hour, Swain resolved to try to convince Vance that it was in the best interest of North Carolina to negotiate for peace. He wrote to Graham suggesting that they go together to Raleigh to persuade the governor. Graham responded that since he had earlier attempted to convince Vance to seek a separate peace, it would serve no purpose for him to return to Raleigh. But he encouraged Swain to proceed and invited him to Hillsborough to discuss a plan for swaying Vance to their point of view. Swain reached Hillsborough on April 9, and he and Graham agreed that he should present to Vance a plan for peace that Graham had written down. The plan called for Vance to convene the legislature and have it pass a resolution calling for a conclusion to the war to discuss peace and inviting the other Confederate states to do likewise. The legislators would also elect commissioners to treat with the Federal government and report to a state convention to be called "to wield the sovereign power of the state in any emergency that may arise out of the changing state of events." If Sherman drew near to Raleigh, however, Vance should dispatch commissioners to the general to request that the Union troops suspend fighting until the governor could determine what further action the state would take regarding continuing the war. Swain arrived in the state capital on April 10 and presented the peace plan to the governor. But Vance again rejected a scheme for unilateral peace negotiations by North Carolina.[78]

Simultaneously with Swain's visit to Raleigh, General Johnston received word that Sherman would soon be advancing toward the capital city, and he gave orders to his corps commanders to begin moving. On April 11, Vance sent the following telegram to President Davis at Greensboro: "Please tell me what of General Lee. Much depends here on a correct knowledge of the situation. Answer tonight."[79] Davis did not respond to Vance's inquiry immediately.

Instead, Davis informed Johnston of unofficial reports that Lee had surrendered at Appomattox two days earlier and ordered Johnston to meet with him and his cabinet at Greensboro. Assigning temporary command of his troops to General Hardee, with orders to continue moving the army westward, Johnston boarded a midnight train for Greensboro, arriving there on the morning of April 12. Prior to leaving Raleigh for Greensboro, Johnston called on Vance to inform him that he was evacuating the city. Vance inquired if the general thought he should remain in Raleigh and negotiate with Sherman. Johnston advised the governor to make the best terms possible with the Union commander. Earlier that day, Kenneth Rayner and Bartholomew F. Moore, both Raleigh residents and former Whig politicians, convinced Swain not to leave Raleigh but to return to the Capitol and try again to persuade Vance to meet with Sherman in order to save the city. Rayner also discussed the surrender of Raleigh with the mayor, William H. Harrison, urging him to appoint a committee to oversee the proceedings.[80] Vance's reaction was to compose the following message for Sherman:

> His honor Mayor Wm. H. Harrison is authorized to surrender to you the City of Raleigh. I have the honor to request the extension of your favor to its defenseless inhabitants generally and especially to ask your protection for the charitable Institutions of the State located here filled as they are with unfortunate inmates, most of whose natural protectors would be unable to take care of them in the event of their destruction.
>
> The Capitol of the State with its Libraries, Museum and much of the public records is also left in your power. I can but entertain the hope that they escape mutilation or destruction in as much as such evidence of learning and taste could advantage neither party in the prosecution of the war whether destroyed or preserved.[81]

At the Greensboro conference, held on the afternoon of April 12 and the morning of the next day, Johnston advised Davis that the war was lost and that peace negotiations should be sought. General Beauregard, Secretary Breckinridge, and the other members of the Confederate cabinet, except Judah P. Benjamin, secretary of state, concurred with Johnston.[82] Davis, however, remained unpersuaded. But he agreed to the drafting of a letter to Sherman on Johnston's behalf, asking that the armies suspend their operations "to permit the civil authorities to enter into the needful arrangements to terminate the existing war." Davis, who wanted no part of capitulation, apparently was convinced that the letter would have no impact on Sherman. As historian William C. Davis has concluded, "Davis was trying to buy time, for a suspension of operations would mean no movement at all by the Yankee armies, thus stalling a junction between Grant and Sherman, and halting Union forces elsewhere in their tracks."[83] Having signed the letter and dispatched it to Sherman, Johnston left Greensboro on April 13 to rejoin his troops, then at Hillsborough.[84] On the same day, Davis finally responded to Vance's request for information on the fate of Lee's army:

I have no official report but scouts said to be reliable and whose statements were circumstantial and corroborative report the disaster as extreme. I have not heard from Genl Lee since sixth inst and have little or no hope from his army as an organized body. I expected to visit you at Raleigh but am accidentally prevented from executing that design and would be very glad to see you here if you can come at once [or] to meet you elsewhere in North Carolina at a future time. We must redouble our efforts to meet present disaster. An army holding its position with determination to fight on and manifest ability to maintain the struggle will attract all the scattered soldiers and daily and rapidly gather strength. Moral influence is wanting and I am sure you can do much now to revive spirit and hope of the people.[85]

Meanwhile, with Sherman's troops steadily approaching the gates of the capital city, Vance had summoned Graham to Raleigh. "This place will not be held longer than tomorrow," read the governor's urgent telegram of April 11.[86]

9

"ALL HELL CAN'T MAKE ME DO IT"

Senator Graham arrived at the Governor's Palace in Raleigh around dawn on April 12. He had departed Hillsborough by train at eleven o'clock the night before. At the executive residence he found Swain, Vance, and Col. James G. Burr of the governor's staff. After breakfast, the four men went to the Capitol. There, in response to the urging of Swain and Graham, Vance composed the following message to General Sherman:

> Understanding that your army is advancing on this capital, I have to request, under proper safe-conduct, a personal interview, in such time as may be agreeable to you, for the purpose of conferring upon the subject of a suspension of hostilities, with a view to further communications with the authorities of the United States, touching the final termination of the existing war. If you concur in the propriety of such a proceeding I shall be obliged by an early reply.[1]

According to Burr, the governor appeared despondent after signing the letter.[2]

Vance instructed Graham and Swain to deliver the missive to Sherman and ordered Burr and another aide, Maj. John Devereux, to accompany them. Surgeon General Edward Warren heard of the plan, and he soon arrived at the Capitol and asked permission to join the party. Having received General Hardee's permission, Swain and Graham, with their three-man escort, departed Raleigh by train in mid-morning. Vance told them to return to the city with a reply from Sherman by four o'clock in the afternoon.[3]

He then busied himself with affairs in his office. The governor told visitors who came to see him for advice to stay at their residences. He continued to sign dispatches and even to respond to his constituents' requests to use his influence in their behalf. For example, he sent a message to General Hardee protesting a Confederate officer's seizure of a horse belonging to Kemp P. Battle, president of the Chatham Railroad Company. Battle had "only two horses which are necessary to business," the governor informed Hardee, and "Our citizens have suffered enough in this way & I beg you to order that it shall not be carried further."[4]

A number of prominent local leaders—including Kenneth Rayner and Bartholomew Moore—arrived to give Vance advice about negotiating with the Federals. The pro-Davis editor Duncan K. McRae stormed into Vance's office to demand if rumors were true that he had dispatched Graham and Swain to arrange his surrender of North Carolina to Sherman. "Governor," he admonished Vance, "If you contemplate being engaged in such a transaction, before you enter on it you had better get some friends to take a grapevine and hang you by the neck until you are dead, for you will thereby avoid a great infamy." Vance calmly responded: "I have no thought of such a thing. . . . I mean to stand on Confederate soil as long as there is ground enough to pirouette on one toe, and under the Confederate flag while there is a rag left to flutter in the breeze."[5] General Hoke, whose division was camped just west of Raleigh, reportedly also visited the governor and asked if rumors were true that he intended to surrender the state. Vance answered: "All hell can't make me do it."[6]

Apparently McRae was not convinced of Vance's resolve to act only in concert with the Davis government, for he walked to the office of Col. Archer Anderson, chief of staff to General Johnston, and told him of the governor's plans to send a message to Sherman. Anderson immediately telegraphed President Davis and General Johnston in Greensboro informing them of Graham and Swain's mission and stating that he had notified Gen. Wade Hampton, commanding troops opposing Sherman's advance, not to allow Vance's commissioners to pass through Confederate lines until he heard from the president.[7]

Simultaneously, Vance explained to Davis the circumstances of his contact with Sherman: "A letter was sent by me to Sherman this morning requesting an interview. It was shown to General Hardee, and the subject-matter was mentioned to General Johnston yesterday. It is not my intention to do anything subversive of your prerogative without consultation with yourself." Davis responded: "I could not attribute to you such purposes as you disclaim, and your military experience and good judgement will render it unnecessary to explain why the commanding general cannot properly allow any intercourse with the enemy except under his authority and with his full knowledge and consent."[8]

A few miles southeast of Raleigh, Hampton halted the train with Graham and Swain aboard. The two commissioners showed him their pass from General Hardee and Vance's letter to Sherman. Hampton said that he did not approve of their mission but that he would abide by the orders of Hardee, his superior. He drafted a message to Sherman, asking for a meeting. He ordered a courier to deliver it, along with a note from Graham and Swain, to the Union commander. Hampton then stepped from the train and allowed it to proceed.

But soon one of Hampton's staff officers stopped the train again. He told Vance's commissioners that Hampton had received orders from General Johnston in Greensboro to halt their mission and send the train back to Raleigh. Graham and Swain refused to move until they talked again with Hampton himself. The general appeared and showed them a message that he had just dispatched to Sherman, telling him that Graham and Swain were returning to Raleigh. The train than began to back up. Within a short distance, however, Federal cavalry attacked the train, firing their weapons as they approached. "They piled down upon us like wild Indians," the young engineer later remembered. When Dr. Warren, who barely avoided a volley, waved a handkerchief as a flag of truce, the cavalrymen ceased fire and ordered the occupants of the train to disembark.[9]

The soldiers escorted their captives to the nearby headquarters of General Judson Kilpatrick. He informed his unwilling guests that Lee had surrendered. Although they had heard rumors to that effect, this was the first confirming evidence that they had received. After a brief detention, which included some humiliating remarks and gibes by the general and his soldiers, Kilpatrick returned the commissioners to the train and ordered it to travel on to Sherman's headquarters at Gulley's Station, near the present-day community of Clayton in Johnston County. As the train approached, Sherman and his staff were waiting, and darkness was falling. Sherman invited the North Carolinians to dinner and treated them with courtesy.[10]

Graham showed Vance's letter to the general and inquired if the governor might have permission to stay in office while the state was under occupation by the Union army. That arrangement evidently was agreeable to Sherman, who composed and sent a message to Vance. "I have the honor to acknowledge receipt of your communication of this date," he wrote, "and enclose you a safeguard for yourself and any members of the late Government that choose to remain in Raleigh. I would have gladly have enabled you to meet me here, but some interruption occurred to the train by General Johnston after it had passed within lines of my Cavalry advance, but as it came out of Raleigh in good faith it shall return in good faith, and will in no measure be claimed by us." The general stated that he doubted "if hostilities can be suspended as [*sic*] between [the] army of the Confederate Govt. and the one I command but I [will] aid you all in my power to contribute to the end you aim to reach, the termination of the existing war."[11]

In another dispatch to Vance the same evening, Sherman advised the governor that "If you conclude to remain in Raleigh you had better send some one out by train to me as quickly as possible, that I may make orders that will prevent any unnecessary confusion resulting from several heads of column, with necessary skirmishes coming in & through the City at the same time. As the Confederate Army is our only Enemy, I must take all possible precautions as you are aware that they do not recognize you as an agent to commit them."[12] According to historian Mark L. Bradley,

> By permitting Vance to remain in the capital, Sherman was repeating the experiment he had attempted the previous September, when he had invited Governor Joseph E. Brown of Georgia to meet him in Atlanta to discuss peace terms. Sherman had proposed to pay for his army's provisions and forage and cease his policy of destruction if Brown ordered the withdrawal of all Georgia troops from the Confederate army. Although Brown never responded, Sherman believed that the Georgia governor desired to cooperate but hesitated for fear of reprisal. Remembering Lincoln's enthusiastic response to the Brown peace overture, Sherman now felt free to act on his own judgment. He hoped to persuade Vance to do what Brown would not—withdraw his state's troops from the Confederate army.[13]

But Sherman never had the opportunity to discuss any terms with Vance, because when Graham and Swain failed to return in the late afternoon of April 12, the Tar Heel governor departed Raleigh. As the day wore on, Vance became increasingly anxious about his commissioners. He remained at his office awaiting word from them while Johnston's troops, under the command of Hardee, evacuated from and through Raleigh. During their movement, the residents of the state capital found the cavalry of Gen. Joseph Wheeler to be particularly rowdy and undisciplined and witnessed them pilfering and stealing from quartermaster stores and retail establishments. At the Capitol, Adjutant General Gatlin and Treasurer Worth packed up the remaining state records, which they accompanied out of town on the state's train, leaving at around nine p.m. Growing more worried about Graham and Swain, Vance first learned that they had been ordered back to Raleigh by General Johnston. Then in the early evening, word came that Kilpatrick's cavalry had captured the two commissioners. Thinking that their mission had thus failed, the governor decided to leave Raleigh.[14] Apparently, Sherman's dispatches to Vance had not reached him by the time he left the capital around midnight.

On the morning of April 13, Graham and Swain entered Raleigh. They sent word to General Wheeler, commanding the rear guard of the retreating Confederate army, that the capital city would be formally surrendered. Wheeler pledged to withdraw his troops quickly. As the vanguard of the Union cavalry drew near to the city, General Hampton sent an officer, under a flag of truce, to inform the advancing Federals that the Confederate army had evacuated Raleigh and the mayor wished to surrender the city. The U.S. cavalrymen moved only a short distance before they encountered the mayor and his delegation, who surrendered the capital and promised cooperation and no resistance. Harrison and his commissioners asked the Federals to safeguard the city residents and property, and Kilpatrick pledged to post guards where needed.[15]

Graham and Swain walked to the Capitol, and there they discovered that Vance had left for Hillsborough. He had stopped for the night at the camp of General Hoke, about eight miles west of Raleigh, and continued on to Hillsborough in the morning. Swain stood by at the Capitol while Graham started for Hillsborough in pursuit of Vance. But Graham was unable to procure transportation and returned to join Swain. When Sherman entered Raleigh, he reviewed his troops as they marched past the Capitol square, and then he established his headquarters at the Governor's Palace. Swain and Graham delivered to him the keys to the Capitol. Sherman provided them with letters of safe conduct that allowed them to return home. He also wrote out and entrusted to Graham and Swain a safe-conduct letter for Vance and any other government officials who wanted to return to Raleigh. On the morning of April 14, the two North Carolinians set out for Hillsborough, riding in a carriage supplied by the Union commander.[16]

On the way, they halted at General Hampton's headquarters, and then they continued on to Hillsborough. When one of the general's staff officers, Maj. W. J. Saunders, pointed out to Hampton that Graham might be carrying a note of safe passage to Vance from Sherman, Hampton ordered the officer to ride after the commissioners, seize the letter, and arrest Graham. But Saunders failed to overtake Graham and Swain before they reached Hillsborough, where Vance had stopped at Graham's house. The two commissioners confirmed for Vance that Lee had indeed surrendered and urged the governor to return to Raleigh to meet with Sherman. Vance, however, refused. Earlier, he had received a request from Davis to meet him in Greensboro, and he intended to keep that appointment. He would not, he said, return to Raleigh without first informing Davis and receiving a pass from General Johnston. When Major Saunders finally arrived at Graham's house, he asked Graham for Sherman's letter to Vance. Graham replied that he had already given it to Vance, but he did not reveal Vance's whereabouts (in a back room of the house). Saunders did not arrest Graham but instead rode on to Johnston's headquarters at Haw River, arriving early the next morning. Also on the morning of April 15, Vance left for Greensboro, and Swain departed for his home in Chapel Hill. Graham remained in Hillsborough.[17]

But Davis and his cabinet had left Greensboro before Vance's arrival. They traveled southwestward toward Salisbury on horseback with a cavalry escort. The party could not travel by rail because Federal cavalry under Gen. George Stoneman, attacking western North Carolina from Tennessee, had severed the track west of Greensboro. "President Davis left this afternoon on horseback for Salisbury," Beauregard telegraphed Vance on April 15. "He regretted not having seen you."[18] When Davis and his cabinet reached Lexington, a town between Greensboro and Salisbury, a telegram from Johnston was waiting for them. The general had returned to Greensboro, and he wanted a conference with Secretary of War Breckinridge to order to discuss the nature of his pending negotiations with Sherman. Davis agreed for Breckinridge to return to Greensboro to confer with Johnston, but he wanted Postmaster General John H. Reagan to accompany him. Believing that Johnston's letter to Sherman—approved by Davis—had produced encouraging possibilities for surrender terms, Breckinridge and Reagan started back to Greensboro, arriving on April 17. There they learned that Johnston had left for Hillsborough. Soon they received a telegram from him, saying that he was meeting with Sherman and would let Breckinridge know if his presence was needed at the talks.[19]

Johnston and Sherman met at the farmhouse of James Bennett, a short distance from Durham Station, near Hillsborough. At their meeting, Sherman informed Johnston that he had just received word that President Lincoln had been assassinated. Both men agreed to keep the news quiet for the time being, lest it excite Sherman's soldiers and hamper their negotiations. The two generals discussed terms for Johnston's surrender but adjourned before agreeing on definite provisions. The chief point of disagreement was Sherman's refusal to grant amnesty to President Davis and his cabi-

10. Union general William T. Sherman and Confederate general Joseph E. Johnston signed a final surrender agreement at the Bennett farmhouse near Durham in April 1865. North Carolina Office of Archives and History, Raleigh.

net. Meanwhile, as he awaited word from Johnston, Breckinridge met with Vance, who was still in Greensboro. Late in the afternoon, the secretary of war received a telegram from Johnston requesting him to come immediately to Hillsborough. Breckinridge invited Vance to accompany him and Reagan, remembering that Sherman had been willing to confer with the Tar Heel governor. Vance's presence might help the negotiations, the secretary believed. After midnight on April 18, the three men arrived at General Hampton's headquarters at the Alexander Dickson House, near Hillsborough, where Johnston awaited them.[20]

After a sumptuous late-night supper, General Hampton suddenly launched a venomous attack on Vance, accusing him of being a traitor because he had sent a letter to Sherman asking for a conference. None of the other men present defended Vance, and Johnston asked the governor to leave the room while those remaining discussed terms to present to the Union commander.[21]

Vance was taken aback by Hampton's attack. After all, the governor's April 12 message to Sherman merely called for a "personal interview" to confer about "a suspension of hostilities" while discussions about ending the war took place. Vance said nothing about agreeing to peace terms without the approval of the Davis government. Furthermore, only the dire situation at the eleventh hour of the war and the persistent pleading of Graham and Swain had led Vance reluctantly to approach Sherman. Later, Graham and Swain's pleas to him at Hillsborough to return to Raleigh and meet with Sherman were answered only by his refusal to return to the capital and his resolve to go on to Greensboro to confer with the president. It is perhaps worth noting that the April 12 letter that Davis and his cabinet had sent to Sherman, with Johnston's signature, contained virtually the same proposal as Vance's message—a suspension of hostilities to allow discussion of terms. If Jefferson Davis, as historian William C. Davis concludes, dispatched his request for talks with Sherman in order to buy time, it is possible that Vance contacted Sherman for the same reason.[22] A pause in hostilities might have given the governor time to find out whether Lee had indeed surrendered, and perhaps to meet with Davis about the situation. But as for the officers at the Dickson House, they shunned Vance because they were convinced that he had been willing to negotiate separately with Sherman.

Dejected by Hampton's attack and Johnston's dismissal at the Dickson house, Vance went out into the yard, where staff officers, including Major Saunders, lay curled under blankets. Vance lay down beside Saunders, a North Carolinian, and shared his blanket. After breakfast the following morning, Vance asked Saunders to take a walk with him. When they strolled beyond the house and yard, the governor, according to Saunders, suddenly and tearfully exclaimed: "I came here to explain that Sherman letter, and they wouldn't hear me. Me in communication with the enemy, me making terms for my State unknown to the authorities! Of all men, sir, I am the last man they can accuse of that infamy." Saunders recalled that "as I gazed on this strong man in his agony of the shame put upon him, I felt a bitterness of resentment, and for the first and only time, I, a soldier of the Confederacy, was untrue and disloyal to its colors."[23]

After the generals and cabinet officers reached an agreement on terms to present to Sherman, they retired for a short rest. Then Reagan began committing the provisions to paper. Before he finished, however, Johnston and Breckinridge were ready to ride to the Bennett farmhouse to meet with Sherman. Reagan promised to send the written terms on to them when the document was completed. Prior to departing, Breckinridge spoke privately to Vance, informing him of Lincoln's assassination and saying that General Johnston wanted him to remain in Hillsborough until the two returned. Vance then rode to Graham's house, where he waited for Johnston and Breckinridge to return.

Breckinridge and Johnston drew near the Bennett house and paused, then Johnston rode on alone. He asked Sherman if the Confederate secretary of war could join their discussion, since he had the authority of the Confederate government. Sherman at first refused, because the Federal government did not recognize the legitimacy of the Davis government and its officials. But Johnston pointed out that Breckinridge was also a Confederate general, and on that basis Sherman agreed to allow him to participate in the negotiations.[24]

Sherman, Johnston, and Breckinridge began their conversation, and soon Reagan's written document arrived by courier. Sherman found the terms contained in it to be too unspecific. After some discussion, Sherman drafted a proposal of his own. His terms were most generous, which surprised and pleased Breckinridge and Johnston. Sherman stipulated that an armistice would remain in effect while negotiations were ongoing. The Confederate armies would disband, and regiments would return to their states and there relinquish their arms to state arsenals. Soldiers would be paroled upon an oath not to take up arms again and acknowledgment of the authority of the state and Federal governments. As soon as the officials of the governments of the former Confederate states swore allegiance to the United States Constitution and government, the states would be returned to the Union. The Federal government would reestablish its courts in the South, and the people of the former Confederacy would have restored to them all their legal rights according to the state and Federal constitutions, as long as they remained peaceful. There was no mention of emancipation or the status of former slaves. Once all of these conditions were met, a universal amnesty would prevail. However, Sherman told Breckinridge privately that he doubted that the United States government would permit amnesty to apply to the high-ranking officials in the Confederacy. He urged them, and especially Davis, to flee the country if possible. Having agreed on the terms of surrender, Sherman and Breckinridge and Johnston now had to seek the approval of their respective superiors.[25]

Sherman returned to Raleigh and wrote to General Grant and Gen. Henry W. Halleck, army chief of staff in Washington, explaining the terms agreed upon at the Bennett farm. He urged quick approval of the agreement, stressing the importance of disbanding the Confederate army.[26]

Johnston and Breckinridge returned to the Dickson house. The secretary of war sent a telegram to Beauregard in Greensboro with a message to be forwarded to Davis, who was en route to Charlotte. He instructed Beauregard to have a train waiting in Greensboro to take him south to join Davis. After a late dinner, Breckinridge, Johnston, and Reagan boarded a train for Greensboro. They waited at the Hillsborough depot for Vance to join them, as they intended to discuss with him the terms of the agreement with Sherman. But apparently a misunderstanding about the time and place that Vance was to meet them resulted in the governor's missing the rendezvous. Thomas Webb, president of the North Carolina Railroad, was aboard the train and ordered the engineer to blow the whistle several times to summon Vance, who evidently believed that the party would send someone to notify him of the departure. When the governor did not appear at the depot, the train left for Greensboro without him.[27] Discovering that he had been left behind, an angry Vance fired off a wire to Webb to send a train to Hillsborough to take him to Greensboro. A testy Webb responded that he had not sent someone to fetch Vance to the train because "I had no one to send after you. I had the whistle sounded again and again and waited for more than three quarters of an hour and you would not come. You ought to have stayed where you were at the Depot. An Engine will start for you at twelve 12 [sic] oclock. Go to the Depot & be ready to come back immed[iatel]y."[28]

Vance arrived in Greensboro on April 19. He was still smarting from the rebuff that he had received at Hampton's headquarters, and he was convinced that his being left behind at Hillsborough was yet another attempt to exclude him from any negotiations or policy involving termination of the war. He immediately dashed off a sarcastic letter to Johnston expressing his resentment at being left out and requesting permission to contact Sherman directly for the purpose of relieving North Carolinians who were suffering the ravages of war. "Being totally uninformed," he said to Johnston,

> of the condition of affairs in this State and being unable to obtain from any one a statement of what is going on or what the Government of the Confederate States intends to do, I respectfully request permission to send by flag of truce a letter to Genl Sherman . . . which shall be submitted to your perusal.
>
> I am induced to take this course for the occasion that the people of my State are now suffering all the horrors of rapine and anarchy and I feel it my duty, in the absence of other authority on whom it might more properly devolve to use my best exertions to protect them.[29]

Johnston responded with an explanation that Vance was not left behind at Hillsborough intentionally, and that the governor was welcome to view the agreement with Sherman at any time. "It was expected by the secretary of War & myself that you would join us at Hillsboro' last night," he told Vance, "[w]hen we intended to show you the agreement entered into with General Sherman. Your letter informs me of your arrival in Greensboro, the bearer says, three hours ago. You can not, therefore, I think, regard me as negligent in not having communicated with you on the subject. I need not remind you that I was not one of those to whom you applied for the information you desire. Had you done so, be assured that every thing concerning North Carolina that I know would have been communicated to you." Johnston said nothing about giving the governor permission to communicate with Sherman.[30]

Still miffed by the treatment that he had received from the Confederate officers, Vance would not let the matter drop. Not only did he feel personally insulted, but he maintained that because North Carolina was bearing the brunt of the war's end, the state's chief executive was entitled to be privy to events affecting its people. He fired back at Johnston that

> The reason why I did not find you last night at Hillsboro was that the President of the Rail Rd. & Genl Breckinridge both agreed to send for me when the train arrived there, it being uncertain at what time it would leave Genl Hampton's Hd Qrs. As it was I waited at the Depot from 4 o'clock the time designated by you until Eight P.M. In this business I make no complaint of you.
>
> Night before last I was invited by Genl Breckinridge to go down to where you were to participate in the consultation there to take place and as I supposed & deserved to accompany the flag of truce to a conference with Genl Sherman, thinking very naturally that I was entitled to know something of and participate in proceedings which arise more immediately to affect my people than those of any other State in the Confederacy.
>
> You cannot be ignorant of the part which I was invited to take at Genl Hampton's Hd. Qrs. Feeling therefore that I was to be excluded from a voice in the decision of the fate of my own people, I thought I could reasonably expect to be informed of the conclusion arrived at by others and make such provision as remained in my power for the welfare of the State. Such was the object of my note this morning.

Vance went on to remind Johnston that he had not answered his request to talk directly with Sherman. "I shall be glad to be informed on this point," he declared.[31]

Johnston answered again by sending Vance a copy of the surrender agreement. He felt that, after reading the terms, the governor would not wish to contact Sherman. But if he did, Johnston would "refer the subject by telegraph to the Secretary of War." Johnston defended his part in Vance's exclusion and made a small attempt to soothe the governor's injured feelings. "I do not think," the general wrote, "that the omissions of Genl. Breckinridge & Mr. Webb ought to be laid at my door. As a mere military officer arranging an armistice, I do not think that it would have been proper on my part, to invite any civilian to join in the conference. Had I been determining the terms on which negotiations were to be based, there is no gentleman whose aid I would have sought sooner than yours. But I had nothing to do but to learn the views of the president, & they were not fully communicated until after my meeting with Sherman."[32]

At Greensboro, Vance attempted to establish a temporary state capital. The state archives and funds from the state treasury and banks had reached Company Shops (present-day Burlington), between Raleigh and Greensboro. As soldiers from Johnston's Army of Tennessee began plundering North Carolina supplies along the westward route from Haw River to Salisbury, Vance hurled a series of heated messages at Johnston, protesting the stealing of supplies that the governor wanted to go first to North Carolina troops. "I respectfully request that you forbid this and place a guard around them to prevent pillage," he wrote Johnston about Greensboro supplies on April 16. Furthermore, "My stores in Raleigh to the amount of nearly 10,000 suits were freely given this army, my stores of leather blankets &c at Graham were pillaged and I confess I am getting tired of it."[33]

When Johnston asked for specific details about the items pilfered by his soldiers, Vance submitted the following report:

> Maj James Sloan Chief Qr. Master of this post [Greensboro] reports that he had on hand on arrival of the troops at this place, two hundred & forty-three (243) Bales of Blankets, cloth and ready made clothing, averaging respectively, (100) Blankets and 500 yards of cloth to the bale and also (4000) pairs of pants, (600) jackets and a small quantity of leather. Of this amount there was issued to the troops 16,028 yds. Cloth, 4458 pairs pants, 2000 pairs of socks, 1143 jackets. Nearly all the remainder, certainly much over half of the whole was violently seized or issued miscellaneously under the threats of the mob to avoid seizure. At the same time the books, papers and private property of the Qr. Masters were stolen & destroyed. A small quantity of blankets and home made cloth yet remains on hand.
>
> Capt. Oliver, Qr Master at Graham N.C. reports that he delivered

under pressure of the mob of soldiers 6300 pairs of pants 7000 lbs. Leather, 21 bales of Blankets (100 to the bale) ten coils of Rope & 2000 yds. of Jeans cloth. There was actually taken by the mob 5000 lbs leather, & 3000 yd. Cloth, in which the citizens participated. In addition to these statements of my Qr Masters, I myself saw the conclusion of the sacking of a train at M[c]leans station [present-day McLeansville] yesterday morning by soldiers laden with blankets and leather. The cars had just been emptied as I got there and the road side & the woods were crowded with soldiers staggering under heavy loads of plunder. It seemed to be an understood & permitted matter as officers of nearly all grades were standing quietly around.

Vance reminded Johnston that, from the beginning of the war, North Carolina had been responsible for equipping its own soldiers. Therefore, he maintained, it was only just that North Carolina troops be supplied first from the state's coffers. In addition, Vance asserted, neither the Confederate government nor the other Southern states would reimburse North Carolina for the supplies it had purchased in Europe. "North Carolina has done five times over more than any other State for the clothing of the Confederate army," the governor claimed. "I think I can appeal the more strongly to you to protect her against plunder and pillage." But he assured the general that he did not hold him personally responsible for the "most complete and outrageous robbery of private citizens" being committed by Confederate soldiers. "When all of this is considered," he concluded, "I am sure you will pardon me for urging upon you, the adoption of [the] most stringent measures in your power for the protection of my State and people against the lawless license of an army about to be disbanded."[34]

When Capt. Thomas White, quartermaster at Salisbury, complained to the governor that Johnston's troops seized some of the state's bacon at that town, Vance ordered him: "Do not give up your stores to any one. Tell Genl. Johnston that I forbid his touching my property without my consent."[35] He also complained to Johnston, who ordered his officers to return the bacon.[36]

As partial payment for the North Carolina supplies appropriated by Johnston's troops, Vance asked the general to turn over to the state at the war's end all of the Confederate property in North Carolina.[37] Johnston responded that "I will readily do all I can to secure to North Carolina the sum due her from the Confederate government. But the course you propose seems to me impracticable." He pointed out to the governor that other states could make similar claims about property impressed by the army. He intended, "as far as practicable," to return impressed property "to its proper owners." Of course, "a very large portion of it was obtained in this State, & I shall confidently ask your excellency's assistance in its restoration."[38] Vance also appealed to Breckinridge for reimbursement. He wrote to the secretary of war that "Recently the entire Army of Tennessee has not only been supplied with Clothing by issues, but large amounts have also been taken violently. As there remains no one to whom we can look for payment in the future, and it bears peculiarly hard upon North Carolina, to be compelled alone to pay for the debts in Europe contracted for the purchase of most of these articles which have inured to the common benefit of the States, I am exceedingly anxious to know if some arrangements cannot be made by which in part the state may be indemnified." He suggested that, because North Carolina had borrowed $700,000 in Europe on cotton and rosin warrants to purchase army supplies, the Confederacy turn over to the state enough cotton to redeem the warrants.[39]

Johnston denied Vance's claims that his army was chiefly responsible for plundering North Carolina supplies. He maintained that when the mob of soldiers raided the Greensboro warehouse, his men had not yet reached that city. He insisted that the only troops in town at the time "were N. Carolina reserves, placed there by Lieut. Genl. [Theophilus H.] Holmes" and soldiers disbanded from Lee's army in Virginia. He acknowledged that "great outrages are committed on your people by Confederate soldiers. . . . But they are the disbanded men of the Army of Northn Va. I regret this as much as you do, but can not, with my little force prevent it. Indeed this army has probably suffered as much, proportionally, as the people of the State, for crowds of these disbanded soldiers seize our subsistence stores wherever they find them."[40]

Vance became concerned about the state archives and funds of the state treasury and banks that were aboard railroad cars at Company Shops. Treasurer Jonathan Worth, who was in charge of the records and money, informed Vance upon the governor's return to Greensboro from Hillsborough on April 19 that he was most concerned that soldiers would raid the cars. Worth asked if Vance could obtain a pass for him to return through Federal lines back to Raleigh, where the treasury and archives could be restored to the safety of the Capitol.[41] Vance immediately contacted Johnston, asking for his permission to remove Worth's cars back to Raleigh and out of harm's way. He stressed that Johnston's troops had "forcibly seized all the property belonging to the state at Haw River" and now threatened to sack the cars containing state records and money.[42]

Johnston answered that "if application had been made, a special guard . . . would have been furnished. I order it now by telegraph." If Vance should find that a guard was "insufficient, I shall be unable to oppose your proposition" to return the records and funds to Raleigh.[43] For the time being, the state archives and treasury under Worth's care remained under guard at Company Shops.

While Vance fussed with Johnston over the loss of state supplies and property, Jefferson Davis and his entourage reached Charlotte, arriving on April 19.[44] After many delays en route, Breckinridge and Reagan finally arrived in the Queen City early in the morning of April 22. They presented the Sherman-Johnston agreement to the president. Davis sought the opinion of his cabinet. All of its members, including Judah P. Benjamin this time, urged him to accept the terms. The president, however, clung to the hope that the Confederate government could escape to the Trans-Mississippi region and fight on for independence. He remembered Vance as an ally who, despite their disagreements, had demonstrated repeatedly his loyalty to the Confederate cause.[45] Therefore, he summoned the governor to come to Charlotte for consultation about the future course of the Confederacy. "I had hoped to see you before this date," he wired the governor on April 23, the same day he met with his cabinet. "Is it convenient for you to come here at this time[?] I desire to confer with you as heretofore expressed."[46] Vance arrived in Charlotte on or about April 25.[47] He found the president "still full of hope." Davis began talking of a plan to join Gen. Edmund Kirby Smith in the Trans-Mississippi, and he wanted Vance and the remaining North Carolina troops to accompany him.[48]

Davis's cabinet was taken aback that the president was once again considering preserving the Confederacy. Like the cabinet, Vance, too, by this time was convinced that the Confederate States of America was doomed, and at first he did not know how to respond to Davis's proposal. But then Breckinridge spoke up, saying that "he did not think they were dealing candidly with Governor Vance." He told the president that his Trans-Mississippi scheme for survival of the Confederacy had no real chance for success, and that Vance should return to his duties as chief executive of North Carolina. Apparently Davis reluctantly agreed. Vance later recalled his own response: "I remarked that General Breckinridge's views coincided with my own sense of duty, and after a very little conversation I arose and offered my hand to President Davis to bid him good-bye. He shook it long and warmly, saying: 'God bless you sir, and the noble old State of North Carolina.' I thus bade farewell to the Southern Confederacy and returned to Greensboro, with the intention of going to Raleigh and resuming my duties as Governor if permitted."[49]

Although still hoping for some sort of miracle for the survival of his government, and doubtful that Washington would endorse the Sherman-Johnston pact, Davis instructed Johnston to accept Sherman's terms. But on the same day, April 24, Sherman received word at Raleigh that Federal authorities had rejected the proposed surrender agreement. Sherman was authorized to offer only the same terms allowed by Grant at Lee's surrender at Appomattox. On that evening, Johnston wired Davis that Washington had refused the Sherman-Johnston terms, and that the Confederate government had forty-eight hours to decide whether to accept the same terms as Lee's before the cease-fire concluded.[50] Johnston also informed Vance, who had returned to Greensboro, of the Federals' decision.[51]

Davis responded to Washington's rejection of the surrender terms by commanding Johnston to begin moving his army southward. The president renewed his scheme to reestablish his government in the Trans-Mississippi. Johnston gave orders for his troops to be ready to move one hour before the cease-fire ended, at noon on April 26. But the general had no intention of setting his men on the march. On April 25, he sent a message to Sherman requesting that they meet again to discuss surrender terms. Johnston notified Breckinridge of his plan but did not inform Davis. Agreeing with Johnston's overture to Sherman, the secretary of war did not tell the president what was about to transpire. With the cease-fire close to an end, Davis and his cabinet and cavalry escort began moving south into South Carolina and Georgia. Federal soldiers would ultimately capture the Confederate president near Irwinville in southern Georgia on May 10, 1865.[52]

On April 26, Johnston and Sherman met again at the Bennett farm. After some discussion, Johnston agreed to the same basic terms as in Lee's surrender, with some supplements approved by Washington authorities. For all practical purposes, Johnston's surrender at the Bennett house embraced the bulk of the Confederate army and ended the war, although some Confederate units in the Southwest, the Trans-Mississippi, and the Indian Territory did not surrender until May and June.[53]

Upon his return to Greensboro, Vance immediately took up the business of operating the state in the aftermath of war. To the extent that he still had power or influence, he made a conscientious effort to avoid a breakdown of law and order and to return the state to as near normalcy as possible. On April 27, he asked Sherman to allow Worth to return the state records to Raleigh.[54] On the same day, he also requested an interview with the Union general. Vance explained that the pass that Sherman had issued him on April 12 for a meeting was probably no longer valid. "I shall therefore be obliged to you," he continued, "if you will either renew the safe conduct or grant me an interview under a Flag of Truce, at as early a day as practicable. The objects to be obtained can be more fully set forth when we meet; but I will intimate that they refer most particularly to the immediate arriving of the Legislature of the State & the adoption of prompt measures to save the people from a condition of anarchy which now threatens them." Apparently, Vance was hoping that Federal authorities would allow the state legislature to convene and civil rule to be restored in the state.[55]

Worth wired the governor from Raleigh on April 28, notifying him that Sherman had left North Carolina and that Gen. John M. Schofield was now in command. "General Schofield declined the interview you solicit here," telegraphed Worth, "but says you can see him in a few days in Greensboro. He directs me to bring here the state records."[56] Denied a return to Raleigh, Vance issued from Greensboro the following proclamation to the people of North Carolina:

Whereas, by the recent surrender of the principal armies of the Confederate States, further resistance to the forces of the United States has become vain, and would result in a useless waste of blood, and whereas, all the natural disorders, attendant upon the disbanding of large armies are upon us, and the country is filled with numerous bands of citizens and soldiers disposed to do violence to persons and property:

Now therefore, I, Zebulon B. Vance, Governor of the State of North Carolina, in the sincere hope of averting some of the many evils which threaten us, do issue this my Proclamation, commanding all such persons to abstain from any and all acts of lawlessness, to avoid assembling together in crowds in all towns and cities, or doing anything whatsoever calculated to cause excitement; and earnestly appealing to all good citizens, who are now at home, to remain there, and to all soldiers of this State to retire quietly to their homes, and exert themselves in preserving order. Should it become necessary for the protection of citizens, I also appeal to the good and true soldiers of North Carolina, whether they have been surrendered and paroled or otherwise, to unite themselves together in sufficient numbers in the various counties of the State, under the superintendence of the civil magistrates thereof, to arrest or slay any bodies of lawless and unauthorized men who may be committing depredations upon the persons or property of peaceable citizens, assuring them that it will be no violation of their paroles to do so. And I would assure my fellow citizens generally, that, under God, I will do all that may be in my power to settle the government of the State, to restore the civil authority in her borders, and to further the great ends of peace, domestic tranquility and the general welfare of the people. Without their aid I am powerless to do anything.[57]

To facilitate the movement of displaced people and relief supplies, the governor asked Schofield to allow the trains that had accumulated at Greensboro to resume operations.[58]

Vance also summoned William A. Graham to Greensboro. After a consultation with him, he asked Graham, John A. Gilmer, and Caswell County politician and former Unionist and senator Bedford Brown to form a commission to visit Washington and confer with President Andrew Johnson, "relative to superseding the State Gov't[,] garrisoning the country with troops, test oaths, etc." Brown declined to serve on the commission, but Graham and Gilmer were prepared to journey to Washington to meet with Johnson.[59]

On May 2, General Schofield and his subordinate Gen. Jacob D. Cox, whose corps would occupy the Greensboro area, arrived in Greensboro to oversee the final surrender and disbanding of Johnston's army. That evening they went to Blandwood, the home of former governor John M. Morehead, to spend the night. Vance was waiting for them there. Schofield told the governor that the United States government did not recognize him and other state officials as legitimate authorities. He further told Vance that sending his commissioners—Graham and Gilmer—to the Federal capital would have to be approved by President Johnson. A telegram from Washington quickly announced the president's rejection of meeting with the North Carolina representatives. Vance beseeched Schofield to ensure the protection of North Carolina's people and property. He offered his surrender to Schofield, who replied that, because he had no orders to detain Vance, the governor was free to leave. Vance then departed for Statesville, where his wife and four sons awaited him.[60]

Vance was having dinner with his family at their house in Statesville on May 13 when a detachment of Union cavalry, under the command of Maj. John M. Porter, rode into the yard. It was the governor's thirty-fifth birthday, and Secretary of War Edwin M. Stanton had ordered his arrest. Porter agreed that Vance could surrender to his detachment on the following morning, to begin a journey to his ultimate destination of Washington, D.C. For transportation to the railroad depot in Salisbury, a local Jewish citizen, Samuel Wittkowsky, volunteered to drive Vance in his own carriage. They started about nine o'clock in the morning, with the cavalrymen surrounding the carriage. Before reaching the edge of Statesville, Vance suddenly broke down and began to weep. He composed himself, and wiping his eyes, he turned to Wittkowsky and said: "This will not do; I must not allow my feelings to unman me, but it is so hard to bear. I am not so much concerned about what may be in store for me, but my poor wife and little children—they have not a cent of money to live on. And then poor old North Carolina. God knows what indignities she may yet be subjected to." He consoled himself that his honor was intact because he had not profited personally from the war, as he might have done through the state's blockade-running activity. By the time the party halted for lunch, Vance had recovered his spirits and joked with the Union officers.

Porter permitted Vance to ride for a while on horseback to break the monotony. About two miles from Salisbury, the detachment halted, and Porter allowed Vance to enter the town without a cavalry escort. The governor spent the night in Salisbury, where he visited with friends and, having no money, borrowed sixty-five dollars. "The next morning I went to the depot to bid him good bye," recalled Wittkowsky, "and found him surrounded by quite a number of Federal officers, all as jolly as if the governor and they had been old friends, starting on a pleasure trip."[61] When Vance's train stopped in Raleigh, he visited with his friend Kemp P. Battle and managed to borrow an additional forty dollars.[62] En route to Washington, he was accompanied by David L. Swain, whom President Johnson had summoned to the capital to consult on Reconstruction policy.[63]

Vance arrived at Washington's Old Capitol Prison on May 20, where he shared a cell with Virginia governor John Letcher. Their cell was located on the first floor of the facility, and each man had a bed and a chair. They had to pay for their meals. The superintendent later recalled that he occasionally supplied the governors with whiskey and brandy.[64] Vance also had the company of Governor Brown of Georgia. "I am glad to hear you have Gov. Brown as a companion," Hattie wrote him on June 5. "I trust you will be a mutual benefit to one another in a spiritual as well as a temporal point of view." She was pleased to learn that "you have all necessary comforts & are able to exercise on account of your health."[65] News soon reached her that her husband had received daily paroles, on which he was "allowed the privileges of the city." She hoped the news was true, "tho' I don't permit it to influence me too much, fearing it may not be so," she lamented.[66] At the end of June, Vance wrote to his wife that he had applied for a pardon and "was still quite well" and "anxious to return to you as soon as possible."[67] Since his imprisonment, Hattie, who frequently suffered from bad health, had become severely ill.

On June 3, 1865, Vance submitted his petition for a pardon to President Andrew Johnson. He stated in 1,200 words that he had been devoted to the Federal Union prior to the war. Only Lincoln's call for troops in 1861 had swayed him to back Confederate independence. He supported the Confederacy because he wanted to defend his state against invasion and to prevent the abolition of slavery, which would bring on social chaos. Now that the war was over, he accepted "the actual condition of affairs" and would offer "no further resistance whatever to the authority of the United States." Vance acknowledged the restoration of the Union and the abolition of slavery and would willingly swear the president's amnesty oath. He desired to return home to care for his wife and four children, who were "living upon the charity of personal friends." He also wanted to "assist an almost ruined people in the restoration of law, and assume all the duties of a quiet and law abiding American citizen." A number of persons supported Vance's application for a pardon, but William W. Holden, who had been appointed provisional governor of North Carolina by President Johnson, refused to endorse it. Apparently Secretary of War Edwin M. Stanton also opposed a pardon. He is said to have denounced Vance as "the worst of the whole batch" of Confederate governors.[68]

On July 6, 1865, Vance was released from the Old Capitol Prison and paroled to remain in Statesville. "So I am here, a prisoner still," he wrote to a friend. "Mrs. Vance during my confinement was seized with hemorrhage of the lungs and came near dying. She is now, however, after much suffering, mental and bodily, restored to her usual health. We are living very poorly and quietly, as I can do no business until I am pardoned or released from my parole."[69] While on parole, Vance requested an interview with President Johnson. His request was denied, although the privilege had been granted to Governor Brown of Georgia and Governor Letcher of Virginia. Vance blamed Holden for the president's refusal to see him.[70] As the former war governor awaited "release from my bonds" or a pardon at Statesville, he faced an uncertain future, and Federal Reconstruction got under way in the Tar Heel State.

EPILOGUE

"To the Last Gasp with Truth and Loyalty"

As Vance contemplated his future, he toyed with the idea of leaving North Carolina for Australia or New Zealand, where an old Asheville friend, John Evans Brown, had established himself as a sheep rancher, miner, businessman, and minister of education. But the former governor decided that a return to the practice of law was the best plan for his future. He considered establishing a practice in Baltimore or Wilmington. In February 1866 he fell victim to a mild stroke, which partially paralyzed him for a brief period. Upon his recovery, he established a law firm in Charlotte with a junior partner, Clement Dowd, who served in Vance's regiment during the war and would compile his biography in 1897.[1]

Vance longed for a return to politics during Presidential Reconstruction, but without a pardon from the president, he had to remain content with his law practice and other public activities, including speaking out against Republican Reconstruction policies. He assisted Cornelia Phillips Spencer in the preparation of her book *The Last Ninety Days of the War in North Carolina* (1866), which was in large part a defense of Vance's performance as governor during the conflict. In 1866 he delivered the commencement address at the University of North Carolina in Chapel Hill. Directed at only three graduates but a sizable crowd of visitors, the speech, titled "The Duties of Defeat," called upon North Carolinians to dismiss bitter feelings about the war, accept their situation, and begin to rebuild the state.[2]

In a speech to the Young Men of Raleigh in January 1867—about two months before he finally received a pardon—he denounced Republican Reconstruction and equality for the freedmen. He declared that the former slaves were not equipped for economic, social, or political equality. In fact, "the emancipation of the negro has made his condition worse" than it had been under slavery. But the South had to face the reality of an end to slavery and make the most of it. Perhaps, Vance noted, "The abolition of slavery will do wonders here" by putting "an end to the reign of those lordly, landed proprietors, planters and farmers who constituted so striking and so pleasant a feature in our rural population. . . . Agriculture will then pass gradually into the hands of small farmers, and the great farms will, forever, disappear." He personally, however, would regret to see such a change in Southern society: "Peace to the memory of the southern country gentlemen! To them were we indebted for the foundations of our once free government, and for its preservation against the assaults of democratic anarchy for more than three-fourths of a century."[3]

During Congressional Reconstruction, which followed the Reconstruction Acts of 1867, Vance—who then held no political office—worked to bolster the efforts of the Conservatives (eventually called Democrats) to wrest power from the Republicans. Their tactics included using the Ku Klux Klan, a violent arm of the Conservative Party. Vance urged retaliation against Republican governor William W. Holden for his attempts to suppress the Klan's violent campaign to prevent black voters and their white Republican allies from going to the polls. When Holden permitted his militia commander, Col. George W. Kirk, to arrest and hold suspected Klansmen without trial, Vance called for the state courts to issue bench warrants for the arrest of Holden and Kirk for violating the habeas corpus act. Vance hoped to remove Holden from office and thereby give complete control of state government to the Conservatives. "I have little or no doubt now that we have carried the state & the legislature," he wrote William A. Graham on August 6, 1870, from Charlotte. "Much depends on our using our victory wisely. I will start all the papers in this section after Holden."[4] To Vance's delight, Holden, his old nemesis from the gubernatorial campaign of 1864, was impeached, convicted, and removed from office by the Conservative legislature in 1871.

Prior to Holden's removal, Vance won election to the U.S. Senate. But Congress, invoking the authority given it by the Fourteenth Amendment, refused to admit him. A division in North Carolina's Democratic ranks in 1872 denied him a second nomination to the national Senate. Vance then launched a career as a public speaker, delivering his orations throughout the eastern United States. His most popular public lecture was "The Scattered Nation," in which he outlined the biblical history of the Jewish people and called for an end to the anti-Semitism prevalent in late-nineteenth-century America. One theory holds that Vance's defense of the Jews and their history stemmed at least partly from his friendship with Samuel Wittkowsky—the man who had provided him with transportation by buggy when he was arrested shortly after the war—and other Jewish merchants of Statesville.[5] "The Jews are our spiritual fathers," proclaimed Vance, "the authors of our morals, the founders of our civilization, with all the power and dominion arising therefrom, and the great peoples professing Christianity and imbued with any of its noble spirit should see to it that justice and protection are afforded them."[6]

Among Vance's other popular public lectures was the one that he delivered to the Southern Historical Society in White Sulphur Springs, West Virginia, in 1875. In that speech he defended both his support for the war and the cause of an independent Confederate States of America. The Tar Heel State, he claimed, had contributed more troops than any other Southern state. He had successfully managed the state's blockade-running to keep North Carolina troops well supplied. In that regard, he had been much more effective than the Confederate government. Any failure of the Confederacy to win its independence rested not with him and North Carolina but with the central government in Richmond. Vance maintained that unpopular Confederate laws and policies—such as conscription and tax-in-kind—never really had the support of the ordinary people of the South.[7] This speech may have been the first time that Vance alluded publicly to ordinary Carolinians' lack of support for the Confederate cause. As noted in chapter 8, however, he had stated privately to his mentor David L. Swain in September 1864 that he had "always believed that the great *popular heart* is not now & never has been in this war! It was a revolution of the *politicians* not *the people*."[8]

Vance's war record became a major campaign issue in 1876 when he ran for Tar Heel governor against Republican Thomas Settle Jr., a state supreme court justice. In a bitter campaign that included debates throughout the state, Settle charged Vance with bringing devastation and ruin on North Carolina through his undying support for the Confederate war effort. He also accused Vance of personally profiting from blockade-running, of approving violence against Unionists and deserters and their families, and of squandering the state treasury by investing in Confederate bonds.

As Vance defended his role as war governor against Settle's accusations, he resorted to his customary public portrayal of himself as both a loyal

Confederate and a protector of states' rights and individual liberty. True, he had cooperated with the War Department in the effort to round up deserters and to enforce the conscription laws. But in doing so, he had prevented a larger involvement of the Confederate government in the state. He also had been obeying the law of the land and performing his duty. He never denied that he had been loyal to the Confederacy, but he implied that his support for the Davis government was rendered to preserve and protect the interests of North Carolinians. Vance attempted to discredit Settle by painting him with the brush of secessionism, despite the justice's record as a Unionist and a postwar Republican. He also accused Settle, as a circuit court judge during the war, of failing to prosecute those inhabitants who violently attacked the families of deserters in Randolph County. He capped off his denunciation of Settle by labeling him a deserter for resigning his commission in a Confederate regiment in 1862.[9]

Vance's dual approach in campaign rhetoric, combined with his oratorical skill, paid off for him again, just as it had in the election of 1864. He further improved his chances of winning the 1876 election by appealing to the racism of white voters. He portrayed himself as the "candidate of the white people of the state." The Democratic Party assisted by having large groups of mounted white men present at the debates to intimidate white Republicans and African Americans. The Democrats also successfully created a "racial disturbance" in Raleigh on the eve of the election. According to historian Gordon B. McKinney, "While Vance did not direct any of these activities, he endorsed their use as a general principle."[10] Nevertheless, there was enough public dissatisfaction with Vance to result in a close election. Vance's margin of victory was only 13,928 of 233,278 votes cast. The Democrats also carried the state in the vote for legislators, congressmen, and president, thereby ending Republican Reconstruction.[11]

Compared to his Civil War governorship, Vance's postwar years in the state capital were relatively uneventful and unimpressive. He lent his support to the completion of railroads and public projects and the use of convict labor. During his administration, the legislature established an insane asylum for whites in the east and one for blacks in the west. The state also created two normal schools—one for whites at Chapel Hill and one for blacks at Fayetteville. Vance did not serve his full four-year term as governor, because the state legislature voted him into the U.S. Senate in 1878 when the incumbent senator, Augustus S. Merrimon, declined to stand for reelection. Merrimon had won the Senate seat in 1872, when the Democrats had divided over Vance's nomination. Before Vance took office in

Washington in early 1879, however, tragedy struck when both his mother and his wife, Hattie, died, in October and November 1878, respectively. Vance married again in 1880. His new bride was Florence Steele Martin, a native of St. Louis, a Washington socialite, and a Catholic. He was reelected to the Senate in 1884 and served for another decade.[12]

Vance's career in the Senate was not distinguished. He supported the "redeemers" and white supremacy in the South and opposed the internal revenue system and reform of the federal civil service system. He became a leading spokesman for tariff reforms that would benefit farmers. His opposition to the repeal of the Sherman Silver Purchase Act won him popularity with the Farmers' Alliance in the 1890s. Vance also proved to be an effective and entertaining advocate for Democratic candidates and legislation in North Carolina. Large crowds gathered to hear him speak. On the eve of the 1882 election, for example, he traveled to distant Pamlico County to promote the state Democrats' prohibition platform, to endorse their regressive county government plan, and to discredit the federal tariff and internal revenue system as self-serving and corrupt devices of the Republican Party. The *Pamlico Enterprise* of October 20, 1882, described his visit:

> Fully one thousand persons were present to hear the issues of the day discussed by this eloquent Carolinian, and the ringing remarks made in behalf of democracy, the clear elucidation of the tariff and internal revenue question and the faithful description of the present system of county government compared with that instituted under the republican regime, captured the hearts of all unbiased hearers, and made favorable impressions on the minds of the most intelligent of those who have followed so long the false principles of republicanism. In regard to the vaunted prohibition scare Gov. Vance showed conclusively that there was nothing in it, and that the question, though a dead social and moral one, was put forward by the radicals solely for the purpose of ensnaring the unwary. . . . In regard to county government Senator Vance proved that the old system was taxation without representation, while under the present system every one, white and black, was benefited. . . . Governor Vance's remarks were interspersed throughout with timely anecdotes, and were received with round after round of applause and laughter.[13]

As the years went by after the Civil War, Vance's public attempts to explain and defend his performance as war governor diminished. He delivered his last address on the war and his role in it to the Boston Grand Army of the Republic chapter in 1886. In that speech, he stressed that a Federal campaign against the Constitution's guarantee of states' rights and the ownership of slaves led to the war. He never denied the right of secession but had questioned the wisdom of seceding. He and other southern Unionists had embraced secession only when, as they saw it, Lincoln's call for troops after Fort Sumter meant an aggressive attack on the South. Vance unfolded for the audience his customary dual claim that he had remained loyal to the Confederacy but at the same time had defended the rights of North Carolinians against the dictates of Confederate laws that might have usurped their liberties. He implied that the Confederate Congress bore the blame for those laws. On the other hand, he vindicated Jefferson Davis of any accusations that the Confederate president had infringed on the rights of the people. "Simple justice requires me," he informed his listeners, "to say that there was no disposition on the part of the President of the Confederacy to violate these rights *per se*. He never abused the extraordinary powers given by Congress; in fact, scarcely resorted to them at all."[14]

While serving in the Senate, Vance endured a number of health problems. In 1889 he developed an ocular infection, and a surgeon removed one of his eyes. Two years later he fell seriously ill with an uncertain malady and traveled to Europe in an effort to recover. He improved for a time but never completely recuperated. He subsequently weakened, and his legs became paralyzed. In April 1894 Vance suffered a stroke and died in Washington, D.C. Funeral services were held in the Senate chamber, and then his casket was transported to Raleigh, where a large crowd viewed his body in the Capitol. When it was moved to its final resting place in Asheville, another large crowd turned out to mourn him prior to his burial.[15]

· · ·

A close examination of Zebulon Vance's career as North Carolina's governor during the Civil War leads to the conclusion that no matter how much he initially rejected secession or at times during the war blamed Jefferson Davis and Confederate policies for unrest on the home front and ultimately Southern defeat, he nevertheless brought the full power of his office to bear in support for the Confederacy and Southern independence. Vance can rightfully be called a Confederate nationalist. Historian George C. Rable has perhaps best defined Confederate nationalism. "To the extent that Confederate nationalism existed," writes Rable, "it meant primarily the struggle for Confederate independence with a strong (though not always consistent) emphasis on national unity and, as the war dragged on, the necessity for expanded government power."[16] Certainly, Vance was "not always consistent" in what he said and did in response to the war policies of the Confederate government. As a clever and perceptive politician, he realized that he could not ignore his people's dissatisfaction with the burdens laid on them by the Davis government. If he was to lead his state in the struggle for Confederate independence, he had to retain the support of a majority of North Carolinians. To keep that support, Vance reasoned, he had to acknowledge publicly and express to the central government in Richmond the resentment felt by Tar Heels over expanding Confederate power as exhibited in such policies as conscription, impressment, tax-in-kind, and the suspension of the writ of habeas corpus. But in the end, Vance inevitably cooperated with the national authorities in waging war for an independent Confederate States of America, even when cooperation meant expanded power for the central government.

Vance's overwhelming reelection in 1864 on largely a pro-Confederate platform was an indication that the majority of voters in North Carolina—despite their protesting some Confederate laws—endorsed the governor's position of supporting expanded national power. As Drew Gilpin Faust in her in-depth discussion of Confederate nationalism has written, "The ideological foundations of nationalism required popular consent; nationalism, not to mention total war, necessarily involved and thus empowered the people at large."[17]

If one accepts that Vance, a former Unionist, took on the mantle of Confederate nationalism after Lincoln's call for troops in April 1861, one is still left to ponder his motivation for upholding and sustaining Confederate laws and policies that many North Carolinians considered a violation of their state autonomy and individual rights. In large part, he was motivated by an absolute belief that, after Lincoln issued his Emancipation Proclamation, the only way slavery would survive was for the Confederacy to achieve its independence. If the Confederate nation collapsed, so too would the South's social and economic system, based on black servitude. Racial warfare might result. "Knowing perfectly well," he explained shortly after the war,

> that war and defeat were equivalent to not only the abolition of Slavery, but to the subjugation—and all which that carries with it—of our country, when I found that by the action of my State I could no longer avert war, I thought it my duty to do everything in my power as a citizen of North Carolina and a patriot to avert *defeat*.

For however much it was denied, and however much stress was laid upon the *Union*, and minor causes of irritation, the result has conclusively shown that the great desire of the North was to abolish Slavery and to humiliate the Slaveholders whom they had been taught to hate.

I concluded therefore to go with my state and to fight—not for secession—not for the Confederate States [as] an object desirable in itself—but to avert the *consequences*—the abolition of slavery.[18]

Vance consistently maintained during the war that the Southern states must remain united under a central authority in order to prevent a breakdown of law and order, which was certain to take place if the Confederacy crumbled piece by piece, state by state, through separate peace negotiations. As he confessed to South Carolina governor Andrew G. Magrath in January 1865, the result might be a "revolution within revolution," rife with "domestic violence and civil feuds."[19] If North Carolina negotiated a separate peace with the Lincoln government, the state would find itself clashing with the Southern states in a "new war, a bloodier conflict" than the present one. At best, the Tar Heel State would be ravaged by both Confederate and Federal troops.[20]

Furthermore, Vance was convinced that only by remaining united could the Confederate states negotiate favorable terms when they lost the war, which by the fall of 1864 seemed to him to be the likely outcome. In January 1865 he wrote to Governor Brown: "I frankly confess to you that I regard it as our chief aim at this time to hold the demoralized and trembling fragments of society and law together and prevent them from dropping to pieces until the rapidly hastening end of our struggle shall be developed. To do this is not only humane and in every respect our duty but also puts off the evil day and keeps us in position to take advantage of any fortunate circumstances tending to redeem our losses, to inspire our people or even to secure better terms in case all should be lost."[21]

In the final analysis, Vance's professed sympathy for states' rights and individual liberties never overshadowed his respect for civil authority and his belief in a strong central government that could maintain stability in the South. He affirmed as much shortly after his reelection as governor in 1864 when he proclaimed that he was standing by the Confederacy with the same devotion with which he had stood by the Federal Union prior to secession. "Duty called me," he explained, "to resist to the uttermost the dissolution of the Union; duty calls me to stand by the new union [the Confederacy] 'to the last gasp with truth and loyalty.'"[22]

True to his word, the Tar Heel war governor stood by the Confederacy until its last gasp. He did not abandon the struggle for Southern independence until the Confederate cabinet met for the last time in Charlotte in April 1865, and Jefferson Davis himself led him to believe that defeat had come and the cause was lost.

NOTES

ABBREVIATIONS USED IN THE NOTES

PC   Private Collections, State Archives, North Carolina Office of Archives and History, Raleigh

SHC   Southern Historical Collection, University of North Carolina Library, Chapel Hill

VGL   Vance, Governors Letter Books, State Archives, North Carolina Office of Archives and History, Raleigh

VGP   Vance, Governors Papers, State Archives, North Carolina Office of Archives and History, Raleigh

INTRODUCTION

1. Yearns, *Confederate Governors*. A number of master's theses, doctoral dissertations, and journal articles about the governors have been written over the years. But the most recently published full treatments of Confederate governors are Hill, *Joseph E. Brown and the Confederacy*; Cassidy and Simpson, *Henry Watkins Allen of Louisiana*; Tucker, *Zeb Vance*; McKinney, *Zeb Vance*; Boney, *John Letcher of Virginia*; Dubay, *John Jones Pettus, Mississippi Fire-Eater*; Parks, *Joseph E. Brown of Georgia*; and Edmunds, *Francis W. Pickens and the Politics of Destruction*. Yates, *Confederacy and Zeb Vance*, is a brief account of Zebulon B. Vance's two terms as Confederate governor of North Carolina.

2. Yearns, *Confederate Governors*, 6–7.

3. Ibid., passim. See also the brief biographies of the governors in Current et al., *Encyclopedia of the Confederacy*.

4. Spencer, *Last Ninety Days of the War in North Carolina*.

5. Powell, *Dictionary of North Carolina Biography*, s.v. "Clarke, Mary Bayard Devereux"; Clarke, "Autobiography of Vance." Vance's autobiography is in the possession of Mary Barden, the great-granddaughter of nineteenth-century writer and

journalist Mary Bayard Clarke, and has passed to her through generations of her family.

6. Weeks, "University of North Carolina in the Civil War," 35–36. On the Lost Cause movement, see Foster, *Ghosts of the Confederacy*.

7. Dowd, *Life of Vance*, 72.

8. Ashe, *History of North Carolina*; Ashe, Weeks, and Van Noppen, *Biographical History of North Carolina*.

9. Connor, *North Carolina*; Hamilton, *History of North Carolina*; Dodd, *Jefferson Davis*.

10. Dodd, *Jefferson Davis*, 337.

11. Owsley, *State Rights in the Confederacy*, 1–4, 38. The war careers of Stephens and Toombs have recently been recounted in Davis, *Union That Shaped the Confederacy*. Unlike these two politicians, however, Vance did not deliberately attempt to thwart Confederate president Jefferson Davis.

12. Moore, *Conscription and Conflict in the Confederacy*, 296.

13. Ramsdell, review of *State Rights in the Confederacy*.

14. Ramsdell, *Behind the Lines in the Southern Confederacy*.

15. Beringer et al., *Why the South Lost the Civil War*, 6.

16. Tatum, *Disloyalty in the Confederacy*.

17. Pressly, *Americans Interpret Their Civil War*, 280–83.

18. Freeman, *R. E. Lee*, 3:498, 4:181.

19. Yates, "Zebulon B. Vance as War Governor of North Carolina"; Yates, "Governor Vance and the Peace Movement"; Yates, "Governor Vance and the End of the War in North Carolina"; Yates, *Confederacy and Zeb Vance*.

20. Coulter, *Confederate States of America*, 387–89, 398.

21. Randall and Donald, *Civil War and Reconstruction*, 267–68.

22. Donald, *Why the North Won the Civil War*, 79–90.

23. Eaton, *History of the Southern Confederacy*, 256.

24. Eaton, *Jefferson Davis*, 225–28.

25. Lefler and Newsome, *North Carolina*, 465–77; Powell, *North Carolina through Four Centuries*, 366–70.

26. Lefler and Newsome, *North Carolina*, 477.

27. Barrett, *Civil War in North Carolina*, 242–43.

28. Tucker, *Zeb Vance*, 392.

29. Johnston and Mobley, *Papers of Vance*, 1:lxxiii.

30. Escott, *After Secession*, 89, 202, 265–66.

31. Scarboro, "North Carolina and the Confederacy."

32. Kruman, *Parties and Politics in North Carolina*, 264–65.

33. Harris, *William Woods Holden*, 148, 149.

34. Beringer et al., *Why the South Lost the Civil War*, 6. For the extent to which these co-authors refute Owsley, see especially appendix 1, "The Politics of Local Defense: Owsley's State Rights Thesis," 443–57.

35. McPherson, *Battle Cry of Freedom*, 431, 615, 699.

36. Davis, *Jefferson Davis*, 535.

37. Cooper, *Jefferson Davis*, 512–13.

38. Rable, "Beyond State Rights," 150. See also Rable, *Confederate Republic*, for a number of perceptive observations and insights into Vance and his performance as war governor.

39. McKinney, "Vance and His Reconstruction of the Civil War in North Carolina."

40. Clarke, "Autobiography of Vance," 24–25.

CHAPTER 1. "MY HAND FELL SLOWLY AND SADLY BY THE SIDE OF A SECESSIONIST"

1. Tucker, *Zeb Vance*, 24–25; McKinney and McMurry, *Guide to the Papers of Vance*, xiii; Powell, *Dictionary of North Carolina Biography*, s.v. "Vance, Zebulon Baird."

2. Clarke, "Autobiography of Vance," 2.

3. Powell, *North Carolina Gazetteer*, 313.

4. Estate of David Vance, 1852, Madison County Estates Records, State Archives.

5. Clarke, "Autobiography of Vance," 2.

6. Johnston, "Biographical Sketch," in Johnston and Mobley, *Papers of Vance*, 1:xxii–xxiii.

7. Ibid.

8. Frances Gray Patton's introduction in Cannon, *My Beloved Zebulon*, xvii–xviii.

9. Ibid., xviii–xix, xxiii.

10. Vance to Harriett N. Espy, March 15, 1851, in Cannon, *My Beloved Zebulon*, 3.

11. See, for example, Cannon, *My Beloved Zebulon*, 22, 24, 25, 43, 71, 103, 160, 188.

12. Clarke, "Autobiography of Vance," 3.

13. Kemp P. Battle in Dowd, *Life of Vance*, 22.

14. Kemp P. Battle and Richard H. Battle in Dowd, *Life of Vance*, 16–30, 163–64; Tucker, *Zeb Vance*, 35–61.

15. Clarke, "Autobiography of Vance," 3.

16. Johnston, "Biographical Sketch," in Johnston and Mobley, *Papers of Vance*, 1:xxv–xxvi; McKinney and McMurry, *Guide to the Papers of Vance*, xvi.

17. Tucker, *Zeb Vance*, 63–64; Johnston, "Biographical Sketch," in Johnston and Mobley, *Papers of Vance*, 1:xxvi–xxviii.

18. Clarke, "Autobiography of Vance," 4.

19. Harris, *North Carolina and the Coming of the Civil War*, 14–25; Kruman, *Parties and Politics in North Carolina*, 143. For details of the rise and fall of the American Party in North Carolina, see Kruman, *Parties and Politics in North Carolina*, 159–79.

20. Clarke, "Autobiography of Vance," 5.

21. Johnston, "Biographical Sketch," in Johnston and Mobley, *Papers of Vance*, 1:xxx–xxxi.

22. Ibid., 1:xxxi–xxxii.

23. Ibid., 1:xxxii–xxxiii.

24. James S. T. Baird to Vance, July 9, 1855, in Johnston and Mobley, *Papers of Vance*, 1:29–30.

25. Tucker, *Zeb Vance*, 64–65. For details on the free suffrage issue, see Jeffrey, "Free Suffrage Revisited."

26. Vance to David F. Caldwell, February 2, 1858, as quoted in McKinney and McMurry, *Guide to the Papers of Vance*, xlii; Vance to David L. Swain, July 6, 1857, David Lowry Swain Papers, SHC. On Clingman, see Jeffrey, "Thunder from the Mountains," and Kruman, "Thomas L. Clingman and the Whig Party."

27. Tucker, *Zeb Vance*, 65–69.

28. Johnston, "Biographical Sketch," in Johnston and Mobley, *Papers of Vance*, 1:xxxvi; Dowd, *Life of Vance*, 41–61.

29. Samuel S. Cox, *Three Decades of Federal Legislation* (1888), as quoted in Johnston, "Biographical Sketch," in Johnston and Mobley, *Papers of Vance*, 1:xxxvi.

30. Robert B. Vance in Dowd, *Life of Vance*, 34–38; Tucker, *Zeb Vance*, 77–80.

31. Johnston, "Biographical Sketch," in Johnston and Mobley, *Papers of Vance*, 1:xxxviii.

32. Clarke, "Autobiography of Vance," 5.

33. Ibid., 6.

34. Randall and Donald, *Civil War and Reconstruction*, 127–34; Johnston, "Biographical Sketch," in Johnston and Mobley, *Papers of Vance*, 1:xxxvii.

35. Clarke, "Autobiography of Vance," 6.

36. Kruman, *Parties and Politics in North Carolina*, 199–200; Potter, *Impending Crisis*, 491–92.

37. Clarke, "Autobiography of Vance," 6–7.

38. Vance to William H. Dickson, December 11, 1860, William Dickson Papers, SHC.

39. Harris, *North Carolina and the Coming of the Civil War*, 37.

40. Vance to William Dickson, December 11, 1860, William Dickson Papers, SHC.

41. Harris, *North Carolina and the Coming of the Civil War*, 39.

42. Randall and Donald, *Civil War and Reconstruction*, 150.

43. Vance to Walter W. Lenoir, December 26, 1860, Lenoir Family Papers, SHC.

44. Eaton, *History of the Southern Confederacy*, 51–61; Thomas, *Confederate Nation*, 37–66.

45. Harris, *North Carolina and the Coming of the Civil War*, 35–46.

46. Vance, "Lecture—The Political and Social South during the War" (1886), in Dowd, *Life of Vance*, 441–42.

47. Clarke, "Autobiography of Vance," 13–14.

48. Barrett, *Civil War in North Carolina*, 10–16.

49. Clarke, "Autobiography of Vance," 15.

50. Gragg, *Covered with Glory*, 11.

51. Tucker, *Zeb Vance*, 22, 34, 474–75.

52. Gragg, *Covered with Glory*, 15.

53. Ibid., 17–22.

54. Ibid., 23–30.

55. Escott, *Many Excellent People*, 36–39.

56. Harris, *William Woods Holden*, 116–20; Johnston, "Biographical Sketch," in Johnston and Mobley, *Papers of Vance*, 1:xli; Kruman, *Parties and Politics in North Carolina*, 230–38.

57. Harris, *William Woods Holden*, 116–20; Johnston, "Biographical Sketch," in Johnston and Mobley, *Papers of Vance*, 1:xlii–xliv.

58. *Spirit of the Age*, August 11, 1862.

59. *Milton Chronicle*, as excerpted in the *Daily Bulletin*, August 11, 1862.

60. *Asheville News*, July 24, 31, 1862.

61. *Daily Bulletin*, August 8, 1862.

62. Kruman, *Parties and Politics in North Carolina*, 237–40.

63. Tucker, *Zeb Vance*, 157.

64. *Raleigh Register*, September 10, 1862.

65. Ibid.

66. Ibid.

67. *Daily Bulletin*, August 19, 1862.

CHAPTER 2. "LET EVERY PATRIOT IN THE LAND ASSIST"

1. Barrett, *Civil War in North Carolina*, 48–130 passim.

2. Click, *Time Full of Trial*; Mobley, *James City*.

3. Browning, "'Little Souled Mercenaries'?"

4. Harris, "Lincoln and Wartime Reconstruction in North Carolina."

5. Vance to James A. Seddon, January 20, 1863, VGL.

6. James A. Seddon to Vance, January 8, 1863, Zebulon Baird Vance Papers, PC.

7. Barrett, *Civil War in North Carolina*, 128–29; Boatner, *Civil War Dictionary*, 107.

8. Robert E. Lee to James A. Seddon, January 5, 1863, Zebulon Baird Vance Papers, PC.

9. Inscoe and McKinney, *Heart of Confederate Appalachia*, 106–10.

10. Ibid., 114.

11. Barrett, *Civil War in North Carolina*, 197–98; Inscoe and McKinney, *Heart of Confederate Appalachia*, 116–20; Boatner, *Civil War Dictionary*, 398. The most complete account of the Shelton Laurel massacre is Paludan, *Victims*.

12. Augustus S. Merrimon to Vance, January 31, 1863, VGP.

13. Henry Heth to Vance, January 21, 1863, VGP.

14. Boatner, *Civil War Dictionary*, 227, 398.

15. Vance to William George M. Davis, February 2, 1863, VGL.

16. Vance to Augustus S. Merrimon, February 9, 1863, VGL.

17. Vance to William George M. Davis, February 27, 1863, VGL.

18. Vance to James A. Seddon, February 28, 1863, VGL.

19. Ibid., May 18, 1863.

20. Augustus S. Merrimon to Vance, May 18, 1863, Zebulon Baird Vance Papers, PC.

21. James A. Seddon to Vance, May 23, 1863, VGP.

22. Auman, "Neighbor against Neighbor," 60–64.

23. Ibid., 64–66.

24. Ibid., 70–71.

25. Ibid., 71–74.

26. Daniel H. Hill to Vance, April 21, 1863, VGL.

27. Vance to Daniel H. Hill, April 23, 1863, VGL.

28. "By the Governor of North Carolina, a Proclamation," May 11, 1863, VGL. See also proclamation of January 26, 1863, VGL.

29. Vance to Shubal G. Worth, October 12, 1863, Marmaduke Swaim Robins Papers, SHC.

30. James A. Seddon to Vance, May 5, 1863, including enclosure of William D. Pender to Walter H. Taylor, April 23, 1863, VGP.

31. Robert E. Lee to James A. Seddon, May 21, 1863, enclosed in James A. Seddon to Vance, May 23, 1863, VGP.

32. Hamilton, "North Carolina Courts and the Confederacy," 368–70; Bardolph, "Confederate Dilemma," 183–84.

33. Mitchell, *Legal Aspects of Conscription and Exemption*, 3–60; Hamilton, "North Carolina Courts and the Confederacy," 366–71.

34. Vance to Jefferson Davis, May 13, 1863, VGL.

35. Mitchell, *Legal Aspects of Conscription and Exemption*, 59; Hamilton, "North Carolina Courts and the Confederacy," 367–77; *Public Laws of North Carolina, 1863* (called session), ch. 10. When troops in the militia were drafted into the Confederate army, the militia diminished as a "fighting force," but depleted units "continued to operate parallel to and intermeshed with the Home Guard." Bradley, *North Carolina Confederate Home Guard Examinations*, i. See also Manarin, *Guide to Military Organizations and Installations*, 1–4.

36. Barrett, *Civil War in North Carolina*, 129–94; Auman, "Neighbor against Neighbor," 77–79.

37. As quoted in Auman, "Neighbor against Neighbor," 79.

38. Auman, "Neighbor against Neighbor," 81–93. Only three counties, including Johnston County, voted for Holden. For a full discussion of the election, see chapter 5.

39. Auman, "Neighbor against Neighbor," 87–88.

40. Robert E. Lee to Vance, February 24, 1865, VGP.

41. "By the Governor of North Carolina, a Proclamation," February 14, 1865, VGL.

42. Vance to Robert E. Lee, March 2, 1865, VGL.

43. Robert E. Lee to Vance, March 9, 1865, VGP.

44. Bardolph, "Confederate Dilemma"; Reid, "Test Case of 'Crying Evil.'"

45. Moore, *Conscription and Conflict in the Confederacy*, 12–19.

46. As quoted in Moore, *Conscription and Conflict in the Confederacy*, 20–21.

47. Moore, *Conscription and Conflict in the Confederacy*, 44–45.

48. Ibid., 52–53 (quotation), 54–67.

49. Ibid., 67–68 (quotation), 308.

50. Ibid., 68.

51. L. K. Walker to Vance, January 16, 1863, VGP.

52. As quoted in Moore, *Conscription and Conflict in the Confederacy*, 71.

53. Moore, *Conscription and Conflict in the Confederacy*, 73–74, 83–84.

54. Eaton, *History of the Southern Confederacy*, 91.

55. *Public Laws of North Carolina, 1862–1863*, as quoted in Yearns and Barrett, *North Carolina Civil War Documentary*, 139.

56. Jesse G. Shepherd to Vance, April 3, 1865, VGP. Vance's reply is written as an endorsement at the end of Shepherd's letter.

57. Ollin Goddin to Vance, February 27, 1863, VGP.

58. Vance, "Lecture—The Political and Social South during the War" (1886), in Dowd, *Life of Vance*, 447–48.

59. Vance to Thomas P. August, March 20, 1863, VGP.

60. Gabriel J. Rains to Vance, March 25, 1863, VGP.

61. Vance to Gabriel J. Rains, March 31, 1863, VGP.

62. Vance to Jefferson Davis, March 31, 1863, Harvard College Library, cited from McKinney and McMurry, *Papers of Vance*, reel 39.

63. Thomas S. Ashe to Vance, April 24, 1863, Library of Congress, cited from McKinney and McMurry, *Papers of Vance*, reel 39.

64. Vance to James A. Seddon, April 22, 1863, VGP.

65. *Raleigh Register*, September 10, 1862.

66. Frederick J. Lord to Vance, August 22, 1863, VGP. Vance's response is written as an endorsement at the end of Lord's letter.

67. Vance to Jefferson Davis, May 13, 1863, VGL.

68. James A. Seddon to Vance, May 23, 1863, and Vance to James A. Seddon, May 25, 1863, both in VGP.

69. Hamilton, "North Carolina Courts and the Confederacy," 372, 396; Tucker, *Zeb Vance*, 291–92.

70. Peter Mallett to Vance, May 18, 1863, VGP; George W. Long to Peter Mallett, May 11, 1863, Zebulon Baird Vance Papers, PC.

71. Hamilton, "North Carolina Courts and the Confederacy," 369.

72. Daniel H. Hill to Vance, June 13, 1863, Zebulon Baird Vance Papers, PC.

73. *In re* [J. C.] *Bryan, North Carolina Reports* 60 (1863), 1; Mitchell, *Legal Aspects of Conscription and Exemption*, 40–43; Hamilton, "North Carolina Courts and the Confederacy," 373–74; Neely, *Southern Rights*, 68–69.

74. Hamilton, "North Carolina Courts and the Confederacy," 375; Neely, *Southern Rights*, 69–70; *Fayetteville Observer*, October 5, 1863.

75. Hamilton, "North Carolina Courts and the Confederacy," 376–77; Mitchell, *Legal Aspects of Conscription and Exemption*, 59.

76. Richmond M. Pearson to Vance, October 3, 1863, VGP.

77. Vance to Richmond M. Pearson, October 7, 1863, VGL.

78. Vance to William H. Battle, October 6, 1863, VGP.

79. William H. Battle to Vance, November 12, 1863, VGP.

80. Vance to Richmond M. Pearson, October 26, 1863, VGL.

81. Sion H. Rogers to Vance, November 2, 1863, VGP.

82. Richmond M. Pearson to Vance, November 2, 1863, VGP.

83. William H. Battle to Vance, November 12, 1863, VGP.

84. *Public Laws of North Carolina, 1863* (called session), ch. 10.

85. Vance to Richmond M. Pearson, November 12, 1863, VGL.

86. Richmond M. Pearson to Vance, December 7, 1863, VGP.

87. Vance to Richmond M. Pearson, December 26, 1863, VGL.

88. Richmond M. Pearson to Vance, January 11, 1864, VGP.

89. Mitchell, *Legal Aspects of Conscription and Exemption*, 61; Coulter, *Confederate States of America*, 319.

90. Hamilton, "North Carolina Courts and the Confederacy," 389; Van Zant, "Confederate Conscription and the North Carolina Supreme Court," 67.

91. Yates, "Governor Vance and the Peace Movement," 92–93.

92. Vance to Jefferson Davis, February 9, 1864, VGP.

93. Jefferson Davis to Vance, February 29, 1864, VGP.

94. Cooper, *Jefferson Davis*, 415.

95. Yates, "Governor Vance and the Peace Movement," 92–93, 95, 109.

96. Vance to James A. Seddon, February 29, 1864, VGP.

97. Van Zant, "Confederate Conscription and the North Carolina Supreme Court," 68.

98. Neely, *Southern Rights*, 72.

99. Van Zant, "Confederate Conscription and the North Carolina Supreme Court," 72.

100. Crow and Durden, *Maverick Republican*, 4.

101. Ibid., 5–7.

102. Ibid., 7; Neely, *Southern Rights*, 70; Vance to Peter Mallett, March 11, 1864, Daniel Lindsay Russell Papers, SHC (quotation).

103. Vance to James A. Seddon, May 19, 1864, Daniel Lindsay Russell Papers, SHC.

104. Vance to William H. C. Whiting, July 5, 1864, Daniel Lindsay Russell Papers, SHC.

105. Mitchell, *Legal Aspects of Conscription and Exemption*, 83–86; Crow and Durden, *Maverick Republican*, 9.

106. Neely, *Southern Rights*, 70.

107. McPherson, *Battle Cry of Freedom*, 616–17; Coulter, *Confederate States of America*, 249–54; Faust et al., *Encyclopedia of the Civil War*, 379.

108. Vance to James A. Seddon, January 22, February 25, March 21, 1863, all three in VGP; Vance to Gustavus W. Smith, January 24, 1863, Zebulon Baird Vance Papers, PC; Vance to Albert G. Jenkins, February 2, 1863, and Vance to Samuel G. French, February 4, 1863, both in VGL; Vance to Richard S. Donnell, February 9, 1863, Zebulon Baird Vance Papers, Special Collections, Duke University Library.

109. Vance to James A. Seddon, April 27, 1863, VGL.

110. Ibid., February 12, 1863.

111. Vance to William H. C. Whiting, April 23, 1863, VGL.

112. Ibid., May 21, 1863.

113. Vance to James A. Seddon, July 1, 1863, VGP.

114. Bradley, "'This Monstrous Proposition,'" 153, 171–73, 179–81, 184; *Milton Chronicle*, November 4, 1864.

115. James A. Seddon to Vance, December 21, 1863, VGP.

116. Daniel Locklar to Vance, July 28, 1863, VGP. Vance's response to Locklar is written as an endorsement at the end of Locklar's letter.

117. Vance to James A. Seddon, July 3, 1863, VGL.

118. James A. Seddon to Vance, July 23, 1863, VGP. Lee's response is quoted in Seddon's letter.

119. Vance to James A. Seddon, July 26, 1863, VGL.

120. Vance to Jefferson Davis, July 6, 1863, VGL.

121. John G. Barrett, "North Carolina," in Yearns, *Confederate Governors*, 152; Powell, *Dictionary of North Carolina Biography*, s.v. "Davis, George."

122. Vance to Jefferson Davis, March 9, 1864, Jefferson Davis Papers, Special Collections, Duke University Library.

123. Vance to James A. Seddon, March 5, 1863, Peter Mallett Papers, SHC.

124. Vance to Jefferson Davis, July 6, 1863, VGL.

125. Philip Hodnett to Vance, July 30, 1863, VGP.

126. Gabriel J. Rains to Vance, March 25, 1863, VGP.

127. Jefferson Davis to Vance, August 18, 1863, VGP.

128. Ibid., August 19, 1863.

129. Vance to Jefferson Davis, August 28, 1863, Harvard College Library, cited from McKinney and McMurry, *Papers of Vance*, reel 39.

130. Tucker, *Zeb Vance*, 223, 226.

131. Vance to Jefferson Davis, July 6, 1863, VGL.

132. William H. C. Whiting to Vance, July 1, 1863, VGL.

133. Vance to Jefferson Davis, July 6, 1863, VGL.

134. Vance to James A. Seddon, January 6, 1863, VGL; Vance to Edward J. Hale, August 11, 1863, Edward Jones Hale Papers, PC. Ostensibly, Vance's trip to Richmond in 1862 was to deliver medical supplies to North Carolina troops following the Battle of Antietam. But he used that opportunity to talk with Davis. Tucker, *Zeb Vance*, 207.

135. The two most thorough treatments of Davis and his personality are Cooper, *Jefferson Davis*, and Davis, *Jefferson Davis*. See also Woodworth, *Davis and Lee at War*, and Beringer, "Jefferson Davis's Pursuit of Ambition."

CHAPTER 3. "HUMANITY SHUDDERS AT WHAT MAY TAKE PLACE"

1. *Public Laws of North Carolina, 1863*, ch. 35, sec. 1. On December 23, 1864, "An Act in Relation to Courts of Oyer and Terminer" supplemented the 1863 act by giving judges of courts of oyer and terminer the "power to extend the term of the said court from week to week until all business of said court is disposed of." *Public Laws of North Carolina, 1864*, ch. 13, sec. 1.

2. *Revised Code of North Carolina, 1854*, ch. 107, secs. 37, 41; McCain, "Magistrates' Courts in Early North Carolina"; Stevenson and Arnold, "North Carolina Courts of Law and Equity prior to 1868," 8, 10.

3. Crow, Escott, and Hatley, *History of African Americans in North Carolina*, 48–51.

4. As quoted in Crow, Escott, and Hatley, *History of African Americans in North Carolina*, 59.

5. Morris, "Panic and Reprisal."

6. Crow, Escott, and Hatley, *History of African Americans in North Carolina*, 48–49; Franklin, *Free Negro in North Carolina*, 192–93; Marshall, "Legendary Thomas Day," 55; Berlin, *Slaves without Masters*, 95.

7. For a thorough description of the slavery controversy and the events leading to the Civil War, see Potter, *Impending Crisis*.

8. E. J. Blount to Vance, October 18, 1864, VGP.

9. "Proceedings of the Confederate Congress," cited and quoted in Moser, "Reaction in North Carolina to the Emancipation Proclamation," 58–59; Coulter, *Confederate States of America*, 265–66; Cooper, *Jefferson Davis*, 439–40.

10. *North Carolina Standard*, October 8, 1864.

11. Ibid.

12. As quoted in Moser, "Reaction in North Carolina to the Emancipation Proclamation," 56–57, 60.

13. Barrett, *Civil War in North Carolina*, 171–201; Escott, *After Secession*, 94–134.

14. Mobley, *James City*, 1–12.

15. Ibid., 16–20; Reid, "Raising the African Brigade."

16. Glatthaar, *Forged in Battle*, 6–10. For the organization of African American troops, see also Cornish, *Sable Arm*, and Quarles, *Negro in the Civil War*.

17. Edmondston, "*Journal of a Secesh Lady*," 226–27, 357.

18. James J. Pettigrew to Vance, February 5, 1863, Zebulon Baird Vance Papers, PC.

19. William T. Dortch to Vance, January 7, 1863, VGP. In the phrase "our President," Dortch is referring to Jefferson Davis's response to Lincoln's Emancipation Proclamation. See note 9 of this chapter.

20. Auman and Scarboro, "Heroes of America in North Carolina"; Auman, "Neighbor against Neighbor."

21. Paul C. Cameron to Vance, February 19, 1863, and Cameron to David A. Barnes (Vance's aide), February 23, 1863, both in VGP.

22. Henry K. Nash to Vance, February 20, 1863, VGP.

23. William A. Graham to Vance, February 21, 23, 1863, both in VGP.

24. Vance to Robert B. Gilliam, February 25, 1863, VGL.

25. *State v. Solomon, Daniel, and America*, and *State v. Lucian and Allen*, and *State v. Solomon*, Orange County Superior Court Minutes, March and September terms, 1863, State Archives.

26. Lincoln County justice of the peace to Vance, March 16, 1863, VGP.

27. Vance to Robert R. Heath, March 23, 1863, VGL; *State v. Bill and Frank*, Lincoln County Superior Court Minutes, special term, April 1863, State Archives.

28. Augustus S. Merrimon to Vance, April 4, 1863, VGP.

29. Rutherford County Court of Pleas and Quarter Sessions Minutes, March term, 1863, State Archives.

30. Augustus S. Merrimon to Vance, December 9, 28, 1864, both in VGP.

31. Inscoe and McKinney, *Heart of Confederate Appalachia*, 222, 226, 230.

32. Horace James, *Annual Report of the Superintendent of Negro Affairs in North Carolina*, 11–12.

33. George F. Winston to a friend or neighbor, February 15, 1863, New Bern Occupation Papers, SHC.

34. Ralph P. Buxton to Vance, April 11, 1863, VGP.

35. Ralph P. Buxton, certification of acquittal of Benjamin A. Howell, November 23, 1863, copy in VGP.

36. B. B. Bulla to Vance, June 16, 1864, VGP.

37. Duplin County Court petition to Vance, April 29, 1863, VGP.

38. Vance to Jefferson Davis, May 30, 1863, VGP.

39. Jefferson Davis to Vance, May 30, 1863, VGP.

40. Daniel H. Hill to Vance, July 10, 1863, VGP.

41. John Pool to Vance, July 25, 1863, VGP.

42. Barrett, *Civil War in North Carolina*, 177–79.

43. Vance to Robert Ould, December 29, 1863, VGL.

44. Meekins, "Caught between Scylla and Charybdis," 207.

45. "Petition of 523 Citizens of Pasquotank, December 26, 1863," enclosure in Benjamin F. Butler to Edwin M. Stanton, December 31, 1863, in *War of the Rebellion*, ser. 1, vol. 19, pt. 2, pp. 597–98. The author acknowledges Alex Christopher Meekins for bringing this document to his attention.

46. Vance to James W. Hinton, November 24, 1863, Edward Clements Yellowley Papers, SHC.

47. Manarin and Jordan, *North Carolina Troops*, 4:521, 523; Clark, *Histories of the Several Regiments and Battalions from North Carolina*, 3:713–18.

48. Jordan and Thomas, "Massacre at Plymouth."

49. Sion H. Rogers to Vance, May 28, 1864, VGP; *State v. Sam and Sam*, Franklin County Superior Court Minutes, spring term, June 3, 1864, State Archives.

50. Sion H. Rogers to Vance, January 2, 1865, VGL; *State v. Ben*, Franklin County Superior Court Minutes, oyer and terminer term, January 9, 10, 1865, State Archives.

51. Richmond County justices of the peace to Vance, December 9, 1864, VGP.

52. Ralph P. Buxton to Vance, December 14, 1864, VGP; *State v. Jack, Asa, Aaron, Bob, Milton, Daniel, Peter, and Willis*, Richmond County Superior Court Minutes, term of January 2, 1865, State Archives.

53. *State v. Jack, Asa, Aaron, Bob, Milton, Daniel, Peter, and Willis*, Richmond County Superior Court Minutes, term of January 2, 1865, State Archives.

54. William Easton Jr. et al. to Vance, June 23, 1864, and Franklin County petition for pardon, June 23, 1864, both in VGP.

55. Robert R. Heath to Vance, June 27, 1864, VGP.

56. Pardons by Vance, July 1, 1864, March 2, 1865, both in VGL.

57. Ralph P. Buxton to Vance, September 8, 1864, VGP.

58. Ibid.

59. Pardon by Vance, September 8, 1864, VGL.

60. See "Calendar of Papers Not Printed in This Volume," in Johnston and Mobley, *Papers of Vance*, 2:361–436.

61. Ibid.

62. As quoted in Grimsley, *Hard Hand of War*, 123, and McPherson, *Struggle for Equality*, 62.

63. Boritt, *Of the People, by the People, for the People*, 46.

64. McPherson, *Drawn with the Sword*, 79.

CHAPTER 4. "TO THEIR HANDS I AM CONTENT TO LEAVE IT"

1. Harris, *With Charity for All*, 58–59.

2. Powell, *Dictionary of North Carolina Biography*, s.v. "Stanly, Edward." For the most complete biography of Stanly, see Brown, *Edward Stanly*.

3. Harris, *With Charity for All*, 59.

4. Harris, "Lincoln and Wartime Reconstruction in North Carolina," 156–58.

5. As quoted in Harris, *With Charity for All*, 63.

6. Harris, "Lincoln and Wartime Reconstruction in North Carolina," 165.

7. As quoted in Harris, "Lincoln and Wartime Reconstruction in North Carolina," 165.

8. Edward Stanly to Vance, October 21, 1862, VGL.

9. Vance to Edward Stanly, October 29, 1862, VGL.

10. Edward Stanly to Vance, November 7, 1862, Zebulon Baird Vance Papers, PC.

11. Vance to Edward Stanly, November 24, 1862, Zebulon Baird Vance Papers, PC.

12. Edward Stanly to Edwin M. Stanton, November 20, 1862, in *War of the Rebellion*, ser. 3, vol. 2, p. 845.

13. Harris, "Lincoln and Wartime Reconstruction in North Carolina," 166–67; Delany, "Charles Henry Foster and the Unionists of Eastern North Carolina."

14. Brown, *Edward Stanly*, 202–3, 208–13; Barrett, *Civil War in North Carolina*, 127–28.

15. Edward Stanly to Edwin M. Stanton, June 12, 1862, *War of the Rebellion*, ser. 1, vol. 9, pp. 399–402.

16. Harris, *With Charity for All*, 70.

17. Raper, "William W. Holden and the Peace Movement"; Yates, "Governor Vance and the Peace Movement"; Harris, *William Woods Holden*, 127–36.

18. As quoted in Harris, *With Charity for All*, 65.

19. *North Carolina Standard*, July 17, 1863.

20. Vance to William A. Graham, August 13, 1863, William Alexander Graham Papers, PC.

21. Jefferson Davis to Vance, July 24, 1863, Zebulon Baird Vance Papers, PC.

22. Vance to Edward J. Hale, August 11, 1863, Edward Jones Hale Papers, PC; Yates, *Confederacy and Zeb Vance*, 88.

23. Vance to John H. Haughton, August 17, 1863, Zebulon Baird Vance Papers, PC.

24. Vance to William A. Graham, August 19, 1863, William Alexander Graham Papers, PC; William A. Graham to Vance, August 21, 1863, in Hamilton, Williams, and Peacock, *Papers of Graham*, 5:522–23; Vance to Edward J. Hale, September 7, 1863, Edward Jones Hale Papers, PC.

25. "By the Governor of North Carolina, a Proclamation," September 7, 1863, VGL.

26. Harris, *William Woods Holden*, 138–40.

27. *North Carolina Standard*, November 17, 1863; Yearns, "North Carolina in the Confederate Congress," 373–74; Cheney, *North Carolina Government*, 388–89.

28. Harris, *William Woods Holden*, 140–42.

29. Vance to Jefferson Davis, December 30, 1863, Zebulon Baird Vance Papers, PC.

30. Ibid.

31. Jefferson Davis to Vance, January 8, 1864, VGP.

32. Ibid.

33. Congressional delegation to Vance, January 25, 1864, VGP.

34. Jefferson Davis to Vance, January 30, 1864, Zebulon Baird Vance Papers, SHC.

35. Vance to Burgess Gaither et al., February 4, 1864, VGL.

36. Jefferson Davis to Vance, February 17, 1864, Zebulon Baird Vance Papers, PC.

CHAPTER 5. "MY LIFE POPULARITY AND EVERYTHING SHALL GO INTO THIS CONTEST"

1. Vance to Edward J. Hale, December 21, 1863, Edward Jones Hale Papers, PC.

2. Vance to David L. Swain, January 2, 1864, Zebulon Baird Vance Papers, PC.

3. Vance to William A. Graham, January 1, 1864, William Alexander Graham Papers, PC.

4. Vance to David L. Swain, January 2, 1864, Zebulon Baird Vance Papers, PC.

5. Vance to Edward J. Hale, August 11, 1863, Edward Jones Hale Papers, PC.

6. Ibid., February 11, 1864.

7. Ibid.

8. John D. Hyman to Vance, February 17, 1864, Zebulon Baird Vance Papers, PC.

9. Yates, "Governor Vance and the Peace Movement," 92–93.

10. Vance to Jefferson Davis, February 9, 1864, VGP.

11. Jefferson Davis to Vance, February 29, 1864, VGP.

12. See, for example, Vance to Jefferson Davis, March 9, 1864, Jefferson Davis Papers, Special Collections, Duke University Library, and Jefferson Davis to Vance, March 31, 1864, VGP.

13. Harris, *William Woods Holden*, 144–45.

14. William W. Holden to Calvin J. Cowles, March 18, 1864, and Jonathan Worth to William W. Holden, April 23, 1864, both in Raper and Mitchell, *Papers of Holden*, 1:154 (quotation), 156.

15. *Conservative*, April 16, 20, 1864.

16. Yates, "Governor Vance and the Peace Movement," 96–97.

17. *North Carolina Standard*, March 3, 1864.

18. Vance to William A. Graham, March 3, 1864, in Hamilton, Williams, and Peacock, *Papers of Graham*, 6:36.

19. *North Carolina Standard*, April 20, 1864.

20. Harris, *William Woods Holden*, 146–47.

21. *Conservative*, April 27, June 8, July 6, 20, 1864.

22. Vance to Edward J. Hale, December 30, 1863, Edward Jones Hale Papers, PC.

23. Harris, *William Woods Holden*, 147; Kruman, *Parties and Politics in North Carolina*, 262.

24. Yates, *Confederacy and Zeb Vance*, 102–3; *Fayetteville Observer*, April 14, 1864.

25. *Conservative*, April 27, 1864.

26. Ibid., July 2, 4, 6, 1864.

27. *Iredell Express*, March 3, 1864.

28. Yates, "Governor Vance and the Peace Movement," 92–93, 95; Kruman, *Parties and Politics in North Carolina*, 264.

29. Kruman, *Parties and Politics in North Carolina*, 264; *Fayetteville Observer*, March 3, 1864; Coulter, *Confederate States of America*, 535–36.

30. Harris, *William Woods Holden*, 148–49; *North Carolina Standard*, May 20, 1864; McPherson, *Battle Cry of Freedom*, 693–94.

31. John A. Gilmer to Vance, April 14, 1864, Zebulon Baird Vance Papers, PC.

32. Harris, *William Woods Holden*, 151.

33. North Carolina Gubernatorial Election Returns, 1864, Miscellaneous Papers, State Archives.

34. Edmondston, *"Journal of a Secesh Lady,"* 599.

35. North Carolina Gubernatorial Election Returns, 1864, Miscellaneous Papers, State Archives.

36. Milledge L. Bonham to Vance, August 6, 1864, Zebulon Baird Vance Papers, PC.

37. Edward J. Hale to Vance, August 11, 1864, Zebulon Baird Vance Papers, PC.

38. Robert E. Lee to Vance, August 12, 1864, Zebulon Baird Vance Papers, PC.

39. Cornelia P. Spencer to Vance, August 22, 1864, Zebulon Baird Vance Papers, PC.

40. *Confederate*, August 6, 1864.

CHAPTER 6. "THROUGH A MOST RIGOROUS AND DANGEROUS BLOCKADE"

1. Johnston, "Biographical Sketch," in Johnston and Mobley, *Papers of Vance*, 1:li–liii.

2. Wise, *Lifeline of the Confederacy*, 105.

3. Vance to John White, November 1, 1862, VGP.

4. Johnston, "Biographical Sketch," in Johnston and Mobley, *Papers of Vance*, 1:lii; Wise, *Lifeline of the Confederacy*, 105–6; Powell, *Dictionary of North Carolina Biography*, s.v. "Crossan, Thomas Morrow."

5. Vance to John White, March 12, 1863, VGP.

6. John White to Vance, May 20, 1863, VGP.

7. Wise, *Lifeline of the Confederacy*, 106.

8. John White to Vance, May 20, 1863, VGP.

9. Wise, *Lifeline of the Confederacy*, 105–6.

10. Vance to John White, July 10, 1863, VGP.

11. Ibid.

12. Fuller, *Anna Long Thomas Fuller's Journal*, 26.

13. Edmondston, *"Journal of a Secesh Lady,"* 425–26.

14. John White to Vance, August 7, 1863, VGP.

15. Vance to Alexander Collie, August 5, 1864, VGL.

16. Wise, *Lifeline of the Confederacy*, 157, 199–200, 242–49; Vance to John J. Guthrie, October 18, 1863, VGL.

17. Vance to Edward J. Hale, October 26, 1863, Edward Jones Hale Papers, PC.

18. Vance to John White, October 18, 1863, VGL.

19. Vance to John White, July 10, September 3, 1863, both in VGP.

20. John White to Vance, September 4, October 31 (quotation), 1863, both in VGP.

21. Joseph E. Brown to Vance, February 4, 1863, VGP.

22. William A. Graham to Vance, February 21, 1863, VGP.

23. Joseph E. Brown to Vance, March 14, 1863, VGL.

24. Johnston and Mobley, *Papers of Vance*, 1:420n–421n; Powell, *Dictionary of North Carolina Biography*, s.v. "McRae, Duncan Kirkland," s.v. "Sanders, George Nicholas."

25. Duncan K. McRae to Vance, January 19, 1863, VGP.

26. Vance to Duncan K. McRae, March 12, 1863, VGL.

27. Vance to Duncan K. McRae, July 10, 1863, VGP.

28. Vance to Duncan K. McRae, September 6, 1863, VGL.

29. Vance to Duncan K. McRae, July 10, 1863, VGP.

30. Vance to Duncan K. McRae, September 6, 1863, VGL.

31. George N. Sanders to Vance, July 16, December 7, 1863, both in VGL; Duncan K. McRae to Vance, July 17, 1863, VGP.

32. Vance to Duncan K. McRae, October 3, 1863, VGL.

33. Duncan K. McRae to Vance, October 3, 1863, VGL.

34. Vance to Duncan K. McRae, October 6, 1863, VGL.

35. Vance to Alexander Collie, February 1, 1864, and Vance to Thomas J. Boykin, February 1, 1864, both in VGL; Manarin and Jordan, *North Carolina Troops*, 7:464.

36. Vance to Joseph H. Flanner, February 1, 1864, VGL.

37. Vance to Kemp P. Battle and Sion H. Rogers, February 1, 1864, Battle Family Papers, SHC.

38. Powell, *Dictionary of North Carolina Biography*, s.v. "McRae, Duncan Kirkland."

39. Vance to John White, October 22, 1864, VGP; Arrington, "John White of Warrenton," 1; Powell, *Dictionary of North Carolina Biography*, s.v. "White, John."

40. Wise, *Lifeline of the Confederacy*, 288, 294, 296, 297, 299, 303, 305, 317, 318.

41. Ibid., 157; Vance to Theodore Andreae, December 28, 1863, VGL; Alexander Collie to John White, October 1, 1863, and Vance to James A. Seddon, January 7, 1864, both in VGP.

42. Vance to Edward J. Hale, February 11, 1864, Edward Jones Hale Papers, PC.

43. Vance to James A. Seddon, January 7, 1864, VGP.

44. Theodore Andreae to Vance, February 8, 1864, VGP.

45. Vance to Theodore Andreae, February 11, 1864, VGL.

46. Vance to Alexander Collie, February 8, 1864, VGL.

47. Ibid., February 18, 1864.

48. Ibid., February 8, 1864.

49. Vance to John White, September 3, 1863, VGP.

50. Vance to James A. Seddon, January 7, 1864, VGP.

51. Vance to Alexander Collie, February 18, 1864, VGL.

52. Ibid.

53. James A. Seddon to Vance, January 6, 1864, VGP.

54. Vance to Theodore Andreae, January 6, 1864, VGL.

55. Vance to James A. Seddon, January 7, 1864, VGP.

56. Ibid., January 25, 1864.

57. Ibid., February 12, 1864.

58. William H. Peters to Theodore Andreae, March 5, 1864, copy enclosed in Vance to James A. Seddon, March 8, 1864, VGP.

59. Vance to James A. Seddon, March 8, 1864, VGP.

60. James A. Seddon to Vance, March 15, 1864, VGP.

61. Joseph E. Brown to Vance, April 13, 1864, VGL.

62. Vance to William A. Graham, May 11, 1864, William Alexander Graham Papers, PC.

63. Owsley, *State Rights in the Confederacy*, 141–46.

64. Coulter, *Confederate States of America*, 293; Owsley, *State Rights in the Confederacy*, 149.

65. Vance to Jefferson Davis, March 17, 1864, Harvard College Library, cited from McKinney and McMurry, *Papers of Vance*, reel 39.

66. Jefferson Davis to Vance, March 26, 1864, VGP.

67. Vance to Jefferson Davis, April 5, 1864, VGP.

68. Christopher M. Memminger to Vance, April 14, 1864, VGP.

69. Vance to Christopher M. Memminger, July 4, 1864, VGP.

70. Vance to John White, September 21, 1864, VGP.

71. Wise, *Lifeline of the Confederacy*, 199–200. See also Stephen R. Mallory to Vance, December 28, 1864, VGP, and Mallory to Vance, January 3, 1865, VGL.

72. Butler, *Pirates, Privateers, and Rebel Raiders*, 194, 199–200.

73. Vance to Alexander Collie, November 2, 1864, VGL.

74. Johnston, "Biographical Sketch," in Johnston and Mobley, *Papers of Vance*, 1:liv.

75. Owsley, *State Rights in the Confederacy*, 110, 112–13.

76. Vance to James Mason, March 11, 1863, VGL; Vance to John White, March 12, 1863, and White to Vance, May 20, 1863, both in VGP.

77. Quoted in Dowd, *Life of Vance*, 71.

78. James A. Seddon to Vance, December 15, 1864, VGP.

79. Ibid., December 15, 31, 1864. See especially Vance's endorsement at the bottom of Seddon's December 15 letter.

80. Dowd, *Life of Vance*, 71; Vance to Joseph E. Johnston, April 16, 1865, Zebulon Baird Vance Papers, PC.

81. Vance to George A. Trenholm, October 25, 1864, VGL.

82. Owsley, *State Rights in the Confederacy*, 126.

83. Dowd, *Life of Vance*, 71.

84. Bradley, *This Astounding Close*, 14–15.

CHAPTER 7. "WOMEN HAS NERVED THE ARM OF THE STALWART SOLDIER"

1. Barrett, *Civil War in North Carolina*, 188; Michael Brown to Vance, March 18, 1863, VGP; *Carolina Watchman*, March 23, 1863.

2. Soldiers' wives to Vance, March 21, 1863, VGP.

3. Nancy Mangum to Vance, April 9, 1863, in Yearns and Barrett, *North Carolina Civil War Documentary*, 220–21.

4. *Greensboro Patriot*, as quoted in Bynum, *Unruly Women*, 126.

5. Escott, *Many Excellent People*, 66–67.

6. Yearns and Barrett, *North Carolina Civil War Documentary*, 219.

7. Escott, "Poverty and Governmental Aid for the Poor in Confederate North Carolina," 468–69, 475–77.

8. Martha Futch to John Futch, February 19, 1863 (quotation), and John Futch to Martha Futch, July 19, August 6, 1863, all three in Futch Letters, PC; Manarin and Jordan, *North Carolina Troops*, 3:593.

9. Nancy Mangum to Vance, April 9, 1863, in Yearns and Barrett, *North Carolina Civil War Documentary*, 220–21; Bynum, *Unruly Women*, 128–29, 134, 146.

10. Mary Lutterloh to Vance, November 19, 1864, VGP.

11. Martha Coltrane to Vance, November 18, 1862, in Johnston and Mobley, *Papers of Vance*, 1:374–75.

12. Carbone, *Civil War in Coastal North Carolina*, 126–27.

13. Barrett, *Civil War in North Carolina*, 260.

14. Norris, "'For the Benefit of Our Gallant Volunteers,'" 315.

15. Ibid., 319–20.

16. Barrett, *Civil War in North Carolina*, 260–61; Mary Anne Buie to Vance, September 21, 1862, in Johnston and Mobley, *Papers of Vance*, 1:212–16.

17. Mary Anne Buie to Vance, September 21, 1862, in Johnston and Mobley, *Papers of Vance*, 1:213.

18. Barrett, *Civil War in North Carolina*, 260–61.

19. Mary Anne Buie to Vance, August 23, 1864, VGP.

20. Delia Jones to Vance, January 6, 1863, VGP.

21. Vance to Robert E. Lee, March 2, 1865, VGL.

22. McKee, "'Home and Friends,'" 369–71, 375, 387.

23. Poor woman and children to Vance, January 10, 1865, VGP.

24. Berlin, "Did Confederate Women Lose the War?" 188. Over a number of decades, historians have offered various interpretations of the role of women in the Confederacy. Some have argued that women made a substantial contribution to the struggle for Southern independence. Others have concluded that the dissatisfaction of women contributed to Confederate defeat. From recent historical scholarship has emerged a multifaceted view of the role of women during the war—a role that depended on location, social class, community support, family relationships, and prior economic and other circumstances in which individual women found themselves while the conflict raged. Among the many recent works that reveal the complexity of women's role in the war are Faust, *Mothers of Invention*; Rable, *Civil Wars*; Whites, *Civil War as a Crisis in Gender*; and Clinton and Silber, *Divided Houses*. Pertinent sources dealing specifically with North Carolina include Bynum, *Unruly Women*; Escott, *Many Excellent People*; McKinney, "Women's Role in Civil War Western North Carolina"; Inscoe, "Coping in Confederate Appalachia"; and McKee, "'Home and Friends.'"

25. As quoted in Inscoe, "Coping in Confederate Appalachia," 396.

26. Berlin, "Did Confederate Women Lose the War?" 172–73, 178.

27. William A. Smith to Vance, January 3, 1863, VGP.

28. Edmondston, *"Journal of a Secesh Lady,"* 330–31.

29. Ibid., 708.

30. Ibid., 176.

31. Cooper, *Jefferson Davis*, 96–97.

32. Edmondston, *"Journal of a Secesh Lady,"* 180.

33. Soldiers' wives to Vance, March 21, 1863, VGP.

34. Bynum, *Unruly Women*, 144–45.

35. As quoted in Auman, "Neighbor against Neighbor," 83.

36. Fuller, *Anna Long Thomas Fuller's Journal*, 43.

37. Poor woman and children to Vance, January 10, 1865, VGP.

38. Escott, *Many Excellent People*, 67.

39. See, for example, Michael Brown to Vance, March 18, 1863, VGP.

40. Soldiers' wives to Vance, March 21, 1863, VGP.

41. J. R. Robertson to Vance, January 13, 1864, Zebulon Baird Vance Papers, PC.

42. Regulators to Vance, February 18, 1863, VGP.

43. "By the Governor of North Carolina . . . Proclamation[s]," November 26, 1862, April 13, May 8, July 10, August 10, 1863, all five in VGL.

44. Joseph C. Pinnex to Vance, April 17, 20, 1863, and James P. Dillard to Vance, June 1, 1863, all three in VGP.

45. Powell, *Dictionary of North Carolina Biography*, s.v. "Morehead, John Motley," s.v. "Swepson, George William."

46. See Vance's endorsements at the bottom of James C. Pinnex to Vance, April 20, 1863, and James P. Dillard to Vance, June 1, 1863, both in VGP.

47. John M. Worth to Vance, January 12, 1863, VGP.

48. David G. Worth to Vance, September 16, 1863, VGP.

49. Vance to Gustavus W. Smith, January 24, 1863, Zebulon Baird Vance Papers, PC.

50. William H. C. Whiting to Vance, June 7, 1864, VGP; H. H. Clay to William H. C. Whiting, June 18, 1864, enclosed in Pierre G. T. Beauregard to Vance, September 22, 1864, VGL.

51. Vance to James A. Seddon, June 27, 1864, VGP.

52. Vance to Nicholas W. Woodfin, March 4, 1863, VGL.

53. William H. C. Whiting to David G. Worth, November 15, 1864, VGL.

54. Vance to William Smith, December 2, 1864, Vance to J. G. Dent, December 2, 1864, and Vance to P. B. Hawkins, December 2, 1864, all three in VGL.

55. Vance to James A. Seddon, December 5, 1864, VGP.

56. Many complaints about distillation can be found in VGP.

57. As quoted in Tucker, *Zeb Vance*, 174.

58. Vance to James A. Seddon, December 31, 1863, VGL.

59. James A. Seddon to Vance, January 12, 1864, VGP.

60. Barrett, *Civil War in North Carolina*, 197–98; Bynum, *Unruly Women*, 135. On the Shelton Laurel episode, see Paludan, *Victims*.

61. As reported in Thomas Settle to Vance, October 4, 1864, in Yearns and Barrett, *North Carolina Civil War Documentary*, 104.

62. Thomas Settle to Vance, October 4, 1864, in Yearns and Barrett, *North Carolina Civil War Documentary*, 104.

63. Vance to James A. Seddon, February 28, 1863, VGL.

64. James A. Seddon to Vance, February 25, 1863, VGP.

65. Charles S. Carrington to Abraham C. Myers, February 24, 1863, enclosed in James A. Seddon to Vance, February 25, 1863, VGP.

66. Vance to James A. Seddon, February 28, 1863, VGL.

67. Vance to James A. Seddon, January 22, 1863, VGP.

68. Ibid., February 25, 1863.

69. James A. Seddon to Vance, March 7, 1863, VGP.

70. Vance to James A. Seddon, March 21, 1863, VGP.

71. Samuel Jones to James A. Seddon, April 2, 1863, as excerpted in Seddon to Vance, April 8, 1863, VGP.

72. Vance to James A. Seddon, December 21, 1863, VGP.

73. Vance to James A. Seddon, April 27, 1863, VGL.

74. McKinney, "Women's Role in Civil War Western North Carolina," 48.

75. Clarke, "South Expects Every Woman to Do Her Duty."

76. Vance, "Lecture—The Political and Social South during the War" (1886), in Dowd, *Life of Vance*, 456.

CHAPTER 8. "I AM NOT OUT OF HEART"

1. Edward J. Hale to Vance, August 11, 1864, Zebulon Baird Vance Papers, PC.

2. "By the Governor of North Carolina, a Proclamation," August 24, 1864, VGL.

3. Vance to James A. Seddon, August 3, 1864, VGL.

4. Vance to David L. Swain, September 22, 1864, Zebulon Baird Vance Papers, PC.

5. See, for example, Vance to Milledge L. Bonham, September 23, 1864, VGL.

6. William Smith to Vance, September 27, 1864, VGP.

7. Milledge L. Bonham to Vance, September 28, 1864, VGP.

8. Joseph E. Brown to Vance, October 1, 1864, Harvard College Library, cited from McKinney and McMurry, *Papers of Vance*, reel 39.

9. John Milton to Vance, October 11, 1864, VGL.

10. Robert E. Lee to Vance, October 8, 1864, Zebulon Baird Vance Papers, PC.

11. Fenner B. Satterthwaite to Vance, October 6, 1864, VGP.

12. Vance to Edward J. Hale, October 11, 1864, Edward Jones Hale Papers, PC.

13. Edward J. Hale to Vance, October 13, 1864, Zebulon Baird Vance Papers, PC.

14. Joseph E. Brown to Vance, October 1, 1864, Harvard College Library, cited from McKinney and McMurry, *Papers of Vance*, reel 39; John Milton to Vance, October 11, 1864, VGL; Coulter, *Confederate States of America*, 293–94; Tucker, *Zeb Vance*, 369–70; Faust et al., *Encyclopedia of the Civil War*, 118, 344.

15. Coulter, *Confederate States of America*, 292–93.

16. William A. Graham to Vance, November 29, 1864, Zebulon Baird Vance Papers, PC.

17. *Hillsborough Recorder*, December 14, 1864, as printed in Hamilton, Williams, and Peacock, *Papers of Graham*, 6:197–98.

18. Vance to Andrew G. Magrath, January 18, 1865, VGL; *Laws of North Carolina, 1864*, cited in Yates, "Governor Vance and the End of the War in North Carolina," 316; *Journal of the Senate of North Carolina, 1864–1865*, 26–27; *Journal of the House of Representatives of North Carolina, 1864–1865*, 55.

19. McPherson, *Battle Cry of Freedom*, 803–6, 808–9; Davis, *Look Away!* 402.

20. Wise, *Lifeline of the Confederacy*, 201, 209–10; Browning, *From Cape Charles to Cape Fear*, 266–67, 305.

21. Vance to Jefferson Davis, November 15, 1864, VGL.

22. Jefferson Davis to Vance, November 21, 1864, Zebulon Baird Vance Papers, PC.

23. Braxton Bragg to Vance, December 20, 1864, VGP.

24. "By the Governor of North Carolina, a Proclamation," December 20, 1864, VGL.

25. "Inaugural Address," December 22, 1864, Zebulon Baird Vance Papers, PC.

26. Tucker, *Zeb Vance*, 383; Gragg, *Confederate Goliath*, 60–61.

27. Barrett, *Civil War in North Carolina*, 263–70; Tucker, *Zeb Vance*, 383.

28. Vance to Jefferson Davis, January 7, 1865, VGL.

29. The battle for the fort is thoroughly recounted in Gragg, *Confederate Goliath*.

30. Faust et al., *Encyclopedia of the Civil War*, 652–53.

31. Vance to Bradley T. Johnson, February 1, 1865, VGL.

32. Vance to James A. Seddon, February 1, 1865, VGL.

33. John C. Breckinridge to Vance, February 8, 1865, VGP.

34. G. W. Booth to Vance, February 3, 1865, VGL.

35. Bradley T. Johnson to Vance, February 12, 1865, VGP.

36. Faust et al., *Encyclopedia of the Civil War*, 653.

37. Vance to Joseph E. Brown, January 18, 1865, VGL.

38. Vance to Andrew G. Magrath, January 18, 1865, VGL.

39. Vance to anonymous, January 31, 1865, Zebulon Baird Vance Papers, PC.

40. McPherson, *Battle Cry of Freedom*, 822–24; Donald, *Lincoln*, 556–61.

41. The most thorough account of the Wilmington campaign and its aftermath is Fonvielle, *Wilmington Campaign*.

42. Robert E. Lee to Vance, February 16, 1865, VGP.

43. Ibid., February 19, 1865.

44. Vance to Robert E. Lee, February 20, 1865, VGL.

45. Fonvielle, *Wilmington Campaign*, 377–78, 428–29; Vance to John White, February 28, 1865, VGL.

46. "By the Governor of North Carolina, a Proclamation," February 14, 1865, VGL.

47. Bradley, *This Astounding Close*, 76.

48. Jefferson Davis to Vance, February 21, 1865, VGP.

49. Robert E. Lee to Vance, February 24, 1865, VGP.

50. John C. Breckinridge to Vance, February 24, 1865, and Isaac M. St. John to Vance, February 24, 1865, both in VGP.

51. Vance to Pierre G. T. Beauregard, February 25, 1865, and Vance to Braxton Bragg, February 25, 1865, both in VGL.

52. Joseph E. Johnston to Vance, February 28, 1865, VGP.

53. Bradley, *This Astounding Close*, 11–12.

54. "To the People of North Carolina," February 28, 1865, VGL.

55. Vance to Robert E. Lee, March 2, 1865, VGL.

56. Robert E. Lee to Vance, March 9, 1865, VGP.

57. Coulter, *Confederate States of America*, 273–74.

58. Black, *Railroads of the Confederacy*, 148–59.

59. Vance to Joseph E. Johnston, March 1, 1865, VGL.

60. Joseph E. Johnston to Vance, March 2, 1865, VGP.

61. Robert E. Lee to Vance, March 2, 1865, VGP.

62. John C. Breckinridge to Vance, March 3, 1865, VGP.

63. Vance to Jeremy F. Gilmer, March 3, 1865, VGL.

64. Vance to John C. Breckinridge, March 18, 1865, VGL.

65. John C. Breckinridge to Vance, March 24, 1865, VGP. Vance's response appears as an endorsement at the bottom of Breckinridge's telegram.

66. Joseph E. Johnston to Vance, March 3, 1865, VGP.

67. Bradley, *This Astounding Close*, 13.

68. Vance to Joseph E. Johnston, March 4, 1865, VGL.

69. Bradley, *This Astounding Close*, 13.

70. Vance to Fayetteville commandant, March 8, 1865, VGL.

71. Bradley, *This Astounding Close*, 12–40. See also Bradley, *Last Stand in the Carolinas*.

72. Patrick H. Winston to Vance, March 14, 1865, VGP.

73. Bradley, *This Astounding Close*, 95.

74. Barrett, *Civil War in North Carolina*, 348–49, 367–70.

75. William A. Graham to David L. Swain, March 26, April 8, 1865, both in Hamilton, Williams, and Peacock, *Papers of Graham*, 6:289–91, 294–97.

76. Bradley, *This Astounding Close*, 78.

77. William A. Graham to David L. Swain, April 8, 1865, in Hamilton, Williams, and Peacock, *Papers of Graham*, 6:294–97.

78. David L. Swain to William A. Graham, April 8, 1865, and Graham to Swain, April 8, 9, 1865, all three in Hamilton, Williams, and Peacock, *Papers of Graham*, 6:292–97.

79. Vance to Jefferson Davis, April 11, 1865, in *War of the Rebellion*, ser. 1, vol. 46, pt. 3, p. 1393.

80. Bradley, *This Astounding Close*, 80, 94, 95.

81. Vance to William T. Sherman, April 11, 1865, Cornelia P. Spencer Papers, SHC.

82. Davis, *Honorable Defeat*, 134–36; Cooper, *Jefferson Davis*, 565.

83. Davis, *Honorable Defeat*, 135–39.

84. Bradley, *This Astounding Close*, 145.

85. Jefferson Davis to Vance, April 13, 1865, VGP.

86. Vance to William A. Graham, April 11, 1865, in Hamilton, Williams, and Peacock, *Papers of Graham*, 6:298.

CHAPTER 9. "ALL HELL CAN'T MAKE ME DO IT"

1. Vance to William T. Sherman, April 12, 1865, in *War of the Rebellion*, ser. 1, vol. 47, pt. 3, p. 178.

2. Bradley, *This Astounding Close*, 108.

3. Tucker, *Zeb Vance*, 394–95.

4. Vance to William J. Hardee, April 12, 1865, Battle Family Papers, SHC.

5. Bradley, *This Astounding Close*, 109.

6. Ibid., 325n.

7. Archer Anderson to Joseph E. Johnston and Jefferson Davis, April 12, 1865, in *War of the Rebellion*, ser. 1, vol. 47, pt. 3, p. 791.

8. Vance to Jefferson Davis, April 12, 1865, and Davis to Vance, April 12, 1865, both in *War of the Rebellion*, ser. 1, vol. 47, pt. 3, p. 792.

9. Bradley, *This Astounding Close*, 110–11.

10. Ibid., 114–15.

11. William T. Sherman to Vance, April 12, 1865 (no. 1), Zebulon Baird Vance Papers, PC.

12. William T. Sherman to Vance, April 12, 1865 (no. 2), Zebulon Baird Vance Papers, PC.

13. Bradley, *This Astounding Close*, 114.

14. Ibid., 118; Tucker, *Zeb Vance*, 393–94, 401–3; Yates, "Governor Vance and the End of the War in North Carolina," 325–28.

15. Bradley, *This Astounding Close*, 119–22.

16. Ibid., 126–27; Tucker, *Zeb Vance*, 401–2; William T. Sherman to all officers and soldiers of the U.S. Army, April 13, 1865, Zebulon Baird Vance Papers, PC.

17. Bradley, *This Astounding Close*, 147–48; Tucker, *Zeb Vance*, 402–4.

18. Pierre G. T. Beauregard to Vance, April 15, 1865, VGP.

19. Davis, *Honorable Defeat*, 150–54.

20. Barrett, *Civil War in North Carolina*, 382–83; Davis, *Honorable Defeat*, 154–55; John C. Breckinridge to Vance, April 17, 1865, Zebulon Baird Vance Papers, PC.

21. Bradley, *This Astounding Close*, 166–67; Davis, *Honorable Defeat*, 154–55.

22. Davis, *Honorable Defeat*, 137–38.

23. As quoted in Tucker, *Zeb Vance*, 24.

24. Davis, *Honorable Defeat*, 158–59; Bradley, *This Astounding Close*, 167.

25. Davis, *Honorable Defeat*, 160–68; Bradley, *This Astounding Close*, 172; Barrett, *Civil War in North Carolina*, 385.

26. Barrett, *Civil War in North Carolina*, 385.

27. Davis, *Honorable Defeat*, 169.

28. Thomas Webb to Vance, April 18, 1865, Zebulon Baird Vance Papers, PC.

29. Vance to Joseph E. Johnston, April 19, 1865 (no. 1), Zebulon Baird Vance Papers, PC.

30. Joseph E. Johnston to Vance, April 19, 1865 (no. 1), Zebulon Baird Vance Papers, PC.

31. Vance to Joseph E. Johnston, April 19, 1865 (no. 2), Zebulon Baird Vance Papers, PC.

32. Joseph E. Johnston to Vance, April 19, 1865 (no. 2), Zebulon Baird Vance Papers, PC.

33. Vance to Joseph E. Johnston, April 16, 1865, Zebulon Baird Vance Papers, PC.

34. Ibid., April 20, 1865.

35. Vance to Thomas White, April 21, 1865, Zebulon Baird Vance Papers, PC.

36. Vance to Joseph E. Johnston, April 21, 1865, and Johnston to Vance, April 21, 1865, both in Zebulon Baird Vance Papers, PC.

37. Vance to Joseph E. Johnston, April 22, 1865, Zebulon Baird Vance Papers, PC.

38. Joseph E. Johnston to Vance, April 24, 1865, Zebulon Baird Vance Papers, PC.

39. Vance to John C. Breckinridge, April 22, 1865, Zebulon Baird Vance Papers, PC.

40. Joseph E. Johnston to Vance, April 14, 1865, Zebulon Baird Vance Papers, PC.

41. Jonathan Worth to Vance, April 19, 1865, Zebulon Baird Vance Papers, PC.

42. Vance to Joseph E. Johnston, April 19, 1865 (no. 1), Zebulon Baird Vance Papers, PC.

43. Joseph E. Johnston to Vance, April 19, 1865 (no. 1), Zebulon Baird Vance Papers, PC.

44. Cooper, *Jefferson Davis*, 567.

45. Davis, *Honorable Defeat*, 180–89.

46. Jefferson Davis to Vance, April 23, 1865, VGP.

47. Bradley, *This Astounding Close*, 348n.

48. Vance, "Lecture—The Last Days of the War in North Carolina," in Dowd, *Life of Vance*, 485–86.

49. Vance, "Lecture—The Last Days of the War in North Carolina," 486.

50. Cooper, *Jefferson Davis*, 568–69; Barrett, *Civil War in North Carolina*, 385; Davis, *Honorable Defeat*, 192–93.

51. Joseph E. Johnston to Vance, April 24, 1865, Zebulon Baird Vance Papers, PC.

52. Davis, *Honorable Defeat*, 194–95; Cooper, *Jefferson Davis*, 569–75.

53. Bradley, *This Astounding Close*, 214–17.

54. Vance to William T. Sherman, April 27, 1865, Zebulon Baird Vance Papers, PC.

55. Ibid.

56. Jonathan Worth to Vance, April 28, 1865, Zebulon Baird Vance Papers, PC.

57. "By the Governor of North Carolina, a Proclamation," April 28, 1865, Zebulon Baird Vance Papers, PC.

58. Vance to John M. Schofield, April 30, 1865, John D. Whitford Papers, PC.

59. William A. Graham to David L. Swain, May 11, 1865, in Hamilton, Williams, and Peacock, *Papers of Graham*, 6:310–11 (quotation); Bedford Brown to Vance, May 2, 1865, Zebulon Baird Vance Papers, PC.

60. Bradley, *This Astounding Close*, 240; William A. Graham to David L. Swain, May 11, 1865, in Hamilton, Williams, and Peacock, *Papers of Graham*, 6:311.

61. Dowd, *Life of Vance*, 95–97.

62. Tucker, *Zeb Vance*, 415; Bradley, *This Astounding Close*, 260.

63. Harriett E. Vance to Vance, May 19, 1865, Zebulon Baird Vance Papers, PC; Powell, *Dictionary of North Carolina Biography*, s.v. "Swain, David Lowry."

64. Dowd, *Life of Vance*, 97.

65. Harriett E. Vance to Vance, June 5, 1865, Zebulon Baird Vance Papers, PC.

66. Ibid., June 9, 1865.

67. Vance to Harriett E. Vance, June 30, 1865, Zebulon Baird Vance Papers, PC.

68. Dorris, "Pardoning North Carolinians," 379–80, 397–98.

69. As quoted in Tucker, *Zeb Vance*, 429.

70. Dorris, "Pardoning North Carolinians," 397–98.

EPILOGUE: "TO THE LAST GASP WITH TRUTH AND LOYALTY"

1. McKinney and McMurry, *Guide to the Papers of Vance*, xxix–xxx; Tucker, *Zeb Vance*, 431–33; Powell, *Dictionary of North Carolina Biography*, s.v. "Dowd, Clement."

2. McKinney and McMurry, *Guide to the Papers of Vance*, xxx–xxi; Tucker, *Zeb Vance*, 437.

3. Vance, "Lecture Delivered before the Young Men of Raleigh," 365–66.

4. Vance to William A. Graham, August 6, 1870, William Alexander Graham Papers, PC.

5. McKinney, "Vance and His Reconstruction of the Civil War in North Carolina," 74–75; Tucker, *Zeb Vance*, 412–13, 470.

6. Vance, *Scattered Nation*, 36.

7. Vance, "Address Delivered by Governor Vance before the Southern Historical Society."

8. Vance to David L. Swain, September 22, 1864, Zebulon Baird Vance Papers, PC.

9. Crow, "Thomas Settle Jr., Reconstruction, and the Meaning of the Civil War"; McKinney, "Vance and His Reconstruction of the Civil War in North Carolina," 77–80.

10. McKinney, "Vance and His Reconstruction of the Civil War in North Carolina," 81–82.

11. Lefler and Newsome, *North Carolina*, 501.

12. Tucker, *Zeb Vance*, 461, 463; McKinney and McMurry, *Guide to the Papers of Vance*, xxxiv; Powell, *Dictionary of North Carolina Biography*, s.v. "Merrimon, Augustus S."

13. *Pamlico Enterprise*, October 20, 1882.

14. Vance, "Lecture—The Political and Social South during the War" (1886), in Dowd, *Life of Vance*, 452–53.

15. McKinney and McMurry, *Guide to the Papers of Vance*, xi; Tucker, *Zeb Vance*, 471, 478–79; *Charlotte Democrat*, April 20, 1894.

16. Rable, *Confederate Republic*, 2.

17. Faust, *Creation of Confederate Nationalism*, 83.

18. Clarke, "Autobiography of Vance," 24–25.

19. Vance to Andrew G. Magrath, January 18, 1865, VGL.

20. *Fayetteville Observer*, March 3, 1864; Escott, *After Secession*, 203.

21. Vance to Joseph E. Brown, January 18, 1865, VGL.

22. Vance to David L. Swain, September 22, 1864, Zebulon Baird Vance Papers, PC.

BIBLIOGRAPHY

PRIMARY SOURCES

Manuscripts

Southern Historical Collection, University of North Carolina Library, Chapel Hill

Battle Family Papers
William Dickson Papers
Lenoir Family Papers
Peter Mallett Papers
New Bern Occupation Papers
Marmaduke Swaim Robins Papers
Daniel Lindsay Russell Papers
Cornelia P. Spencer Papers
David Lowry Swain Papers
Zebulon Baird Vance Papers
Edward Clements Yellowley Papers

Special Collections, Duke University Library, Durham, N.C.

Jefferson Davis Papers
Zebulon Baird Vance Papers

State Archives, North Carolina Office of Archives and History, Raleigh

County Records
    Franklin County Superior Court Minutes, 1864–1865
    Madison County Estates Records, 1852

Lincoln County Superior Court Minutes, 1863
Orange County Superior Court Minutes, 1863
Richmond County Superior Court Minutes, 1865
Rutherford County Court of Pleas and Quarter Sessions Minutes, 1863
Governors Office
Governors Letter Books
Governors Papers
Miscellaneous Papers
North Carolina Gubernatorial Election Returns, 1864
Private Collections
Futch Letters
William Alexander Graham Papers
Edward Jones Hale Papers
Zebulon Baird Vance Papers
John D. Whitford Papers

North Carolina Newspapers

Asheville News, 1862
Carolina Watchman (Salisbury), 1863
Charlotte Democrat, 1894
Confederate (Raleigh), 1864
Conservative (Raleigh), 1864
Daily Bulletin (Charlotte), 1862
Fayetteville Observer, 1863–1864
Iredell Express (Statesville), 1864
Milton Chronicle, 1864
North Carolina Standard (Raleigh), 1863–1864
Pamlico Enterprise (Stonewall), 1882
Raleigh Register, 1862
Spirit of the Age (Raleigh), 1862

State Laws and Reports

Journal of the House of Representatives of North Carolina, 1864–1865
Journal of the Senate of North Carolina, 1864–1865
North Carolina Reports, 1863
Public Laws of North Carolina, 1862–1864
Revised Code of North Carolina, 1854

Published Documents and Diaries

Cannon, Elizabeth R., ed. *My Beloved Zebulon: The Correspondence of Zebulon
    Baird Vance and Harriett Newell Espy.* With an introduction by Frances Gray
    Patton. Chapel Hill: University of North Carolina Press, 1971.
Cheney, John L., Jr. *North Carolina Government, 1585–1979: A Narrative and*

Statistical History. Raleigh: North Carolina Department of Secretary of State, 1981.

Clark, Walter, ed. *Histories of the Several Regiments and Battalions from North Carolina in the Great War, 1861–'65*. 5 vols. Raleigh: State of North Carolina, 1901.

Clarke, Mary Bayard. "The South Expects Every Woman to Do Her Duty." In *Live Your Own Life: The Papers of Mary Bayard Clarke*. Ed. Terrell Armistead Crow and Mary Moulton Barden. Columbia: University of South Carolina Press, 2003, 222–28.

Dowd, Clement. *Life of Zebulon B. Vance*. Charlotte: Observer Printing and Publishing House, 1897.

Edmondston, Catherine Ann Devereux. *"Journal of a Secesh Lady": The Diary of Catherine Ann Devereux Edmondston, 1860–1866*. Ed. Beth G. Crabtree and James W. Patton. Raleigh: Office of Archives and History, North Carolina Department of Cultural Resources, 1995.

Fuller, Anna Long Thomas. *Anna Long Thomas Fuller's Journal, 1856–1890: A Civil War Diary*. Ed. Myrtle C. King. Alpharetta, Ga.: Priority Publishing, 1999.

Hamilton, J. G. de Roulhac, Max R. Williams, and Mary Reynolds Peacock, eds. *The Papers of William Alexander Graham*. 8 vols. Raleigh: Office of Archives and History, North Carolina Department of Cultural Resources, 1957–1992.

James, Horace. *Annual Report of the Superintendent of Negro Affairs in North Carolina, 1864. With an Appendix, Containing the History and Management of the Freedmen in This Department up to June 1st, 1865*. Boston: W. P. Brown Printers, n.d.

Johnston, Frontis W., and Joe A. Mobley, eds. *The Papers of Zebulon Baird Vance*. 2 vols. to date. Raleigh: Office of Archives and History, North Carolina Department of Cultural Resources, 1963–.

McKinney, Gordon, and Richard McMurry, eds. *The Papers of Zebulon Vance*. Microfilm. 39 reels. Frederick, Md.: University Publications of America, 1987.

Raper, Horace W., and Thornton W. Mitchell, eds. *The Papers of William Woods Holden*. 1 vol. to date. Raleigh: Office of Archives and History, North Carolina Department of Cultural Resources, 2000–.

Vance, Zebulon B. "Address Delivered by Governor Vance before the Southern Historical Society." *Our Living and Our Dead* 3 (November 1875): 619–24.

———. "A Lecture Delivered before the Young Men of Raleigh, January 1867." *Land We Loved* 6 (March 1869): 363–83.

———. *The Scattered Nation*. New York: Rational Publishing Co., 1904.

The War of the Rebellion: A Compilation of the Official Records of the Union and Confederate Armies. 128 vols. Washington, D.C.: Government Printing Office, 1880–1901.

Unpublished Contemporary Accounts

Arrington, Hannah Bolton. "John White of Warrenton, N.C.: A Sketch of His Life by His Daughter." 1923. Manuscript in the possession of the author.

Clarke, Mary Bayard Devereux. "Autobiography of the Hon. Zebulon B. Vance, Copied from the Original Notes in His Own Handwriting." 1868. Manuscript in the possession of Mary Moulton Barden.

SECONDARY SOURCES

Books

Ashe, Samuel A. *History of North Carolina*. 2 vols. Greensboro: Charles L. Van Noppen, 1908–1929.
Ashe, Samuel A., Stephen B. Weeks, and Charles L. Van Noppen, eds. *Biographical History of North Carolina*. 8 vols. Greensboro: Charles L. Van Noppen, 1905–1917.
Barrett, John G. *The Civil War in North Carolina*. Chapel Hill: University of North Carolina Press, 1963.
Beringer, Richard E., Herman Hattaway, Archer Jones, and William N. Still Jr. *Why the South Lost the Civil War*. Athens: University of Georgia Press, 1986.
Berlin, Ira. *Slaves without Masters: The Free Negro in the Antebellum South*. New York: Pantheon Books, 1974.
Black, Robert C. *The Railroads of the Confederacy*. Chapel Hill: University of North Carolina Press, 1952.
Boatner, Mark M., III. *The Civil War Dictionary*. New York: David McKay, 1959.
Boney, F. N. *John Letcher of Virginia: The Story of Virginia's Civil War Governor*. Tuscaloosa: University of Alabama Press, 1966.
Boritt, Gabor S., et al., comps. *Of the People, by the People, for the People and Other Quotations by Abraham Lincoln*. New York: Columbia University Press, 1996.
Bradley, Mark L. *Last Stand in the Carolinas: The Battle of Bentonville*. Campbell, Calif.: Savas Publishing, 1996.
———. *This Astounding Close: The Road to Bennett Place*. Chapel Hill: University of North Carolina Press, 2000.
Bradley, Stephen E., Jr., comp. *North Carolina Confederate Home Guard Examinations, 1863–1864*. Keysville, Va.: n.p., 1993.
Brown, Norman D. *Edward Stanly: Whiggery's Tarheel "Conqueror."* Tuscaloosa: University of Alabama Press, 1974.
Browning, Robert M., Jr. *From Cape Charles to Cape Fear: The North Atlantic Blockading Squadron during the Civil War*. Tuscaloosa: University of Alabama Press, 1993.
Butler, Lindley S. *Pirates, Privateers, and Rebel Raiders of the North Carolina Coast*. Chapel Hill: University of North Carolina Press, 2000.
Bynum, Victoria E. *Unruly Women: The Politics of Social and Sexual Control in the Old South*. Chapel Hill: University of North Carolina Press, 1992.
Carbone, John S. *The Civil War in Coastal North Carolina*. Raleigh: Office of Archives and History, North Carolina Department of Cultural Resources, 2001.

Cassidy, Vincent H., and Amos E. Simpson. *Henry Watkins Allen of Louisiana*. Baton Rouge: Louisiana State University Press, 1964.

Click, Patricia C. *Time Full of Trial: The Roanoke Island Freedmen's Colony, 1862–1867*. Chapel Hill: University of North Carolina Press, 2001.

Clinton, Catherine, and Nina Silber, eds. *Divided Houses: Gender and the Civil War*. New York: Oxford University Press, 1992.

Connor, Robert D. W. *North Carolina: Rebuilding an Ancient Commonwealth, 1584–1925*. 4 vols. New York: American Historical Society, 1929.

Cooper, William J., Jr. *Jefferson Davis, American*. New York: Vintage Books, 2001.

Cornish, Dudley Taylor. *The Sable Arm: Negro Troops in the Union Army, 1861–1865*. New York: Longmans, Green, 1956.

Coulter, E. Merton. *The Confederate States of America, 1861–1865*. Baton Rouge: Louisiana State University Press, 1950.

Crow, Jeffrey J., and Robert F. Durden. *Maverick Republican in the Old North State: A Political Biography of Daniel L. Russell*. Baton Rouge: Louisiana State University Press, 1977.

Crow, Jeffrey J., Paul D. Escott, and Flora J. Hatley. *A History of African Americans in North Carolina*. Raleigh: Office of Archives and History, North Carolina Department of Cultural Resources, 1992.

Current, Richard M., et al., eds. *Encyclopedia of the Confederacy*. 5 vols. New York: Simon and Schuster, 1993.

Davis, William C. *An Honorable Defeat: The Last Days of the Confederate Government*. New York: Harcourt, 2001.

———. *Jefferson Davis: The Man and His Hour*. New York: HarperCollins, 1991.

———. *Look Away! A History of the Confederate States of America*. New York: Free Press, 2002.

———. *The Union That Shaped the Confederacy: Robert Toombs and Alexander Stephens*. Lawrence: University Press of Kansas, 2001.

Dodd, William E. *Jefferson Davis*. Philadelphia: George W. Jacobs, 1907.

Donald, David Herbert. *Lincoln*. New York: Simon and Schuster, 1995.

———, ed. *Why the North Won the Civil War*. 1960. Reprint, New York: Collier Books, 1971.

Dubay, Robert W. *John Jones Pettus, Mississippi Fire-Eater: His Life and Times, 1813–1867*. Oxford: University Press of Mississippi, 1975.

Eaton, Clement. *A History of the Southern Confederacy*. 1954. Reprint, New York: Free Press, 1965.

———. *Jefferson Davis*. New York: Free Press, 1977.

Edmunds, John B., Jr. *Francis W. Pickens and the Politics of Destruction*. Chapel Hill: University of North Carolina Press, 1986.

Escott, Paul D. *After Secession: Jefferson Davis and the Failure of Confederate Nationalism*. Baton Rouge: Louisiana State University Press, 1978.

———. *Many Excellent People: Power and Privilege in North Carolina, 1850–1900*. Chapel Hill: University of North Carolina Press, 1985.

Faust, Drew Gilpin. *The Creation of Confederate Nationalism: Ideology and Identity in the Civil War South.* Baton Rouge: Louisiana State University Press, 1988.

———. *Mothers of Invention: Women of the Slaveholding South in the American Civil War.* Chapel Hill: University of North Carolina Press, 1996.

Faust, Patricia L., et al., eds. *Historical Times Illustrated Encyclopedia of the Civil War.* New York: Harper and Row, 1986.

Fonvielle, Chris E., Jr. *The Wilmington Campaign: Last Rays of Departing Hope.* Campbell, Calif.: Savas Publishing, 1997.

Foster, Gaines M. *Ghosts of the Confederacy: Defeat, the Lost Cause, and the Emergence of the New South, 1865–1913.* New York: Oxford University Press, 1987.

Franklin, John Hope. *The Free Negro in North Carolina, 1780–1860.* Chapel Hill: University of North Carolina Press, 1943.

Freeman, Douglas Southall. *R. E. Lee: A Biography.* 4 vols. New York: Charles Scribner's Sons, 1934–1936.

Glatthaar, Joseph T. *Forged in Battle: The Civil War Alliance of Black Soldiers and White Officers.* New York: Free Press, 1990.

Gragg, Rod. *Confederate Goliath: The Battle of Fort Fisher.* New York: HarperCollins, 1991.

———. *Covered with Glory: The 26th North Carolina Infantry at Gettysburg.* New York: HarperCollins, 2000.

Grimsley, Mark. *The Hard Hand of War: Union Military Policy toward Southern Civilians, 1861–1865.* New York: Cambridge University Press, 1995.

Hamilton, J. G. de Roulhac. *History of North Carolina.* 3 vols. New York: Lewis Publishing, 1919.

Harris, William C. *North Carolina and the Coming of the Civil War.* Raleigh: Office of Archives and History, North Carolina Department of Cultural Resources, 1988.

———. *William Woods Holden: Firebrand of North Carolina Politics.* Baton Rouge: Louisiana State University Press, 1987.

———. *With Charity for All: Lincoln and the Restoration of the Union.* Lexington: University Press of Kentucky, 1997.

Hill, Louise Biles. *Joseph E. Brown and the Confederacy.* Chapel Hill: University of North Carolina Press, 1939.

Inscoe, John C., and Gordon B. McKinney. *The Heart of Confederate Appalachia: Western North Carolina in the Civil War.* Chapel Hill: University of North Carolina Press, 2000.

Kruman, Marc W. *Parties and Politics in North Carolina, 1836–1865.* Baton Rouge: Louisiana State University Press, 1983.

Lefler, Hugh Talmage, and Albert Ray Newsome. *North Carolina: The History of a Southern State.* 3rd ed. Chapel Hill: University of North Carolina Press, 1973.

Manarin, Louis H., comp. *A Guide to Military Organizations and Installations in North Carolina, 1861–1865.* Raleigh: North Carolina Confederate Centennial Commission, 1961.

Manarin, Louis H., and Weymouth T. Jordan Jr., comps. *North Carolina Troops, 1861–1865: A Roster.* 15 vols. to date. Raleigh: Office of Archives and History, North Carolina Department of Cultural Resources, 1966–.

McKinney, Gordon B. *Zeb Vance: North Carolina's Civil War Governor and Gilded Age Political Leader.* Chapel Hill: University of North Carolina Press, 2004.

McKinney, Gordon, and Richard McMurry, eds. *Guide to the Papers of Zebulon Vance.* Frederick, Md.: University Publications of America, 1987.

McPherson, James M. *Battle Cry of Freedom: The Civil War Era.* New York: Oxford University Press, 1988.

———. *Drawn with the Sword: Reflections on the American Civil War.* New York: Oxford University Press, 1996.

———. *The Struggle for Equality: Abolitionists and the Negro in the Civil War and Reconstruction.* Princeton: Princeton University Press, 1964.

Mitchell, Memory F. *Legal Aspects of Conscription and Exemption in North Carolina.* Chapel Hill: University of North Carolina Press, 1965.

Mobley, Joe A. *James City: A Black Community in North Carolina, 1863–1900.* Raleigh: Office of Archives and History, North Carolina Department of Cultural Resources, 1981.

Moore, Albert B. *Conscription and Conflict in the Confederacy.* 1924. Reprint, Columbia: University of South Carolina Press, 1996.

Neely, Mark E., Jr. *Southern Rights: Political Prisoners and the Myth of Confederate Constitutionalism.* Charlottesville: University Press of Virginia, 1999.

Owsley, Frank L. *State Rights in the Confederacy.* Chicago: University of Chicago Press, 1925.

Paludan, Phillip Shaw. *Victims: A True Story of the Civil War.* Knoxville: University of Tennessee Press, 1981.

Parks, Joseph H. *Joseph E. Brown of Georgia.* Baton Rouge: Louisiana State University Press, 1977.

Potter, David M. *The Impending Crisis, 1848–1861.* New York: Harper and Row, 1976.

Powell, William S., ed. *Dictionary of North Carolina Biography.* 6 vols. Chapel Hill: University of North Carolina Press, 1979–1996.

———. *The North Carolina Gazetteer.* Chapel Hill: University of North Carolina Press, 1968.

———. *North Carolina through Four Centuries.* Chapel Hill: University of North Carolina Press, 1989.

Pressly, Thomas J. *Americans Interpret Their Civil War.* 2nd ed. New York: Collier Books, 1962.

Quarles, Benjamin. *The Negro in the Civil War.* Boston: Little, Brown, 1953.

Rable, George C. *Civil Wars: Women and the Crisis of Southern Nationalism.* Urbana: University of Illinois Press, 1989.

———. *The Confederate Republic: A Revolution against Politics.* Chapel Hill: University of North Carolina Press, 1994.

Ramsdell, Charles W. *Behind the Lines in the Southern Confederacy*. Baton Rouge: Louisiana State University Press, 1944.

Randall, J. G., and David Donald. *The Civil War and Reconstruction*. Rev. ed. Lexington, Mass.: D. C. Heath, 1969.

Spencer, Cornelia Phillips. *The Last Ninety Days of the War in North Carolina*. New York: Watchman Publishing, 1866.

Tatum, Georgia Lee. *Disloyalty in the Confederacy*. Chapel Hill: University of North Carolina Press, 1934.

Thomas, Emory M. *The Confederate Nation, 1861–1865*. New York: Harper and Row, 1979.

Tucker, Glenn. *Zeb Vance: Champion of Personal Freedom*. New York: Bobbs-Merrill, 1965.

Whites, Lee Ann. *The Civil War as a Crisis in Gender: Augusta, Georgia, 1860–1890*. Athens: University of Georgia Press, 1995.

Wise, Stephen R. *Lifeline of the Confederacy: Blockade Running during the Civil War*. Columbia: University of South Carolina Press, 1988.

Woodworth, Steven E. *Davis and Lee at War*. Lawrence: University Press of Kansas, 1995.

Yates, Richard E. *The Confederacy and Zeb Vance*. Tuscaloosa, Ala.: Confederate Publishing, 1958.

Yearns, W. Buck, ed. *The Confederate Governors*. Athens: University of Georgia Press, 1985.

Yearns, W. Buck, and John G. Barrett, eds. *North Carolina Civil War Documentary*. Chapel Hill: University of North Carolina Press, 1980.

Articles

Auman, William T. "Neighbor against Neighbor: The Inner Civil War in the Randolph County Area of Confederate North Carolina." *North Carolina Historical Review* 61 (January 1984): 59–92.

Auman, William T., and David D. Scarboro. "The Heroes of America in North Carolina." *North Carolina Historical Review* 58 (October 1981): 327–63.

Bardolph, Richard. "Confederate Dilemma: North Carolina Troops and the Deserter Problem." Parts 1 and 2. *North Carolina Historical Review* 69 (January/April 1989): 61–86, 179–210.

Beringer, Richard E. "Jefferson Davis's Pursuit of Ambition: The Attractive Features of Alternative Decisions." *Civil War History* 38 (March 1992): 5–38.

Berlin, Jean V. "Did Confederate Women Lose the War? Deprivation, Destruction, and Despair on the Home Front." In *The Collapse of the Confederacy*, ed. Mark Grimsley and Brooks D. Simpson, 168–93. Lincoln: University Press of Nebraska, 2001.

Bradley, Mark L. "'This Monstrous Proposition': North Carolina and the Confederate Debate on Arming the Slaves." *North Carolina Historical Review* 80 (April 2003): 153–87.

Browning, Judkin J. "'Little Souled Mercenaries'? The Buffaloes of Eastern North Carolina during the Civil War." *North Carolina Historical Review* 77 (July 2000): 337–63.

Crow, Jeffrey J. "Thomas Settle Jr., Reconstruction, and the Meaning of the Civil War." *Journal of Southern History* 62 (November 1996): 702–16.

Delany, Norman C. "Charles Henry Foster and the Unionists of Eastern North Carolina." *North Carolina Historical Review* 37 (July 1960): 348–66.

Dorris, Jonathan Truman. "Pardoning North Carolinians." *North Carolina Historical Review* 23 (July 1946): 360–401.

Escott, Paul D. "Poverty and Governmental Aid for the Poor in Confederate North Carolina." *North Carolina Historical Review* 61 (October 1984): 462–80.

Hamilton, J. G. de Roulhac. "The North Carolina Courts and the Confederacy." *North Carolina Historical Review* 4 (October 1927): 366–403.

Harris, William C. "Lincoln and Wartime Reconstruction in North Carolina, 1861–1863." *North Carolina Historical Review* 63 (April 1986): 149–68.

Inscoe, John C. "Coping in Confederate Appalachia: Portrait of a Mountain Woman and Her Community at War." *North Carolina Historical Review* 69 (October 1992): 388–413.

Jeffrey, Thomas E. "Free Suffrage Revisited: Party Politics and Constitutional Reform in Antebellum North Carolina." *North Carolina Historical Review* 59 (January 1982): 24–48.

———. "Thunder from the Mountains: Thomas Lanier Clingman and the End of Whig Supremacy in North Carolina." *North Carolina Historical Review* 56 (autumn 1979): 366–95.

Jordan, Weymouth T., Jr., and Gerald W. Thomas. "Massacre at Plymouth: April 20, 1864." *North Carolina Historical Review* 72 (April 1995): 125–93.

Kruman, Marc W. "Thomas L. Clingman and the Whig Party: A Reconsideration." *North Carolina Historical Review* 64 (January 1987): 1–18.

Marshall, Patricia Phillips. "The Legendary Thomas Day: Debunking the Popular Mythology of an African American Craftsman." *North Carolina Historical Review* 78 (January 2001): 32–66.

McCain, Paul M. "Magistrates' Courts in Early North Carolina." *North Carolina Historical Review* 58 (January 1971): 23–30.

McKee, David H. "'Home and Friends': Kinship, Community, and Elite Women in Caldwell County, North Carolina, during the Civil War." *North Carolina Historical Review* 74 (October 1997): 363–88.

McKinney, Gordon B. "Women's Role in Civil War Western North Carolina." *North Carolina Historical Review* 69 (January 1992): 37–56.

———. "Zebulon Vance and His Reconstruction of the Civil War in North Carolina." *North Carolina Historical Review* 75 (January 1998): 69–85.

Morris, Charles Edward. "Panic and Reprisal: Reaction in North Carolina to the Nat Turner Insurrection." *North Carolina Historical Review* 62 (January 1985): 29–52.

Moser, Harold D. "Reaction in North Carolina to the Emancipation Proclamation." *North Carolina Historical Review* 44 (January 1967): 53–71.

Norris, David A. "'For the Benefit of Our Gallant Volunteers': North Carolina's State Medical Department and Civilian Volunteer Efforts, 1861–1862." *North Carolina Historical Review* 75 (July 1998): 297–326.

Rable, George C. "Beyond State Rights: The Shadowy World of Confederate Politics." In *Writing the Civil War: The Quest to Understand,* ed. James M. McPherson and William J. Cooper, 135–53. Columbia: University of South Carolina Press, 1998.

Ramsdell, Charles W. Review of *State Rights in the Confederacy,* by Frank L. Owsley. *Mississippi Valley Historical Review* 14 (June 1927): 107–11.

Raper, Horace W. "William W. Holden and the Peace Movement in North Carolina." *North Carolina Historical Review* 31 (October 1954): 493–515.

Reid, Richard. "Raising the African Brigade: Early Black Recruitment in Civil War North Carolina." *North Carolina Historical Review* 70 (July 1993): 266–97.

———. "A Test Case of 'Crying Evil': Desertion among North Carolina Troops during the Civil War." *North Carolina Historical Review* 58 (July 1981): 234–62.

Scarboro, David D. "North Carolina and the Confederacy: The Weakness of States' Rights during the Civil War." *North Carolina Historical Review* 56 (April 1979): 133–49.

Stevenson, George, and Ruby D. Arnold. "North Carolina Courts of Law and Equity prior to 1868." [North Carolina] *Archives Information Circular* 9 (March 1977).

Van Zant, Jennifer. "Confederate Conscription and the North Carolina Supreme Court." *North Carolina Historical Review* 72 (January 1995): 54–75.

Weeks, Stephen B. "The University of North Carolina in the Civil War." *Southern Historical Society Papers* 24 (January-December 1896): 35–36.

Yates, Richard E. "Governor Vance and the End of the War in North Carolina." *North Carolina Historical Review* 18 (October 1941): 315–38.

———. "Governor Vance and the Peace Movement." Parts 1 and 2. *North Carolina Historical Review* 17 (January/April 1940): 1–25, 89–113.

———. "Zebulon B. Vance as War Governor of North Carolina, 1862–1865." *Journal of Southern History* 3 (February 1937): 43–75.

Yearns, W. Buck, Jr. "North Carolina in the Confederate Congress." *North Carolina Historical Review* 27 (July 1952): 359–78.

Thesis

Meekins, Alex Christopher. "Caught between Scylla and Charybdis: The Civil War in Northeastern North Carolina." Master's thesis, North Carolina State University, 2001.

INDEX

Joe A. Mobley is a former administrator and historian with the North Carolina Office of Archives and History in Raleigh, where he served as editor in chief of the *North Carolina Historical Review* and editor of *The Papers of Zebulon Baird Vance*. He is a visiting lecturer at North Carolina State University, Raleigh, and has authored or edited a number of articles and books related to North Carolina history.